Celebrity Culture and the Entertainment Industry in Asia

Celebrity Culture and the Entertainment Industry in Asia

Use of Celebrity and its Influence on Society, Culture and Communication

Vivienne Leung, Kimmy Cheng and Tommy Tse

intellect Bristol, UK / Chicago, USA

First published in the UK in 2017 by
Intellect, The Mill, Parnall Road, Fishponds, Bristol, BS16 3JG, UK

First published in the USA in 2017 by
Intellect, The University of Chicago Press, 1427 E. 60th Street,
Chicago, IL 60637, USA

A catalogue record for this book is available from the
British Library.

Cover designer: Aleksandra Szumlas
Copy-editor: Michael Eckhardt
Production manager: Katie Evans
Typesetting: Contentra Technologies

Print ISBN: 978-1-78320-807-4
ePDF ISBN: 978-1-78320-808-1
ePUB ISBN: 978-1-78320-809-8

Printed and bound by Hobbs, UK

This is a peer-reviewed publication.

Department of
COMmunication
Studies 傳播系

香 港 浸 會 大 學
HONG KONG BAPTIST UNIVERSITY

Contents

Foreword by Kineta Hung

Celebrity fan culture in Asia is highly vibrant. Fuelled by the explosive growth in the popularity of Chinese and Korean superstars across the region and beyond, as well as the licensing of popular reality shows in markets around the world, celebrity fan culture is turning into a unique worldwide phenomenon. New players (such as cyber-personalities) and new economic values (such as fan economics) are being introduced into the media and entertainment industry, as well as into the world of branding and consumption. Through a negotiation between on- and offline culture and commerce, the relationships among celebrity, fans, media and entertainment are continually evolving and transforming one another.

This book traces the development of this cultural phenomenon as the lines between those who 'make' the celebrity and those who 'use' the celebrity – and how they do so – are blurred. To provide a better appreciation of the current cultural scene, the authors traced the transformation of media and entertainment industries over previous decades. Key industry players in China, Hong Kong and South Korea were interviewed to garner insights from different perspectives. The role of consumer fans and the impact of social media received special emphases due to the important roles they play in developing the celebrity–fans culture. In so doing, exciting issues are examined, including who determines a public figure's celebrity status, how a celebrity's profile is received and recreated, and the impact of these issues on the triangular relationship between society, culture and communication. This book would be of interest to readers excited about the celebrity and entertainment industry in particular and popular culture in general.

The authors are communication and cultural scholars who are well-versed in the areas of celebrity, fashion, luxury brands and the entertainment industry. Each gained substantial experience in the advertising and public relations industries before joining academia, teaching and publishing in their related subject areas.

Foreword by P. David Marshall

In some of my recent writing and research, I have called for the need to advance the study of our public personality systems – including our elaborate and complex celebrity culture – using various different approaches (Marshall, Moore, & Barbour, 2015). As I have developed persona studies over the last five years (in which celebrity can be understood as a subset of a larger and extensive public presentation of the self; cf. Marshall & Barbour, 2015), I have promoted the idea that we have to get much closer to our objects of study: we need to interview celebrities and work out what they imagine they are doing, and then reconstruct our thinking to better express their relationship to our cultures.

This is not an easy process. Researchers such as Kerry Ferris and Scott Harris (2011), who wanted to get close to the Hollywood system of celebrity, downgraded to studying celebrities in mid-sized American cities specifically because they wanted to interview them directly and could not do this successfully with any significant Hollywood stars. A recent study of the psychological implications of fame had to de-identify the famed individuals in their study (Rockwell & Giles 2009), and most of these interviews were conducted by phone or correspondence. Researchers have often been left with the exploration of these public personalities via what I would describe as 'intrinsic' interviews, conducted by the media itself, where the content is serving purposes and strategies other than the research. 'Extrinsic' interviews of celebrities are the goal, whereby the researcher and the celebrity work through the meaning of the celebrity's public presentation of the self in a phenomenological explorative way.

The remarkable achievement of this book is that it accomplished this goal, and in many ways represents the first major work that has achieved this direct connection to celebrities and the industrial apparatus that surrounds them. Through a blend of interviews of industry professionals and self-reflective celebrities, this book makes major inroads into the meaning of celebrity culture via its chapters that include an in-depth study of the media and celebrity, identity and celebrity, and the form of marketing communication that celebrities express. This achievement is certainly dependent on the expertise and industrial connections of the authors of this work; yet it is also work that demonstrates an integration of the growing research on celebrity, both from a media and cultural studies perspective, as well as a marketing, communication and advertising point of view.

It is very possible that the predominant location of this study in Hong Kong presented a peculiarly rich resource for this exploration of the industrial and personal dimensions of celebrity culture. Hong Kong has been an entertainment capital in Asia and beyond for some time. And at its current juncture, it has also become a site where one can observe with intensity the transnational flows of pan-Asian media and entertainment. On one level, the entertainment industry and its associated celebrity culture is contained and visible within Hong Kong itself – a city of just over seven million, but with an interesting history of a very visible and active popular culture within its borders. This intense microcosm of interlocking entertainment industries and celebrities perhaps provided some of the visible and accessible pathways for the authors' investigation of celebrity culture.

Equally significant is that the authors were able to uncover how media professionals and celebrities navigate the changing transnational movements of Asian popular culture. As some of the interviews and analyses in this book reveal, there has been a pragmatically inspired movement of the centre of the entertainment industry to Shanghai, and celebrities are similarly conscious of this shift. As this book reveals, simultaneous to this sensitivity is an understanding of the regional power and aesthetic sensibility of Korean popular culture across Asia. Both of these decades-old transformations are developed and discussed in valuable ways within the context of celebrity culture in the chapters of this book.

Beyond its methodological success and its capacity to directly interview the practitioners and managers of celebrity in the industry, *Celebrity Culture and the Entertainment Industry in Asia* has also begun the significant work that I am hoping will expand with the publication of this work, namely comparative celebrity and persona research. With its nuanced understanding of the Hong Kong scene and its wider reading of East Asian popular culture, this book represents one of the pilots for the development of comparative persona and celebrity research. Each culture has a related but differentiated system of persona, one that is connected to the individuals that are visibly celebrated there. In addition, there is clearly a transnational sense of public and celebrity identity; for example, an idea of glamour that moves between cultures via all sorts of industrial, consumer and popular culture processes enacted by celebrities (Marshall, 2016). Along with a host of other writers and researchers – and an integration of numerous other sources from many national and transnational studies of celebrity – this work certainly is a stimulus to a new generation of research on the fascinating and interlocking world of public personality systems.

Chapter 1

Introduction

W hether living in modern western or Asian societies, we would not be surprised by the fact that we are surrounded by traces of celebrities in our everyday lives: in the news and commercials we watch; the television shows and films we enjoy; the products and images we consume; the role models and media personalities we mimic; the sociocultural issues we tirelessly gossip about; or even the benchmarks we uphold to judge ourselves and others. But what is celebrity? Do we all conceive it similarly across time and space, cultures and contexts? Who produces, propagates and twists its meaning and manifestation?

This book attempts to enrich the existing literature of celebrity studies – which has been predominantly developed from the western cultural context – through in-depth interviews with seasoned practitioners in various entertainment industries and members of media and brand communication teams in Hong Kong, mainland China and South Korea, specifically celebrities, media workers, artist managers and publicists. Through this, we aim to critically understand the divergent definitions of celebrity, analyse the differing manifestations of celebrity cultures, and comprehend the construction of their meaning and cultural positioning. Discussions of celebrity creation and endorsement cases across East Asia over the past three decades can help us understand the multiple facets of celebrity power and culture, such as the construction of self-identity, celebrity-driven consumer behaviour and embedded ideologies, in addition to its analogous and dissimilar impacts on branding, society and consumers in the specified sociocultural contexts. Various western, cross-disciplinary theories that explain the influence of celebrities are also examined for their empirical applicability, and are contextualized to real-life scenarios in Asia in the hopes of bridging the gap between theory and practice.

Data in the book

Through our professional networks, twelve in-depth interviews were conducted in Hong Kong with media, marketing and entertainment industry professionals and prominent celebrities between July 2014 and February 2015. Among them were artist managers, publicists/advertisers, media workers and celebrities from Hong Kong, mainland China and South Korea.

All interviewees were selected using volunteer sampling; as such, they were selected non-randomly, based on availability. After reading an explanatory statement, participants were asked to sign a form consenting to their participation. Interviews were conducted and recorded through exchanges in which the interviewees verbally provided us with information face-to-face in semi-structured interviews. We posed a set of basic questions, but also asked probing follow-up questions to gather specific details or answers that were more complete. Questions were also open-ended in order to encourage in-depth answers from the interviewees. All interviews lasted for between approximately 45 minutes and 90 minutes.

All interviewees participated on a voluntary basis; moreover, they were allowed to decline to participate at any time during the study period. They could also refuse to answer any questions they did not want to answer while still remaining part of the study. Although some interviewees gave permission for their information to be used, selected company names and sensitive data provided by them were anonymized to protect their confidentiality. Furthermore, upon the interviewees' request, audio transcripts and relevant recordings were available for their review.

Structure of the book

The organization of this book is meant to offer a critical discussion of recent cases of, and first-hand interviews with, significant players in the entertainment industry across Asia, particularly in Hong Kong, mainland China and South Korea.

The layout of each chapter follows the same format: an introduction; interviews concerning the major themes and content; and final insights. Direct quotations from the interviews have been incorporated to provide a better representation of the interviewees' perspectives and feelings.

In Chapter 2, we uncover the different facets of celebrity co-creation dynamics in Hong Kong, mainland China and South Korea compared with those in the west and other Asian societies. This is accomplished through interviews with Wallace Kwok (郭啟華), a seasoned media personality and celebrity manager in Hong Kong; Francis Cheng (鄭紹康), CEO of Occasions PR and Marketing Ltd; and Yeong-Beom Jeong (영범정), an experienced celebrity manager in South Korea. The historical changes and hierarchical statuses of major parties/agents involved in the co-creation and publicity process are elucidated. In the specified Asian context, the economic potential and hindrance derived from a distinctive entertainment culture and political environment are discerned and validated by both the primary and secondary data presented.

For Chapter 3, a history of celebrity endorsement and its rising importance in marketing communications strategies is narrated. Anson Shum, marketing and communication director (Greater China) at the Bluebell Group, and June Lee, communication director (Asia-Pacific) at a well-known western cosmetics brand, were interviewed. The pair shed new light on the evolving use and gradually diminishing power of celebrities across various types of marketing communications in Asia amid the rising ubiquity of digital technology, which now renders celebrity endorsement a more challenging and complicated process. The interviewees also shared cross-cultural similarities between how brands and celebrities collaborate and mutually benefit each other, such as by enhancing a celebrity's fame, escalating brand awareness and generating sales. That said, new modes of partnership between celebrities and brands are also introduced.

Chapter 4 offers a critical discussion of the symbiotic yet asymmetrical relationship between celebrity and media in the entertainment industry in Asia, drawing on insights from three seasoned media workers in Hong Kong. They are Francis Mak (麥潤壽), a well-known radio host in Hong Kong; Patrick Suen (宣柏健), a seasoned columnist and film critic in Hong Kong, who is keen on Asian films and Korean pop culture; and Kam Kwok-leung (甘國亮), an experienced practitioner within the Hong Kong entertainment industry. Along with the rapid expansion and development of media conglomerates, the prevalence of celebrity in the media and their symbiotic relationship are discussed. This chapter also takes a look at how digital media alters the celebrity–media relationship. In addition, the interviewees shared how both Chinese and Korean celebrities currently work with traditional and digital media, which is expected to continue to provide tension.

Chapter 5 presents four case studies on celebrity culture and celebrity identity, based on in-depth interviews with Denise Ho (何韻詩), Hilary Tsui (徐濠縈), Pakho Chau (周柏豪) and Bob Lam (林盛斌), all of whom are leading celebrities in Hong Kong across different sectors of the media and entertainment industries. We investigate celebrity as an ever-changing and intertextual sign that is discursively and differently constructed across cultures and societies. Different audiences' and social groups' polarized views on a wide range of celebrity signs in society, and their unprecedented impact on the key agent in the entertainment industry – the celebrities themselves – are discussed and analysed based on the interviewed Chinese celebrities' insider experiences and views. The themes directly addressed and uniquely shared in detail by the key players themselves include self-identity; the chances and challenges posed by the new media environment they face; and how local audiences are fascinated by and strongly identify with these celebrities in forming their subversive social, cultural and gender identities.

Overall, these interviews and case studies bear empirical and theoretical significance. Empirically, this project benefited from direct and individual in-depth accounts from renowned celebrities and professionals. We revealed and analysed not only the recollections of practitioners, but also their reflections, attitudes and perceptions, overcoming the lack of willingness of industry insiders to be interviewed (Stokes, 2013), particularly in this culturally sensitive business. The first-hand, insider information gathered from these diverse sources in the entertainment industry engendered authentic and holistic perspectives, providing a more comprehensive and balanced understanding of celebrity cultures. Theoretically, the up-to-date cases discussed in this book offer a timely examination of the phenomenon of stardom in an East Asian context, forging a dialogue between Asian and western academic discourses.

In the following introductory section, we will introduce various academic disciplinary perspectives to celebrity culture – from sociology, anthropology, media and cultural studies to communication theories and political economy. Such a plethora of interdisciplinary ideas presented at the outset – which mainly originated from the western academic discourse – becomes the theoretical backbone of this book, opening up multiple perspectives of understanding, and complicating the operational mechanisms of the entertainment industry in Hong Kong, mainland China and South Korea, as well as its manifestation in celebrity cultures. It also provides us with a useful set of mental tools to carefully connect and critique the applicability of interdisciplinary theories to the selected empirical data collected in each of the chapters.

Celebrity as a role model

The term 'celebrity' is often used to describe famed and extremely talented individuals in various professions, particularly in the media and entertainment industries. The origin of the star system can be traced back to the emergence of the Hollywood film industry and its public discourse in America in the 1910s (DeCordova, 2007). After its initial entry into the Chinese market in the 1930s, the film star system became widespread and rapidly developed there. Along with the launch in 1967 of Television Broadcasts Limited (TVB), the first free-to-air commercial TV station in Hong Kong, celebrity culture in Hong Kong blossomed swiftly from the late 1960s due to the meteoric rise of local pop songs and TV shows, as well as their high degree of penetration of mass society as a form of free entertainment, gradually overshadowing motion pictures. During the 1980s, an influx of Hong Kong and Taiwanese celebrity images materialized that nurtured an early trend of celebrity worship in the mainland (Yue, 2007). Since then, celebrities have become more like a cultural product for consumption and entertainment than a heroic role model for admiration and apprenticeship. In China, this phenomenon became more prominent, triggering a sophisticated celebrity manufacturing system, a more rapid celebrity cycle (usually about two to three years) and a fervent fan culture (Edwards & Jeffreys, 2010; Yue, 2007). Nowadays, influential celebrities are emerging and being produced in other industries as well, including television, radio, sports, fashion modelling, academia, business and political sectors, and other creative and cultural industries, consequently making our time a glittering 'celebrity era' (Yue, 2007, pp. 3–4). This is evidenced by mainland actresses Fan Bingbing (范冰冰), Li Bingbing (李冰冰), Liu Shishi (劉詩詩) and Yao Chen (姚晨); Taiwanese singers Jay Chou (周杰倫), Jolin Tsai (蔡依林) and Wang Leehom (王力宏); Cantopop singers Eason Chan (陳奕迅) and G.E.M. (鄧紫棋); mainland actors Huang Xiaoming (黃曉明), Deng Chao (鄧超) and Li Chen (李晨); Hong Kong actors Nicholas Tse (謝霆鋒), Jackie Chan (成龍), Louis Koo (古天樂) and Donnie Yen (甄子丹); pianist Lang Lang (郎朗); mainland singer Li Yuchun (李宇春), who was a winner of the Chinese singing contest 超級女聲/*Super Girl* (2005); Hong Kong actresses Carina Lau (劉嘉玲) and Angelababy (楊穎); musical groups Mayday, Sodagreen and TFBOYS; Olympic gold medallists such as badminton player Lin Dan (林丹), gymnast Li Ning (李寧) and hurdler Liu Xiang (劉翔); the tennis player Li Na (李娜); and the NBA basketball player Yao Ming (姚明). All of these have been listed on Forbes' China Celebrity Top 100 List (Forbes, 2015; cf. Edwards & Jeffreys, 2010).

Figure 1: Kam Kwok-leung and Fan Bing bing, a renowned Chinese actress, at the Dior party in 2010.

Figure 2: Kam Kwok-leung and Jay Chou, a popular Taiwan singer and actor, at the Shanghai International Film Festival in 2013.

Celebrities are the quintessence of success and exceptionality, and are seen as distant from the ordinary populace. However, although they may evoke a sense of intimacy and familiarity in us, they have become highly replaceable (Yue, 2007). Some stress the different key roles that celebrities play in society: for instance, celebrity worship can provide teenagers with role models of a similar/older age to look up to or identify with, filling the 'emotional voids' brought on by their gradual emotional detachment from their parents throughout their teen years, as well as a hyperreal, fantasized yet gratifying sentimental/sensual experience with celebrities outside of their humdrum everyday lives (Yue, 2007). Ultimately, their stardom provokes desires, fantasies and vanities in the spiritual world of both teenagers and adults; in extreme cases, such attachments to celebrity culture and its representations can become obsessive and pathological (Yue, 2007). We can also categorize celebrity worship as either superficial or substantial appreciation (Yue & Cheung, 2000). The former idealizes, romanticizes and absolutizes celebrities, mostly valorizing their physical traits and appeals. Celebrities who adhere to this category include Fan Bingbing (范冰冰), Li Bingbing (李冰冰), Liu Shishi (劉詩詩) and Huang Xiaoming (黃曉明) from mainland China; Wang Leehom (王力宏), Godfrey Gao (高以翔) and Lin Chiling (林志玲) from Taiwan; Angelababy (楊穎), Nicholas Tse (謝霆鋒) and Louis Koo (古天樂) from Hong Kong; and Kim Soo Hyun (金秀賢), Jun Ji-Hyun (全智賢) and Si-won Choi (崔始源) from South Korea. The latter takes celebrities as 'relative, rational and ordinary' beings, emphasizing their personality traits and inner strengths (Yue, 2007, pp. 40–41). Examples of this sort of celebrity are effectively represented by Eason Chan (陳奕迅), MC Jin (歐陽靖), Mayday (五月天), Sodagreen (蘇打綠), Ge You (葛優), Sun Honglei (孫紅雷) and Li Yuchun (李宇春).

Celebrity as a system of rationalization

Celebrity can also be seen as resulting from an emergence from the modern mass. From Marshall's (1997) perspective, celebrity is 'an embodiment of a discursive battleground on the norms of individuality and personality within a culture' (p. 65). Various institutions employ celebrity creation, the production of individuality or unique identity as a tactic to contain the intimidation and irrationality of the masses; this individualizes the collective sphere and shows how the masses are defused into concepts of individual behaviours (Marshall, 1997). Similar to the function of social psychology, celebrity celebrates 'the potential of the individual and the mass's support of the individual in mass society' (Marshall, 1997, p. 43). As a negotiated terrain of significance, celebrity is a production of the hegemonic culture sustained by a capitalist commodity system of cultural production, one that is produced to lead and represent; conversely, the subordinate audiences of the culture are also involved in the process, comprehending and identifying it, as well as making it fit into their everyday experiences (Marshall, 1997).

In that sense, celebrity can be regarded as a 'system of rationalization' for different social groups to make sense of the social world, allowing them to articulate the transformation of various cultural values into the rationalizing system of the commodity (Marshall, 1997). Celebrities are being placed in a highly visible position to grab public attention within a circuitry of power, thus becoming models for the rest of the population (van Krieken, 2012a). The famed Chinese pop singer Li Yuchun (李宇春), who was manufactured by a highly commercial reality TV programme *Super Girl* (2005), outshines other typically feminine female pop singers with her tomboyish and rebellious image (Edwards & Jeffreys, 2010). Li quickly struck a chord among hundreds of thousands of young girls in mainland China who strongly identified with her as an able, adventurous and alluring role model. Yet some suggest that celebrities are in fact quite powerless, as they are reliant on the allocation of attention from their audience (van Krieken, 2012a).

As characters who seize various forms of affective power into rationalized configurations, celebrities effectively integrate the notion of personality differences and individuality into a system of exchange; hence, audiences are 'rationalized' to see the represented and idolized celebrity personalities as legitimate forms of identification and cultural value. Consequently, such celebrated formative power rests with the people as an expression of social spirit and popular culture (Marshall, 1997), essentially allowing them to exercise power and govern a population (van Krieken, 2012a). We can also identify strong parallels between celebrity and religion in their similar socially integrative effects. In the production process, a sense of sacredness has been injected into the celebrity signs that lure the masses (van Krieken, 2012b). On the heels of the shocking suicide of Hong Kong actor/singer Leslie Cheung (張國榮), ten fans committed suicide in Beijing and Hong Kong, with psychiatrists terming this series of incidents the 'Leslie Cheung phenomenon' (Wang, 2007). Over the past twelve years, voluntary commemoration activities across Hong Kong, China and Taiwan to embalm Cheung's cultural legacy demonstrate his integrative effects on society even after his death. This collective nostalgia for him in Greater China stems from fans' identification with his candour, sincerity and bravery in staying true to himself (Cheung came out as a homosexual in 1997), which embodies Leslie's extraordinary appeal beyond space and time (Wang, 2007).

Celebrity as institutional charisma

Rather than considering a celebrity as merely a charismatic individual, his or her charisma – their unique personal qualities, creativity and status – is often a mediated and institutionalized element present in the routine functioning of society, in which there is a pervasive disposition to attribute charismatic properties to ordinary secular roles and aggregates of people.

> Charismatic domination in the 'pure' sense [...] is always the offspring of unusual circumstances – either external, especially political or economic, or internal and spiritual, especially religious, or both together. [...]. If the tide which once elevated a

charismatically led group out of the routine of everyday life flows back into everyday channels, then charismatic domination [...] is undermined in most cases.

(Weber, 2006, p. 19)

Paradoxically, this institutional charisma not only trespasses, but also maintains social order. This thus becomes an assessment of the deference-worthiness of one's:

[...] wealth, income, occupation, the power to order by command, prohibition and control over resources, style of life, standard of living, education, primordial connections [...] with persons possessing these properties, and the power to protect or benefit the community or life itself.

(Shils, 2010, pp. 84, 92 & 96)

全民星探/*I am Paparazzi* is a China-based smartphone app that reports the daily life events of celebrities and has become a hit among young people seeking updates on their admired stars. Rather than reporting glamorous entertainment news about walking the red carpet or attending movie premieres, this app captures the very mundane facets of celebrities: shopping in the mall, walking a dog, going on holiday with family, etc. However, these ordinary activities are mediated and institutionalized as 'charismatic' as they are carried out by celebrities and then brought into the public realm. As McNamara (2011) suggested, although technologies bring new dynamics to approaching celebrities, thus making them much more approachable, their glory is still there. This is what lies at the very core of our celebrity culture.

Celebrity as a discursive cultural sign

When we speak about celebrities, we rarely refer to them as a material being or real person who is at the centre of the representation, but rather as celebrity signs whose eminent personalities within the social world are given heightened cultural importance (Marshall, 1997). Classic examples include Marilyn Monroe, Marlon Brando, James Dean and Elvis Presley in 1950s America, who characterized the period's new and contested concepts of morality and sexuality (Dyer, 2004). Since then, a range of legendary film stars and musicians from Hong Kong's media and entertainment industries have had their eminent images sublimated into cultural signs: Bruce Lee (李小龍), who personifies the philosophy of martial arts and Taoism; Jimmy Wang Yu (王羽), who epitomizes modern individualism and ideal masculinity (Jarvie, 1977); Connie Chan (陳寶珠) and Josephine Siao (蕭芳芳), who respectively perpetuate the candour of working-class women and the poise of high-born ladies; Tina Ti (狄娜), the ultimate sex symbol who refuses to be a good girl, is actively sexual, and shatters traditional and virtuous female qualities (Suen, 2000); Samuel Hui (許冠傑), who personifies the wit, thirst for success and bicultural identity of *Hong*

Kong yan ('Hong Konger'/'Hong Kongese'); Leslie Cheung (張國榮), who manifested himself as the soul of androgynous charm (S. H. Chan, 2010); and Anita Mui (梅艷芳), who embodies a subversive femininity and versatile talents. Even so, these celebrity/cultural signs are seldom utterly determined or 'naturalized', but rather subject to negotiation in the intertextual, discursive signification process, with ubiquitous interpretive writings on cultural artefacts deepening and connecting their symbolic meanings to the culture, and fabricating ideological differences between the celebrity and his/her audiences/consumers so as to articulate a form of social power. Audiences are interpellated to see the normatively centred celebrity qualities as distinctive and superior ideal types, which they can adapt and adopt in their formation of social identities (Marshall, 1997).

The operationalization of celebrity power and culture cannot stand without the 'subordinate' audience allowing it to circulate, although this does not mean that the interpellation and rationalization process is always efficacious and everlasting. Such a temporarily coherent constructed audience subjectivity is unstable and unsolidified; the celebrity, as a moving signifier, is regularly configured and transformed by mediatized news and popular texts about their professional and personal life, both in and through the operation of cultural industries and the proliferation of certain discourses of individuality, particularly within contemporary cultures and social contexts (Marshall, 1997).

Celebrity as a para-religion

The significance of a celebrity culture is not so much about who they are, but whom they can influence (and how) in the semi-religious environment we inhabit. Celebrities become 'deities' because it is the collective 'us' in them that is being deified and worshipped, embodying the projected identifications and desires of those who worship them as 'idols' and 'icons'. Although the fans may not realize it, a 'para-religion' is formed through themselves as an agency of their celebrity adoration (Ward, 2011). However, celebrity worship and identification are different from religion as they are 'not a formal system that can order society and structure institutions' (Ward, 2011, p. 19). Through the media's reproduction and representation of the celebrity images, celebrities are sanctified as semi-divine figures to facilitate identity construction and transcendence, forming part of their fans' constructed fantasy worlds: 'Celebrity worship is the sacred without the moral and the totem without the social [...] the sacred is thereby merged with the profane' (Ward, 2011, pp. 64–66). Through Hollywood's continued media productions, Bruce Lee's philosophy of martial arts and traditional Chinese religion sublimated from the films of his time into values and beliefs that are still being espoused today. The long-lasting muse and the inspiration he brought to Hollywood and American society were termed 'cult worship', thereby turning him into 'an object, even a fetish' (Teo, 1997, as cited in Tinkcom & Villarejo, 2003, p. 175). Although not a rigid school of religion, people's worship of Bruce Lee still deifies him as the sage, the immortal, who represents the infinite wisdom of the Orient.

Moreover, celebrity culture has vague religious parallels in that it is dislocated from the chain of meaning in a tradition – the social and the communal – yet persists in a disintegrated and disguised shape in popular culture, propagating a 'worship of the multiple possibilities of the self' (Ward, 2011, pp. 81–82). Fans, who often keep only half an eye on celebrities, do not necessarily have sacred and serious responsibilities to their para-gods; rather than the divine stars, they are the ones who are endowed with the all-seeing power to mix and match their 'polytheistic' identifications with varied celebrities (Ward, 2011).

Celebrity as an interactionalist symbol

Stardom is generated in the social interactions between celebrities and their fans (Ferris & Harris, 2011). Such meanings are not inherent, but based on what things mean to them divergently, thereby creating conflicting patterns of interpretation and interaction beyond a simplistic structuralist approach (Ferris & Harris, 2011). The social norms that govern social interactions with celebrities are flexible, fleeting, emergent and multi-oriented. A more nuanced ethnographic study of how fans actually (dis)identify with stars – and how these (dis)identifications are in conjunction with their lived experiences and habitus – can help comprehend the microstructuralism of celebrity as multiple and interactionalist symbols, and avoid mistaking celebrity culture for a one-dimensional and linear phenomenon (Ferris & Harris, 2011). Social media platforms, such as Twitter and Facebook, are employed globally to facilitate interactions between celebrities and fans, where a horizontal exchange of virtual responses cast significant influences on the image and perception of celebrities (Marwick & Boyd, 2011). In recognition of this, top global celebrities commonly share their personal lives (Stever & Lawson, 2013), as evidenced by Hugh Jackman's Twitter, in which he shares his private pictures (Longhetti, 2015). Globally, fans are becoming more attached to discovering celebrities' day-to-day lives and seeing their 'natural or unmediated picture' (Holmes & Redmond, 2006, p. 4). Hence, an interactionalist approach plays a significant role in shifting celebrities' popularity and reputation. In South Korea, in particular, many celebrities openly share their personal struggles on-air to generate an empathetic appeal to fans (Noh Kelsey, 2014). Many also attempt to project down-to-earth images by participating in television programmes involving low-maintenance activities, such as camping and babysitting. In being 'stripped of all their finery' (Holmes & Redmond, 2006, p. 4), the celebrity naturally increases levels of intimacy between them and their fans.

Celebrity as attention capital

As 'the crowning result of the star system of a society that makes a fetish of competition' (van Krieken, 2012b, pp. 65–66), celebrities occupy a particular position in the distribution of status and prestige. An underlying logic of competition underpins the production of celebrity (van Krieken, 2012a), and in many ways they resemble the traditional aristocracies whose positions were based on power and wealth. So who can become a celebrity and why are some of them more powerful than others? Milner Jr. (2005) suggested that, as a particular kind of status system, celebrity status does not rely exclusively on one's talents and merits, nor is it reducible to economic or political power. A star's immanent attributes can surely attract a multitude, but sometimes one becomes a star simply because that person is already attracting the public's attention. Such attention capital draws the ultimate interest of the mass media to leverage it into sales and viewership (van Krieken, 2012a). Since the late 2000s, 'lang mo' (嘍模) or 'pseudo-models' (female teenage models whose physical attributes fall short of traditional high-fashion catwalk models' attributes) have been propagated by the mass media in Hong Kong as sexually seductive, innocent or even stupid young girls who aspire to instant fame, best exemplifying the growing significance of attention capital in celebrity culture (D. Chu, 2013).

Given how the boundaries around celebrity groups are rather porous (van Krieken, 2012a), the star systems favour a constant turnover and recruitment of new members. A celebrity's fame can be further enhanced through association with higher-profile celebrities; conversely, they can be undermined or ruined by the ongoing surveillance and normative adjudication of their own conduct and identity (such as around ideals of physical appearance, gender roles and behaviour), or by other members of society, revealing a complex and multi-layered power structure within the star systems (van Krieken, 2012a).

Celebrity as a political and humanitarian messiah

Meanwhile, the sovereignty of media celebrity has gradually extended to political and humanitarian arenas. In the post-democratic era, celebrities become quasi-political figures and philanthropists, and have a more influential role on significant global policy issues, ranging from debt to trade, starvation, health conditions, poverty and scarcity of resources (Kapoor, 2013). Celebrities are now the unaccountable political brokers and decision-makers who are even more powerful than most mainstream politicians or diplomats. By gloriously adorning their celebrity identities with good-hearted altruism, they can convert citizens into their devotees, consumers and spectators (Kapoor, 2013). This political–humanitarian stardom is backed by a prevalence of neo-liberal hyperindividualism, public political passivity, and the nature of our networked and media-dominated societies (Debord, 1983; Kapoor, 2013; Stevenson, 2010).

There are polarized opinions to this kind of star power. Although they undeniably draw significant public attention to mediatized social, economic and political problems and celebritized humanitarian works, there is also a tendency for such problems to be 'glossed over', individualized and isolated from broader issues of political economy, cultural imperialism and socio-economic complexity (Kapoor, 2013). Ultimately, audiences delegate their beliefs about political change or charity to the celebrity without 'getting their hands dirty', saving themselves from the guilt and helplessness caused by actually confronting global problems (Kapoor, 2013, p. 42).

Another irony is that celebrities who are deeply immersed in capitalism – often the root cause of the inequality they seek to address – constantly and inevitably showcase their own brand image, strong ties to their professional work and glamorous lives through their apparently altruistic humanitarianism (Kapoor, 2013). Angelina Jolie, a leading celebrity advocate, has been subjected to criticisms despite her efforts to promote humanitarian causes; although her active involvement in UN-affiliated campaigns and conferences is positively received, the tangible impact of her celebritized efforts is often questioned. Her tendency to work with high-profile organizations also suggests that her motivation might lie in having 'psycho-symbolic returns' (Kapoor, 2013, p. 24), as noted by her welcoming receipt of numerous honorary titles such as 'damehood' and 'UNHCR goodwill ambassador'. This suggests that celebrity advocates are ultimately focused on consolidating their brand image (Kapoor, 2013), leading the organizations and the public to 'fall into the celebrity trap'. Similarly, Lady Gaga's philanthropy in youth empowerment and LGBT rights have been perceived as efforts to promote her own self-image rather than produce apparent outcomes. The outrageous ways in which she has promoted these causes, such as wearing revealing costumes and displaying controversial sexual behaviour onstage, suggest that her sensationalization of humanitarian acts and displays of 'moral outrage' were aimed at promoting her own unorthodox image (Kapoor, 2013).

Celebrity as 'celetoid'

In contemporary western societies, we have also witnessed a new type of celebrity alongside a changing ecosystem of celebrity culture, namely the increasing visibility of ordinary persons becoming 'instant/ordinary celebrities' who turn themselves into media content via user-generated websites, reality TV shows, celebrity culture, and so forth. The aura of celebrity has colonized the expectations of everyday life; meanwhile, media industries have transformed and accelerated the star manufacturing system into a formulaic and mechanical process, utilizing the sudden fame radiating from ordinary celebrities for viewership and advertising sales, but then quickly disposing of them due to their short life cycle as public figures (Turner, 2010). In the mediatization process, formations of identity and desire are also invented, popularized and distributed in society, functioning 'like an ideological system but without an ideological project' (Turner, 2010, pp. 224–225). Defined by Chris Rojek (2001) as 'celetoids', this novel type of celebrity is also hierarchically placed in an inferior position, and is not endowed with 'particular talents which might give them expectations of work in the entertainment industry, [and] no specific career objectives beyond the achievement of media visibility' (Turner, 2010, p. 218). The recently controversial, low-budget music video 'Sugar Baby' by FFx (a new Hong Kong girl idol group), released on YouTube in October 2015 (FFx UTO, 2015), scored more than one million views in three days due to their awfully amateur performance. This triggered the local mainstream newspaper *Apple Daily*'s interest in reproducing two music videos for the girl band in order to monetize their publicity for viewership on the media group's online news platform. Such co-creation immensely escalates these celetoids' instant fame, as well as the mass public's and netizens' prosumption of their mediatized celebrity further (Miller, 2011) – not just in Hong Kong, but also across East Asia.

The discussion thus far presents various theoretical paradigms of celebrity as a social and cultural phenomenon: as a system of rationalization; as an institutional charisma; as a discursive cultural sign; as a para-religion; as an interactionalist symbol; as an attention capital; as a political and humanitarian messiah; and even as a 'celetoid'. Yet in order to determine how celebrity culture is discursively manufactured and actually disseminated in and through a capitalist social setting, the intricate relationships between the stars and the entertainment industry should be carefully examined. In the subsequent chapter, we will unveil the production structure and key players (i.e. agent, manager and publicist) in the process of star creation within the entertainment industry. The respective roles, interactions and modes of collaboration among these key players in co-creating a celebrity's stardom will be scrutinized. Such an understanding will help us dissect the similarities and differences of the East Asian entertainment industry and star creation in Asia.

Chapter 2

Co-creation of celebrities

Introduction

Put simply, co-creation is an initiative that brings different parties together so as to jointly produce a mutually valued outcome. In the culture of celebrity, these parties might include – to name just a few – agents, PRs, media practitioners, managers and the celebrity themselves. In other words, they are marrying their efforts together in order to gain monetary and/or non-monetary benefits from establishing a famous celebrity.

However, the manufacturing process of celebrities is complicated: it often involves multiple parties, with each party playing a very significant role in the process. The strategic integrated effort of all involved parties in the creation of a celebrity has never been as difficult as it is in this information age, since any celebrity-to-be is now subjected to unprecedented scrutiny and the increasing expectations of its audience.

In this chapter, we attempt to delineate the functions assumed by three significant players in the process of celebrity creation: (1) the representatives of the celebrities; (2) the media; and (3) the celebrities themselves. Following this section, we will support our observation using face-to-face interviews conducted in Hong Kong with three renowned artist managers from Asia – namely, Wallace Kwok (郭啟華), a seasoned media personnel and celebrity manager in Hong Kong; Francis Cheng (鄭紹康), CEO of Occasions PR and Marketing Ltd; and Yeong-Beom Jeong (영범정), an experienced celebrity manager in South Korea – who will present their views on the co-creation dynamics in the Hong Kong and South Korean entertainment industries. We hope to depict the unique characteristics, cooperation and conflicts found in the process of the co-creation of celebrities using professional quotes and real, vivid, Asian examples.

Development of the celebrity-making mechanism

Early development and background

Celebrities are represented by and understood through texts circulated across various media in which the celebrities' images/personas are created (Dyer, 2004; Evans, 2005). Prior studies have long debated the contradiction of the discourses that construct and define celebrity. Within these controversial debates on celebrity cultures, celebrity is frequently perceived as either deserved or totally arbitrary: the recognition of natural talent or just blind good luck, respectively (Turner, 2004). In the past, only the images of the great and the powerful were disseminated among the public, meaning ordinary people could rarely attain fame. As such, the celebrities' 'real self' was expected to remain behind their on-screen life (Evans, 2005). Media and entertainment companies would only manufacture prospects with talents, skills or achievements before grooming them for stardom (Turner, 2004). In the early years, individuals/talents design their own self-promotion strategies by taking advantage of links to existing institutions or personal networks (Rein, Kotler, & Stoller, 1997). Before nineteenth century, celebrity production and image management were still primitive and unsystematic (Gamson, 1992; van Krieken, 2012a).

The industrialized and mass production of stardom first started in the early nineteenth century. Due to the enormous commercial potential of celebrities, the manufacture of their mediated personas developed into a serious business, with media and entertainment businesses taking control from scratch of the entire process of producing, distributing and marketing their products (as in celebrity-making) to create a vertically integrated production line aided by various public relations (PR) techniques. Media and entertainment industries would discover fresh, 'unspoiled' prospects and then market them to become famous by making audiences believe in the 'desired images' the industries had created. Some of these celebrities did not possess any special abilities or achievements; rather than the individual competence or talents of the celebrities, 'market value' was deemed more important in this era. The commercial intent behind this was to take control of the individual's career, minimize costs and maximize returns to the original investor, regardless of the uniqueness of the individual (Turner, 2004).

Barnum and the early growth of public relations

The control over the manufacturing process continued to shift from celebrities to third parties throughout the nineteenth century (Brockington, 2009; Gamson, 1992; Turner, 2004). The growth of professional PR and film technology gave rise to the 'counsel on public relations' profession (Gamson, 1992). P. T. Barnum and W. H. Betty were two famous pioneers in the field. Barnum, an American showman–publicist, was among the first to create fame using a press agency (Gamson, 1992). Meanwhile, Betty, who was the manager and father of the child actor William Henry West Betty, established several PR techniques to attract public attention and interest for his son. Through these two individuals, the publicist and the publicity system became active parts of the discourse of fame at the time (Gamson, 1992). Publicists employ various means to stimulate public interest and establish an emotional connection with the audience, such as the artificial creation of events or the promotion of particular novelty features to marketing research, product design, packaging, pricing, promotion and distribution (van Krieken, 2012a). At times, the PR professional simply serves as a means of bringing the deserving self to the public; they do not produce or create celebrity themselves.

These PR techniques were further developed in the late nineteenth and early twentieth centuries, when celebrity production became an increasingly organized business (Gamson, 1992; van Krieken, 2012a). Gamson (1992) observed that the celebrity-making mechanism was first adapted by movie manufacturers who wanted to cater to the needs of the entertainment industry when established actors proved to be effective value-added tools for promoting their movies. During the early twentieth century, celebrities were treated as studio-owned commodities; thus, their images were kept under the tight control of the film studios (Gamson, 1992). Studios would design celebrity personas through continuous testing and moulding before being disseminated through various media. The studios' publicity departments often worked hard to match a celebrity's private life with their on-screen character; sometimes such images were even fabricated (Gamson, 1992). At times, audiences not only focused on the screen character a celebrity plays in the movie, but also shifted their attention to entertainers and their personal lives – this marked the changes in the celebrity-building environment in the middle of twentieth century. Celebrities were now at the service of the audience. Studios started to promote the 'ordinariness' of celebrities in order to create a sense of connectedness and intimacy between famous individuals and their admirers: 'The more active the audience, the more celebrity is suspect as an artificial image created and managed to pander to that audience' (Gamson, 1992, p. 11). In the mid-twentieth century, studios primarily produced false or fake public images in celebrity narratives, and celebrities began to partake in product endorsement and became 'merchandise'. It is this highly visible and inauthentic 'simulating glamour' of the celebrity lifestyle increasingly catalyses the pulling down of 'the expensive mask of glamour' (Gamson, 1992, p. 11).

Decentralization of the celebrity industry

Starting in the late twentieth century, celebrities were no longer owned by the film studios, but were instead contracted on a picture-by-picture basis. As a result, the earlier image management activities of the studios were dispersed into several independent sub-industries of celebrity-making (Gamson, 1992). The celebrity-making mechanism became increasingly systematic and sophisticated, and was subsequently named the 'celebrity industry' (Rein et al., 1997). According to Rein et al. (1997), the celebrity industry consists of a group of specialists who design, manufacture and disseminate images of unknown or well-known people, helping them achieve high visibility. During the process, the celebrity industry draws upon support from nine other sub-industries, including the entertainment industry, the representation industry, the publicity industry, the communication industry, the appearance industry, the coaching industry, the legal and business services industry, the endorsement industry and the celebrity service industry (Rein et al., 1997). The various specialists (e.g. publicity agents, venue consultants, business managers, market researchers, specialty coaches, etc.) combine their efforts to produce and promote celebrities (Rein et al., 1997). The decentralized celebrity industry allows celebrities to attain celebrity-hood from virtually any geographic base (Rein et al., 1997).

During this period, two key players were drawn into the narrative: publicity agents and managers. They are responsible for training and coaching the stars for media interviews and public appearances. The more popular the star, the more power the publicist wielded. With this move, control shifted more clearly to the managers, with a large proportion of celebrities' earnings going to the costs of management (van Krieken, 2012).

The rise of the 'ordinary' celebrity

Moving closer to today, with the development of the increasingly advanced technology, through which media have become more and more accessible, the notion of celebrity has expanded to include 'ordinary' citizens. As a result, celebrity is no longer associated exclusively with aristocratic social status or heroic deeds (Evans, 2005; Gamson, 1992). The 'democratic celebration of celebrity' allows everyone to become famous: 'the audience has been invited to take its power further with a new, cynical distance from the production of celebrity and celebrity images' (Gamson, 1992, p. 17). Nowadays, audiences are more interested in the fabrication process (i.e. how the celebrity is being constructed to entertain others), rather than simply viewing the individual behind the image. The explosion of reality TV, confessional talk formats, docu-soaps and reality-based game shows has significantly changed the understanding of celebrity culture. Almost everyone can become now 'famous', and many 'ordinary' celebrities have appeared in various reality shows, thus marking the era of the 'demotic turn' (Turner, 2006).

Based on the history of the development of the celebrity-manufacturing system outlined thus far, we can conclude a crucial insight: celebrities are co-created by a group of industry specialists/agents/professionals/units. Each of their roles is unique, but the relationship among them is complex, with several major parties constantly engaged in a tug of war over the control of the manufacturing process (Turner, 2004). In this chapter, we attempt to delineate the functions assumed by three significant players in the celebrity creation process: (1) the representatives of the celebrities; (2) the media; and (3) the celebrities themselves. Following this section, we will support our observation using face-to-face interviews conducted in Hong Kong with three renowned Hong Kong and South Korean celebrities. We hope to depict the unique characteristics, cooperation and conflicts among these three parties using professional quotes and real, vivid, local examples.

Co-creation of celebrities

Representatives of celebrities

Representatives of celebrities, including agents, managers, publicists and/or PR professionals, are probably the most noteworthy players in the celebrity manufacturing process.

The agent

Agents act as a bridge between the celebrities and those who employ them. The primary functions of agents are to find work for the celebrities, provide marketing advice and developmental coaching (Rein et al., 1997; Turner, 2004). With an eye toward seeking new talent and another looking over contractual details for their clients (celebrities/talents), the agent serves as the liaison for the budding partnership between celebrities and the various networks of directors or producers. This role has evolved analogously with the rapidly changing requirements of the entertainment industry. Nowadays, the agent – more commonly known as the 'new wave' agent or agent manager – is responsible for multifarious facets of their client's life, in which the job specifications are more versatile, stretching to cover those of a manager and publicist (Turner, Bonner, & Marshall, 2000, p. 774). The glitz and glamour of premieres and receptions require the attendance of the agent, but so do the tedious and mundane personal tasks that are called upon by his or her clients. Needless to say, agents are well versed not only with the ever-growing demands of the entertainment industry, but also with the intricate needs of the celebrities at a personal and career level, in which their expertise is commended with '10% of the talent's fees' (Turner et al., 2000). As a critical component in elevating the fame of their clients, an agent's work fully epitomizes the true essence of job hybridization (Turner et al., 2000, p. 774).

As the primordial and most important role of the agent, finding talent is imperative to any agent's success. To truly stand out in the entertainment industry, a successful agent must be able to develop a niche or specialization for recruiting specific types of celebrities, leveraging their network of connections to sign top-tier talents. According to Turner et al. (2000, p. 775), 'depending on the strength of their links with casting services and directors, a specific agent will begin to have a certain amount of influence in a certain sphere of production'. Consequently, dependent on the agent's specialty, they will be required to attend numerous commercial productions, movie launches and theatrical releases in order to seek new stars who already possess an array of polished skill sets. Discovering new, charismatic talents who can cause millions of fans to swoon over them is an extremely difficult task in today's entertainment industry. Along with media organizations, agents look for particular traits and characteristics embedded within these talents, which are perceived as alluring factors that can generate 'hits' (the ultimate economic goal for celebrities and their co-creators of fame) (Croteau & Hoynes, 2003, p. 153). However, the agent's extensive research and scouting of talents may not always materialize into a significant rise in the number of hits. Managers and agents look for aspirants with 'it' or 'star quality', repeatedly stating that finding them is 'a big guessing game' based on visceral responses (Gamson, 1994, p. 70).

Another prominent responsibility of an agent is to look through contracts for their clients to assess if a particular job opportunity is worthy or appealing. Although agents may not possess great legal knowledge, they must pick this skill up on the job in order to protect their clients' interests. Furthermore, in addition to his or her allocated tasks, the agent is also required to manage and control publicity, as they are often considered to be the first line of defence in maintaining their client's privacy (Turner et al., 2000). With numerous business ventures and sponsored media events that their clients must attend, an agent's versatility also comes into play to ensure that those celebrities reap the greatest benefit in terms of image-building and profitability.

The manager
In contrast to agents, who tend to have contact with a large number of celebrities-as-clients and are more closely related to their employers, managers often represent a smaller

number of aspirants, and play a relatively larger strategic role in developing their careers (Rein et al., 1997; Turner, 2004). Managers provide comprehensive management services for the celebrities and sometimes may even take care of their personal lives (Rein et al., 1997; Turner, 2004). When a celebrity rises to stardom and experiences a burgeoning increase in terms of media sponsorships and other enticing offers, they will look into employing a manager – an individual who engages in multifarious tasks devoted to image-building, marketing and bookkeeping for the respective celebrities (Turner et al., 2000). Managers are always fixated upon increasing the number of hits that a celebrity can produce, satisfying the logic of 'hits make money, stars make money, and hits have stars; therefore hits need stars' (Croteau & Hoynes, 2003, p. 155).

The celebrity market traditionally sees three types of managers: (1) the classic manager, being the ultimate task coordinator and decision-maker involved with financial and personal obligations; (2) the role-specific manager, who is associated with scheduling speaking engagements, as well as cultivating and developing the value of the celebrity's 'touch' to a contingent of corporate clients (Turner et al., 2000); and (3) the impresario manager, who oversees the clients' media presence (Turner et al., 2000), such as that of 'Michael Ovitz in the US, Max Clifford in the UK and Harry M. Miller in Australia' (Turner, 2007, p. 201). As a rule of thumb, most managers' salaries supersede that of the agents', garnering approximately 15 per cent of their client's income (Turner et al., 2000).

The publicist

Publicists (e.g. PR practitioners) are responsible for generating publicity and boosting a celebrity's visibility by controlling, coordinating and 'massaging' the images and information about them circulated to the public through various media (Rein et al., 1997; Turner, 2004). Publicists are not merely the purveyor of news; they are the very creators of news, usually favouring the creation of a persuasive image of the celebrities that the public can believe in (Bernays, 1952). They will coach celebrities in handling press interviews, and supervise the correct choice of make-up and clothing for public appearances (Gamson, 1992).

Embedded within a web of connections in the celebrity industry, publicists – as co-creators of celebrities' stardom – are tasked with formulating and monitoring a celebrity's relationship with the media. With the proliferation of numerous social media platforms for celebrities to build and enhance self-promotion opportunities, the true importance of publicists in shaping celebrities' perceived images cannot be understated. As Gamson (1994) reiterated, 'in many cases, developing successful and useful relationships with publicists means developing a reputation for presenting their clients in the desired light' (p. 90). Depending on the customary practices in varying celebrity industries around the globe, celebrities may employ a personal publicist who focuses solely on co-creating stardom and fame. However, certain industries, with their aims of relating to 'products first and personalities second' (Turner et al., 2000, p. 786), only provide an indirect platform for celebrities to achieve a long-lasting imprint on audiences' minds.

Generally, publicists are split into freelance and media corporation subcategories: the former possesses a vast network of industry connections developed from past roles within major media corporations, which help them capitalize on potential opportunities; the latter are a constituency of support staff members working under a singular media company, who facilitate the full circulation of celebrities' personalities (Turner et al., 2000). Ultimately, both types of workers orchestrate media coverage at events and film/television productions (Turner et al., 2000). The efforts put forth by publicists in their attendance at media events hopefully results in free advertising and editorial content, thereby contributing to the enhancement of the celebrity's stardom (Turner et al., 2000). Furthermore, publicists have to work hand in hand with producers to elevate the fame of their celebrities; this is also true of television programmes themselves, in which past hits should be a defining criterion for the selection of creating particular styles of programmes aligned with current market trends (Croteau & Hoynes, 2003).

Diverging from these long-established media platforms, celebrities – with varying degrees of help from their publicists – are now actively involved in personally managing their online/social media presence. A celebrity's authentic engagements through various social media channels elicit further insights for an enhanced understanding of one's portrayal of the self, assembling a greater 'commodity and package' that can consequently elevate their 'hit rate'. Through the emergence of these new media platforms, current digital trends have 'modified the sources of the self as we move from a representational culture epitomized by celebrity to a presentational culture where celebrities are being reworked and reformed in terms of their value and utility by audience and users' (Marshall, 2006a, p. 644).

With a renewed focus on cultivating and showcasing celebrities' personalities through various marketing and promotional campaigns (as an enticement to raise the popularity of their media corporation's television programmes), network publicists retroactively position celebrities as 'spokespersons in one form or another for some further commodity than themselves' (Turner et al., 2000, p. 797). Ultimately, network publicists are perceived to be 'by far the most powerful single factor in shaping the celebrity industry' (Turner et al., 2000, p. 793).

Media

The media play an essential role in the celebrity manufacturing process, with celebrities having always been heavily dependent on it to create and disseminate their images to the public (Braudy, 1997; Burke, 1992; Dyer, 2004; Evans, 2005). Celebrity coverage in the press first appeared in the late nineteenth century and has now become ubiquitous (Evans, 2005).

Gamson (1992) noted that, during the 1930s, the oligopolistic film industry in Hollywood was able to manipulate the news media and exercise tight control over the circulation of celebrities' images. In recent years, celebrities' representatives have become even more powerful and now have considerable influence over news production (Turner, 2004). Hollywood had already become the third largest news source in the United States by the 1930s (Evans, 2005), and today celebrity news continues to dominate the market to the point where it is commonly regarded as a major source of high sales and ratings (Johansson, 2006; Turner, 2004). In order to gain access to A-list celebrities, journalists may therefore need to intermittently sacrifice their right to free speech and cooperate with celebrities' publicists to publish pieces that help build a favourable image (Gamson, 1994; Turner, 2004).

The celebrity-making mechanism is undoubtedly not seamless, and some oppositional forces (such as tabloids and paparazzi) who do not work in the publicists' interests also exist inside the media industry (Turner, 2004). Johansson (2006) argued that the glamorous lives of celebrities highlight the symbolic boundaries between famous people and audiences; by exposing celebrities' misfortunes or corrupted lives, the paparazzi provide audiences with a temporary exercise of power and a chance to vent their dissatisfaction. For this reason, tabloids and paparazzi play an important role in satisfying the alternative desires of audiences to ridicule and mock celebrities by exposing the sleazy aspects of their lives (Turner, 2004).

To counteract the monopoly of Hollywood, some sections of the media have started to manufacture their own celebrities (Turner, 2004, 2006). An explosion of new media content has resulted in significant demands for ordinary people desiring 'celebrification' (Turner, 2006). Turner (2006) coined this phenomenon 'the demotic turn' – the proliferation of 'ordinary' celebrities through reality TV and do-it-yourself (DIY) celebrity websites, talk radio docusoaps, and the like. Couldry (2003) suggested that contestants participated in reality TV programmes not because they want their specific talents to be recognized, but because they want to last long enough in the programmes to become famous.

The media provide a platform for ordinary people to reach a range of audiences. Through repetitive and persistent exposure, the media construct, promote and distribute formations of 'star' identity (the personal, the ordinary and the everyday) and desire as a representation of various societies' core beliefs (Couldry, 2003; Turner, 2006). For instance, through reality TV programmes, ordinary people are given opportunities to compete for fame and popularity (Turner, 2004); yet these shows often openly encourage its participants to merge their personal everyday lives with the lives they have created publicly. Contestants on Hong Kong shows such as 超級巨聲/*The Voice* (Stephen Chan, 2009) and 盛女愛作戰/*Bride Wannabes* (Shum, 2012) are typical examples of this, with the winners of these two television shows often becoming popular afterwards. *The Voice*, a singing competition broadcast by TVB, first aired in 2009, before the rise of the international singing competition franchise, *The Voice of Holland* (although the format is slightly different from the Dutch version). In *The Voice*, aspiring singers are selected from auditions to become contestants in the show. After the competitions, some of the winners and other talented contestants in the show – such as Alfred Hui (許廷鏗), Mag Lam (林欣彤) and Jay Fung (馮允謙) – signed contracts with The Voice Entertainment Group Limited (星夢娛樂集團有限公司), which is a subsidiary company of TVB. Meanwhile, *Bride Wannabes* (2012), also produced by TVB, aims to transform a group of single, ordinary women into more attractive and popular versions of themselves. A group of five single women in their late twenties and thirties were recruited to partake in the programme. They went through a series of transformational processes, such as cosmetic surgery, dieting, hair styling, and make-up and fitness training with the help of a group of professional fashion and styling instructors, including life coaches, nutritionists, stylists, make-up artists and match-makers. After the series' broadcast, the instructors, including Winnie Leung (梁穎妍), Santino (郭政彤) and Mei Ling (吳美玲), became well-known individuals in Hong Kong. Although many contestants/participants received a great deal of media attention, the producers of the programmes only used these ordinary talents to boost ratings and as a selling point for the programmes' advertisers. The producers are not dedicated to developing these individuals (Turner, 2004). Media industries, as a 'mediating' apparatus, still retain control in the celebrity-creation system, and the talents are much dependent on the programmes (Turner, 2006):

> [T]he media industries have transformed and accelerated the star manufacturing system into a formulaic and mechanical process, utilizing the sudden fame radiated from the ordinary celebrities for viewership and advertising sales, but then quickly disposing them due to their short lifecycle as public figures.
>
> (Turner, 2010, p. 216)

In the mediatization process, formations of identity and desire are also invented, popularized and distributed in society, functioning 'like an ideological system but without an ideological project' (Turner, 2010, p. 218).

Celebrities

Dyer (2004) viewed celebrities as a combination of both their labour and the commodities that they produce. Celebrities are only one of the creators of these celebrity-commodities; they do not have complete control over the manufacturing process. Their degree of power varies greatly from case to case (Dyer, 2004). For instance, Marx (2012) observed that celebrities in Japan are under the tight control of their agencies and do not even have a say in the direction of their own careers. Moreover, celebrities are normally at the mercy of media organizations.

Set against this backdrop, along with the development of increasingly sophisticated technology, more and more aspirants are utilizing the media in their own interests to achieve fame on their own terms (Elberse, 2013a; Roberts, 2010; Turner, 2004). Elberse (2013a) observed that digital technology has greatly reduced the cost of selling, producing and reproducing entertainment products, thereby lowering the barriers to entry. Aspiring individuals can now produce and disseminate their creations at a lower price, and then sell their products directly to consumers without the mediation of representatives, producers or even retailers (Elberse, 2013a). For example, some young girls identified as 'cam-girls' are constructing and managing fame themselves through personal websites (Turner, 2004). In China, bloggers such as Furong Jiejie (芙蓉姐姐) are also making themselves into celebrities through the assistance of the Internet (Roberts, 2010); in Hong Kong, famous DIY celebrities include Winnie Leung (梁穎妍) (multimedia writer, instructor on the reality TV show *Bride Wannabes*, newspaper and magazine columnist), Queenie Chan (陳莉敏) (magazine columnist, owner of SO by Queenie Chan, instructor on the reality TV show 求愛大作戰/ *Bachelors at War* (Cheung, 2013), a male version of *Bride Wannabes*), Darren Cheng (nicknamed 熊仔頭) (online director, writer and actor) and Tina Leung (梁伊妮) (famous Hong Kong stylist and blogger). At first glance, the DIY celebrity is perceived as a means of personal or artistic expression, as well as a means of economic gain. It seems that individual celebrities are taking back control over the process of celebrity formation from the representatives and the media. However, Turner (2004) has asserted that, ultimately, these DIY celebrities will be incorporated by the industry. Indeed, Elberse (2013a) argued that a few aspirants have already achieved commercial success using digital technology; they eventually signed big contracts and were incorporated by established producers. In fact, established content producers are more financially and technologically equipped to utilize digital technologies in their interests. Judging from the fact that digital technology usually fosters concentration and a winner-takes-all dynamic (Elberse, 2013a), aspiring individuals only have a slim chance of achieving commercial success through the new media on their own.

In sum, the relationship among the representatives of the celebrities, the news media and the celebrities themselves is very complex. Sometimes the three parties are cooperative and dependent on each other, while at other times they are engaging in a tug of war.

In the following, three renowned artist managers from Hong Kong and South Korea will share their views on the co-creation dynamics in the Hong Kong, mainland China and South Korean entertainment industries, specifically using their own experiences with celebrities to project a realistic picture of the co-creation process of celebrities.

Artist managers interviews

Wallace Kwok (郭啓華)

Wallace Kwok (郭啓華) is a seasoned media personnel and celebrity manager in Hong Kong. He began his career as a DJ at Commercial Radio Hong Kong and, in 2000, became the manager of a renowned Hong Kong female singer, Sammi Cheng (鄭秀文), a role he continues to this day. He also works for East Asia Music (東亞唱片) as a consultant, managing the music business of affiliated singers and bands, including Denise Ho (何韻詩), Anthony Wong (黃耀明), Ellen Joyce Loo (盧凱彤), RubberBand and C Allstar, and is a founding member of independent production company People Mountain People Sea (人山人海). During the interview, Kwok narrated the story of the evolution of entertainment industries in Greater China, and expressed his views on creating/promoting celebrities in the region.

The Hong Kong entertainment industry: From dominance toward marginalization

During the 1980s, the film and music industries in Hong Kong dominated almost all Chinese communities in the world and made huge profits in overseas markets (J. M. Chan, Fung, & Ng, 2009; S. Chu, 2007). As Kwok described, 'this [was] the "golden age" for Hong Kong celebrities and the entertainment industry'. He recounted that it was a time when the industry was the supreme leader of the Chinese-language entertainment market. The

Figure 3: Wallace Kwok, the founding member of an independent production company People Mountain People Sea (人山人海).

Figure 4: Wallace Kwok, a seasoned media practitioner and celebrity manager in Hong Kong, is recounting the entertainment industry development in the interview.

Figure 5: Wallace Kwok and HOCC, a famous Hong Kong-based Cantopop singer/actress.

Figure 6: Wallace Kwok and Sammi Cheng, famous Cantopop female singer/actress in Hong Kong.

situation started to change when the mainland Chinese government launched a programme of economic reforms and the country began to open up to the outside world. Following this, private investment was encouraged in the previously state-funded sector. As a result, the commercial entertainment industry took shape and entered the international market (Montgomery, 2010; Semsel, Chen, & Xia, 1993; Y. Zhang, 2004). Mainland Chinese started to get involved in the entertainment business in China, yet Hong Kong still played an important role in facilitating the development of the mainland Chinese entertainment industry. Kwok illustrated his views with the example of film production: 'Mainland Chinese didn't know how to shoot a movie and had to rely on directors from Hong Kong to transfer the knowledge and technology back to the mainland'. In return, Hong Kong film production teams were given more opportunities to utilize the unexploited resources of the mainland, which motivated more and more people to 'flock back to the mainland to shoot movies'. Thus, co-production became increasingly common in the 2000s (J. M. Chan & Fung, 2010; Montgomery, 2010). The impact was not limited to the development of the movie industry, but also extended to music and concerts.

By the late 1990s, Hong Kong's entertainment industry had begun to decline, as evidenced by the diminishing record sales and box office of local film production (K. Chan et al., 2009; S. Chu, 2007; Y. Zhang, 2004). Kwok suggested one of the reasons behind their downfall was the marginalization of Hong Kong's entertainment products in mainland China.

Today's mainland Chinese entertainment industry has matured enough to develop entertainment products by itself. Kwok noticed that, when given more choices, mainland Chinese shifted their attention to other local productions; for instance, the previously popular co-production movies gave way to other mainland Chinese local productions, such as 中國合夥人/*American Dreams in China* (Peter Chan, 2013), 小時代/*Tiny Times* (Guo, 2013) and 致我們終將逝去的青春/*So Young* (Zhao, 2013), as well as popular reality TV shows such as 爸爸去哪兒/*Where Are We Going, Dad?* (Lyu, Zhang, & Li, 2013) and 最強大腦/*The Brain* (Endemol, 2014) (a Chinese version of the German show *Superhirn*). After this, Mandarin products began to take the place of Cantonese products from Hong Kong. Kwok believed the cultural differences between the mainland and Hong Kong was a major reason why mainland Chinese turned to local productions. He used TV dramas as an example to support his views:

> [The TV industry] needs to provide some TV dramas which can reflect the locals' thoughts and feelings […]. People living in Beijing will not find *Come Home Love* [愛回家 (Tsang, 2012)] appealing, and the drama will not evoke their emotional resonance. After all, entertainment is closely connected with culture.

As many localized large-scale entertainment companies were established on the mainland, and many previous collaborators with Hong Kong now became competitors, Kwok anticipated that the mainland Chinese entertainment industry would be able to catch up within ten years. By then, Hong Kong would be further marginalized in the nation:

> At present, whether you are talking about the TV or film or music industry, mainland China doesn't have enough talents, so they still need Hong Kong. But in less than ten years, they can rely on their own entirely […]. In the future, Hong Kong will be marginalized and changed.

For those local artists working exclusively in Hong Kong, Kwok commented that they were having a hard time because the city was too small to economically support them and the industry. As the home market of the Hong Kong entertainment industry was limited, the industry had to rely on exports for survival; therefore, the collapse of the traditional mainland Chinese market and other overseas markets inevitably led to the downfall of the industry (K. Chan et al., 2009). Kwok pointed out the difficulties facing local Hong Kong singers by comparing their situations to those of their mainland Chinese counterparts:

> In mainland China, the artists can travel from one province to another and go to different cities to perform, but Hong Kong is such a small place […]. For those who sing only Cantonese songs for a living in Hong Kong and do not venture into the international market, their lives will be very hard.

To make matters worse, the Hong Kong entertainment industry increasingly had to compete with strong foreign competitors, such as Hollywood movies and other entertainment products from South Korea and Japan (K. Chan et al., 2009). Hong Kong celebrities faced increasingly intense competition in this small city as foreign artists, especially South Korean singers, were now getting an increasingly bigger piece of the pie.

> The South Korean stars get all the product endorsement deals, and their concert tickets are so expensive that people don't have money left for other artists [...]. Take Pakho Chau [周柏豪] and G-Dragon[1] as an example. I like them both, but if they hold a concert at the same time, and I only have 1000 dollars, I'll probably go for the Korean star. The Hong Kong entertainment industry is now facing this kind of foreign competition.

In order to survive, Kwok believed Hong Kong celebrities had to venture outside Hong Kong. In fact, starting from the 1990s, record companies had already redirected their attention and resources to the vast, thriving mainland Chinese market. By this time, many leading Cantopop singers in Hong Kong were releasing more Mandarin pop songs than Cantopop ones (S. Chu, 2007). Kwok also noted that some local artists have started to shift their attention to the mainland Chinese market and might even ignore the local market as a result. He quoted the example of G.E.M. (鄧紫棋), a female Hong Kong singer, to illustrate:

> G.E.M. [鄧紫棋] got a chance to perform in *The Voice of China* [*中國好聲音* (Canxing Productions, 2012)][2] and attained national fame, and now she wouldn't be bothered with whether Commercial Radio Hong Kong agreed to broadcast her songs or not.

Co-creation of celebrities in Hong Kong and Greater China

As Rein et al. (1997) suggested, most celebrities attain high visibility because of a strategy marketing process supported by a celebrity industry. In the process of producing and promoting celebrities, the industry is supported by several other sub-industries, including the entertainment, representation, publicity and appearance industries. Specialists in these industries are responsible for designing, manufacturing, distributing and managing the images of (potential) celebrities (Rein et al., 1997). Given the unique nature and characteristics of the evolution of the entertainment industry in Hong Kong, three major parties have been involved in the co-creation of the celebrity process in Hong Kong.

Celebrity managers
The celebrity manager is one of the most important specialists in the celebrity industry. Kwok reiterated that there was no professional training for celebrity managers in Hong Kong until about 50 years ago: 'Most of the Canto-movie stars were assisted by their family members, and there were no professional celebrity managers'. The situation was similar

to Rein et al.'s (1997) observation that, in the initial stage of the evolution of the celebrity industry, the industry was less developed, and aspirants might have had to rely on support from family and friends.

As the celebrity industry developed and matured, aspirants were able to solicit help from specialists (Rein et al., 1997). According to Kwok, most of today's celebrity managers have had previous experience working in various sectors of the entertainment industry or media industry, such as television stations, broadcasting corporations and the film industry. These media workers have related experiences and have established relationships with some celebrities, leading to a greater possibility of the celebrities recruiting them to be their managers.

In the west, managers provide comprehensive management services for celebrities and are responsible for organizing practically the entirety of their clients' lives (Rein et al., 1997; Turner, 2004). Similarly, managers in Hong Kong play a strategic role in developing celebrities' careers. For example, celebrity managers arrange and select potential job offers for celebrities through their connections with other celebrities (i.e. songwriters, lyricists, film directors or clients), which provides the celebrities with opportunities to display their abilities. They arrange media interviews for the celebrities and coach them in handling interview questions. Managers might even need to manage the private lives of the celebrities (Rein et al., 1997); many of them even become close friends with the celebrities in reality. Kwok stressed that it is important for celebrity managers to take care of and respond to the psychological needs of celebrities. As he stated, 'sometimes you have to be a counsellor, talk to the artists, and understand their needs in various stages of their lives'.

Mani Fok (霍汶希), artist management director of the Emperor Entertainment Group (英皇娛樂集團 [EEG]) (one of the largest entertainment groups in Hong Kong, founded in 1986), is another famous celebrity manager in Hong Kong. Her artists including famed girl idol duo Twins, singer and actor Nicholas Tse (謝霆鋒) and singer and actress Joey Yung (容祖兒), among others. She is also very close with the company's artists. For instance, she has known Nicholas Tse for more than twenty years – experienced his trials, his relationships and break-ups, and his subsequent marriage and even kids. Her relationship with her artists goes far beyond just a working relationship.

Sometimes managers in Hong Kong are also responsible for managing a celebrity's public image, a role largely carried out by publicists in the west (Rein et al. 1997; Turner, 2004). Kwok explained that, in the past, some old-school celebrity managers might have tried to establish a good relationship with journalists or other media personnel to manipulate how the media portrayed and represented their artists. However, he observed that, in recent years, with an increased number of media channels to disseminate celebrity news/gossip, it became much harder to maintain a good, positive image of celebrities. This perspective echoes that of Gamson (1992), who observed that, in the first half of the twentieth century, it was not difficult for the entertainment industry in the United States to manage images and control information because of the industry's vertically integrated oligopolistic structure. Nowadays, traditional media can no longer monopolize the dissemination of information, as social media platforms play an increasingly important role in society. Kwok noted that it has become very difficult for an artist to disguise themselves as someone they are not, as there are too many channels to reach out to the audience, and thus a celebrity has to expose their true self. He explained that 'artist managers had to spend much time teaching [up-and-coming artists] how to manage their public image in social media'.

Record labels and entertainment corporations

In addition to celebrity managers, record labels and entertainment corporations play a significant role in creating and promoting celebrities in Hong Kong. In the past, celebrity managers and record labels were two separate entities that assisted the celebrities in different aspects. During the 1980s and 1990s, the sales of CDs were very high, and the high profits allowed the record companies to focus solely on music-related production and promotion, while leaving other roles to the celebrity managers. Kwok gave an example of Jacky Cheung (張學友), a famous Hong Kong singer-songwriter and actor who is also known as one of the 'Four Heavenly Kings' of Hong Kong, having sold more than 25 million records as of 2003:

> For years, Jacky Cheung had two managers, Willie Chan [陳自強] and Chan Suk-fan [陳淑芬]. Willie Chan helped Jacky Cheung negotiate film contracts, while Chan Suk-fan was his concert manager. Their job responsibilities were quite independent, and they both earned a lot in their own areas, and everyone was happy.

However, when CD sales started to slow, several local record companies gradually lost their influence. According to Kwok, a structural change occurred in the industry. He believed that the establishment of EEG during the period of dwindling CD sales was a watershed in the history of the Hong Kong entertainment industry. In the initial stage of its establishment, EEG focused on developing talents from a young age and ensured they had the full management rights of its artists. EEG has created many superstars in Hong Kong/Greater China, such as Joey Yung (容祖兒), Nicholas Tse (謝霆鋒) and Twins. Kwok explained that, during that time, it was very rare to have a company like EEG, a company which started from scratch and nurtured its own talents. He pointed out that EEG introduced a new style of management whereby the company had full control over and responsibility for every aspect of the artists' career. It recruited and trained the artists, and helped them produce CDs, organize concerts and even find acting roles in the movies the company made. EEG's management method was in stark contrast to other international record labels, such as Universal Music Hong Kong (Universal):

> Universal is not like that [...]. Universal did not have Eason Chan's [陳奕迅] management agreement – they have Kary Ng's [吳雨霏] and Mr.'s[3]; they have some artists' agreement, but inside the company, there are many others whose agreements they don't have. This kind of management style is inherited from the international companies. Especially for the more established singers, it is very difficult to get their management agreements.

Intriguingly, based on Kwok's observation, local labels in China relied on artists' personal appearances at public and private commercial events to make profits, which meant that, rather than focusing on producing albums, more emphasis has been placed on generating single hits that could lead to lucrative endorsement deals and live performance deals (Montgomery, 2010). It thus became important for the companies to obtain management rights over the artists in a time when CD sales in Hong Kong continued to dwindle.

The media and ordinary celebrities

In the first half of the twentieth century, the entertainment industry had almost full control over celebrities (who were then studio-owned commodities) and their public images (Gamson, 1992). Even now, publicity is powerful and manipulative. Turner (2004) observed that publicity is so powerful in the entertainment industry that it might 'compromise the independence of the news media and its capacity to simply tell the truth as it sees it' (p. 45). As the media continues to rely on publicists or managers to gain access to A-list celebrities in order to boost sales or ratings, publicity has been able to infiltrate into news production (Turner, 2004).

However, the system was not perfectly seamless, and the power of the publicists could be challenged by the tabloids, paparazzi and audience (Turner, 2004). The development of new media in the past few decades has broken down the tight control held by producers in the entertainment industry over the cultural products, and audiences are now able to influence the process of celebrity formation and rework the meanings of celebrity images according to their needs (Dyer, 2004; Marshall, 2006a; Roberts, 2010). For instance, Kwok noted that the emergence of the Internet in mainland China allowed what Turner (2004) called 'DIY celebrity' to construct fame for themselves. These celebrities (akin to Justin Bieber and Esmee Denters in the west) bypassed the institutional structure to communicate directly with potential fans, who launched them toward high visibility. According to Kwok, Internet singers had been attracting national attention for several years before pop music culture and a mature entertainment industry were developed in mainland China. They were producing and uploading simple, low-quality songs on the Internet, like '老鼠愛大米'/'Mouse Loves Rice' (2004), and those singers came into prominence because their songs were favoured and spread by numerous netizens.

Kwok recounted that Internet singers had been the centre of national attention for several years before they were gradually surpassed by locally nurtured singers who were elected on *Super Girl* (2005) and other similar nationwide reality TV singing contests. The competition *Super Girl* (2005), inspired by the UK show *Pop Idol* (Fuller, Lythgoe, Holloway, & Warwick, 2001–03), was open to any female contestant in China. In it, one contestant is eliminated each week based on the votes of the judges and the audiences. In the past, the mass media mainly played the role of mediator in the process of creating celebrities, serving as a link between celebrities and audiences; however, the media has recently begun to manufacture celebrities on its own through, for example, reality TV shows (Turner, 2004, 2006).

Kwok noted that reality TV singing contests are hugely popular in mainland China and Hong Kong, and these shows give audiences the power to crown someone a celebrity. He concluded that the mainland Chinese audience worshipped these contestants because the shows gave the audience a taste of democracy: 'In a society that does not have democracy and elections, […] every mainland Chinese now has an opportunity to vote'. Kwok remarked that, through these 'elections', mainland Chinese could select their own celebrities, and express their love and admiration for them. Kwok did express some doubts about the authenticity of these 'democratic elections'; however, he believed that 'at least what [the audience] feels is real'. In Hong Kong, besides *The Voice* (2009), there is a celebrity version named 星夢傳奇/*The Voice of the Stars* (Mak, 2013), which is also produced by TVB. The show aimed to give contestants (who were all TVB artists) the opportunity to display their singing talents and become singers. Many of the outstanding contestants went on to sign contracts with and become artists of The Voice Entertainment Group Limited.

Francis Cheng (鄭紹康)

Francis Cheng (鄭紹康) is the CEO of Occasions PR and Marketing Ltd. Established in 1987, Occasions is a leading PR and event organization company in Hong Kong that specializes in the luxury lifestyle market. Cheng also holds positions as a renowned columnist for multiple magazines in Hong Kong and China, as well as an artist manager for Hilary Tsui (徐濠縈).

Figure 7: Francis Cheng, the CEO of Occasions PR & Marketing Ltd.

Figure 8: Francis Cheng and Jude Law at the Dunhill party in Hong Kong, 2006.

Figure 9: Tang Wei, a famous international Chinese actress, and Francis Cheng at the Ten Best Dressed event in Hong Kong, 2009.

Figure 10: Francis's birthday in 2012 and his celebrity friends.

Types of celebrities in Hong Kong

Today, the word 'celebrity' is commonly used to refer to famous individuals (Giles, 2000; Marshall, 1997). In the nineteenth century, the term 'celebrity' represented 'a more fleeting, ephemeral connotation of fame' (Marshall, 1997, p. 5). It is no longer associated only with religion and inherited social position, nor does it still reflect heroic achievement (Evans, 2005).

Cheng pointed out that there are three main types of celebrities in Hong Kong. The first type is the 'famous celebrity' – those who are well-known and acclaimed in a particular area, such as sports, entertainment or charity. They are usually very talented and experts in the sector in which they specialize, such as designers, well-known artists or singers, or celebrity sports athletes. The second type is the 'topical celebrity', who are usually good in terms of a sound news value. They are often the talk of the town within a specific time span, such as people involved in a scandal or people who contributed to a good social cause in a community, such as lottery winners, mistresses of public figures and have-a-go heroes. (These people are usually covered in 'celetoids'.) They command media attention one day and are forgotten the next (Turner, 2004). The third type is the 'old money': this group of celebrities includes socialites or the 'who's who' of society. They have high social values

Figure 11: Zhang Ziyi, an international renowned Chinese actress, and Pansy Ho, the managing director of various companies including Shun Tak Holdings, and the Sociedade de Turismo e Diversoes de Macau, together with Francis Cheng at the Armani Dinner, 2013.

Figure 12: Karina Lau, a famous Hong Kong actress, and Francis Cheng at the Cancer Fund Ball, 2008.

because socialites usually have strong, extensive personal networks. They help create noise and attention from media, thereby creating good brand promotional events.

Dual role: Celebrity manager and PR professionals

Cheng is the manager of several artists, including fashionista Hilary Tsui (徐濠縈). At the same time, he is the chief executive officer of a PR and event organization company in Hong Kong. Being a PR specialist, he represents the interests of his clients and invites appropriate celebrities to participate in PR events. He admitted that sometimes the two roles might overlap and conflict with each other, although he did not specify how. However, he explained that: 'Both roles do not overlap much. I have been working in the PR industry for many years [and] there is a clearly marked price for everything, and I won't force [the celebrities I manage to do it cheap for me]'. Cheng reckoned that ultimately the effects of synergy arise and the celebrities he manages/represents would help his work as a PR specialist.

As a celebrity manager, Cheng realized that communication between managers and artists is one of the most important components in the celebrity-making process. He noted that the chemistry between the two parties determines the success of a celebrity. He explained:

> It's like seeking treatment from a doctor or seeking advice from a feng shui master. Not every doctor or every feng shui master is able to help you. You have to see whether the relationship between the artist and the manager is synergetic or not [...]. Sometimes it depends on fate.

Cheng thus believes that a particular formula for creating a star does not exist. Different management firms in Hong Kong have their own unique styles, and 'every manager and every management firm use a different formula to create celebrity'. For instance, he observed that some management companies only seek to make quick money and hence lack a long-term or detailed plan in star production. He described this kind of management style as an 'instant-noodles approach' (aka a 'fast-food approach'): 'They put forward three or five aspirants simultaneously, and publish their photo books [at the] Hong Kong Book Fair. After that, they keep the ones who successfully grab media attention and come to prominence, and abandon those who cannot'.

Cheng believed that looking for quick money and seeking instant popularity were distinctive features that set Hong Kong celebrity culture apart from its Hollywood counterpart. He commented that people in Hong Kong tend to overemphasize a quick return and fail to acquire a long-term perspective in creating celebrities: 'There are too many people seeking quick money in the entertainment industry [...]. They don't have a clear vision nor a long-term perspective, but only a short-term one'.

Cheng has adopted a different approach to respond to this unique and localized sociocultural environment. Although he rejected the existence of a particular formula for creating a celebrity in Hong Kong, he realized that continuous media exposure is the most essential foundation of an artist's fame, and the artists should receive regular exposure on various media platforms: 'I always aim for a "holistic package", which means, in addition to the digital – even digital media has various platforms, such as Facebook, Instagram, Weibo – you have to secure much media attention, like exposure in weeklies and monthlies'.

Moreover, Cheng believed that an artist should be able to continually generate and produce noise and exposure – such as publishing CDs or participating in film production – to prove that they are still active in the entertainment industry. Nowadays in China, producing albums or acting in films is no longer the most lucrative parts of a celebrity's job, and so celebrities and their representatives have to rely on endorsement and live performance deals to make profits (Montgomery, 2010). Therefore, Cheng reckoned that the continuously active exposure of an artist is an important indicator of a celebrity's value, with their constant exposure potentially bringing endorsement deals to the artist: 'Nowadays, even advertisements of instant noodles and intruder alarms are using celebrity endorsers, and these are all chances for celebrities to make money. So the celebrities need to capitalize on their ongoing careers in this way to generate profits'.

Dynamics between publicists/celebrity managers and the media in Hong Kong

Cheng observed that the media in Hong Kong sometimes cooperate with the representatives of celebrities to generate visibility for them by making up news. Cheng explained that 'love scandals are the most effective way to boost popularity [...]. Almost every scandal nowadays is fabricated'. However, Cheng believed that the fame of these types of celebrities is not sustainable because long-lasting fame ultimately depends on real talent: 'The singers have to know how to sing, and the actors/actresses have to know how to act; only then can they be long-lasting'.

Notwithstanding that media cooperation is imperative for the fame of a celebrity, the existence of tabloids and paparazzi, which are outside the realm of mainstream media, are deemed potential forces challenging the power of publicists/celebrity managers (Turner, 2004). For instance, Cheng recognized that tabloid stories in Hong Kong disrupted all the rules and guidelines of the entertainment industry. He was often shocked by some trivial media coverage on insignificant celebrities, which in turn suddenly and unexpectedly turned them into the talk of the town in one day. He concluded that the current entertainment industry in Hong Kong is disorderly and formless:

The only rule is no rules [...]. For example, photos [in the entertainment sections of newspapers and magazines] which should be made larger are downsized, and the unimportant photos are occupying a large amount of space. As a celebrity manager/

publicist, all I can do is expect the unexpected [...]. Of course I'll still be very guarded, but nowadays there are so many things you cannot control.

Having said that, Cheng believed that celebrities should establish a 'non-rivalry' if not friendly relationship with the paparazzi or even cooperate with them to make news. He recounted an occasion when he went shopping with local socialite Laurinda Ho (何超蓮), sister of Pansy Ho (何超瓊) founding partner and executive director of Occasions HK in Hong Kong. When Laurinda Ho discovered that they were being followed by the paparazzi, she took the initiative to approach the journalists directly and allowed them to take pictures of her. The act shocked Cheng, as Ho, even as a famed local socialite, refused to avoid paparazzi. Interestingly, when the paparazzi said they did not have enough pictures to cover a proper news story on Ho, she suggested that they travel to her next destination together, giving them permission to take more photos on the way. Cheng perceived her response and cooperation with the paparazzi as a new form of celebrity–media communication.

Yeong-Beom Jeong (영범정)

Yeong-Beom Jeong (영범정) is an experienced celebrity manager in South Korea. He has been working in the entertainment industry for the past twenty years, and has discovered and managed numerous renowned South Korean actors/actresses, such as Dong-gun Jang (張東健), Eun-ha Shim (沈銀河) and Won-bin (元斌). He founded Star J Entertainment and co-founded United Asia Management in 1996 and 2011, respectively. He is currently the CEO of the two entertainment companies.

Entertainment industry development and celebrity culture in South Korea

In order to delineate the major parties involved in the celebrity co-creation process in South Korea, we should first briefly mention the development of the entertainment industry and celebrity culture in the area.

The 1970s and 1980s: The entertainment industry as political propaganda

Similar to the situation in mainland China, decades of political upheaval have profoundly affected the development of the entertainment industry in South Korea. Under the rule of the military regime led by Park Chung-hee (朴正熙), South Korea underwent a process of rapid modernization and industrialization throughout the 1960s and 1970s (C. Kim, 2012). Although the government strongly promoted the development of the economy, freedom of expression was restrained and entertainment production was put under political control (C. Kim, 2012). For example, the Motion Picture Law was revised in 1979 to create the Korean Ethics Committee of Public Performance, which censored both political and sexual content;

the government also imposed stern control over the contents of TV dramas, and TV stations were required to produce more news and educational programmes (A. Chung, 2011). In the mid-1970s, the government even arrested a large number of professionals in the industry, including singers, composers and film directors (C. Kim, 2012).

This political censorship suppressed the creativity and imagination of many media workers, which profoundly affected the development of the entertainment industry. According to Jeong, during this time, the country was in a 'very bad situation'. He stated that 'the South Korean government had stern control over the contents of entertainment products circulating in the country, and everybody was controlled by the government'. He described the 1970s and 1980s as a 'very bad period' because these strict censorship laws limited the development of popular culture and the entertainment industry in the country. Jeong explained that 'the entertainment products are mainly used as political propaganda, I would say, for serving the government'.

The 'Great 90s'

South Korea entered the era of civilian governance in 1992, and the preliminary censorship of entertainment production was fully abolished in 1996 (C. Kim, 2012). President Kim Dae-jung (金大中), who called himself the 'President of Culture', fully supported the development of South Korean popular culture and adopted policies favourable to the development of the cultural industry. He established the Culture Industry Bureau and enacted the Motion Picture Promotion Law to encourage investment in the cultural industry (Yang, 2012). As a result, instead of political authority, the entertainment industry was operated entirely under the logic of capital and the markets (C. Kim, 2012). Popular culture exports became a new economic initiative and were utilized as a kind of soft power to elevate the status of South Korea in the world (Cai, 2008; A. Chung, 2011; The Korea Herald, 2008).

Jeong revealed that the 1990s was a golden period for the entertainment industry and has been generally referred to as the 'Great 90s'. He pointed out that, as the government relaxed its control over the media and entertainment production, Koreans had a very good time with some freedom given by the government, and this new-found freedom led to the revival of the entertainment industry. Indeed, Jeong described the 1990s as the true beginning of the development of the entertainment industry in South Korea, in which many talented artists emerged in the market. Jeong singles out singer Seo Taiji (徐太志) as the most significant example: 'Seo Taiji changed everything. He influenced everyone in Korea because all the lyrics he wrote were fresh and liberal back then'.

Moreover, the licensing of a new terrestrial broadcaster, Seoul Broadcasting System, in 1990 and the emergence of paid TV platforms in 1996 triggered a ratings battle in the TV industry, which in turn motivated producers to strive for higher-quality entertainment production (A. Chung, 2011). Jeong noted that more TV stations were established during the 1990s, including the country's third major station, several source stations and even some cable stations, and this intense competition vastly improved the quality of the entertainment products. In sum, Jeong commented that the 'Great 90s' provided a firm foundation for the vibrant entertainment industry in modern-day South Korea, with many of the era's emerging managers and artists eventually becoming heads of entertainment companies. These people – which includes Jeong himself – were strong leaders:

> We have profound experience […]. Like the SM entertainment [also named Star Museum] and the YG entertainment [also named Yang-Gun], I think [people who work in SM entertainment and the YG entertainment] all sort of have a kind of relationship or experience like me. I have a vision to tell: to produce actors and actresses. Maybe there are other singers and producers who have their own visions too […]. Many of them have great experiences in the entertainment industry.[4]

2000s to present: Venturing into global markets

The South Korean entertainment industry has developed rapidly in recent decades. From 1999 to 2003, the value of South Korea's entertainment industry experienced a fivefold increase, surging from US$8.5 billion to US$43.5 billion (A. Chung, 2011). At the same time, the industry is also exporting its products and spreading its influence extensively to Asia and beyond (A. Chung, 2011; Yang, 2012). The exports of South Korean entertainment products, which totalled merely US$1 million in 1997, reached US$29 million in 2002 (Park, 2004); between 2006 and 2010, the export of South Korean pop culture products continued to expand and grew by more than 30 per cent (Yang, 2012).

As such, Jeong strongly believed that venturing into global markets was the only way out for the South Korean entertainment industry. He explained that, because the country's domestic market was too small to support a vibrant and dynamic entertainment industry, the industry had to go global in order to survive. He compared the South Korean entertainment industry with that in Switzerland, pointing out that both countries are small: 'We do have many press [media outlets] that can sell our entertainment content […]. We have a very limited market. You have to expand. Expand for survival'.

Therefore, celebrity and entertainment production in South Korea increasingly emphasizes the importance of appealing to international audiences; for instance, the composition of idol groups (such as Big Bang, Super Junior, SHINee, Girls Generation, EXO, 2NE1, TVXO, Infinite) have become more multinational. Celebrities are required to learn foreign languages, and international composers have been invited to compose songs for the artists (C. Kim, 2012; Yang, 2012).

The emergence of video streaming websites and social networking during the 2000s further accelerated the spread of South Korean entertainment products throughout the world (A. Chung, 2011; Yang, 2012). Jeong observed that South Korea, which had 'one of the best Internet services in the field' (ITU-D, 2015), was able to utilize the Internet effectively, and how it played a significant role in circulating South Korean entertainment products in overseas markets: 'It is easy too. Our contents go overseas […] and people like it'.

Although the present entertainment industry only started to develop in the late 1980s, Jeong believes that the short historical development of this entertainment offered its own advantage for South Korea's entertainment industry. In Jeong's opinion, as South Korea did not have enough time to develop a unique entertainment culture, the country became more adaptable to changes, and could more easily cater to the tastes of overseas audiences. He contrasted the situation in South Korea with that in Japan:

> The Japanese are quite satisfied with their market. They do not go out that much. They are afraid to go out. They are too comfortable with their own entertainment, circumstances and culture. Sometimes it doesn't work [if you want to expand into] the international market. Japan is a very weird context, right? Compared to Japan, Korea does not have that much time to build up our own culture [to appeal] to the international market [...]. Somehow, through the Internet, we can extend to other markets. Easy. You know? What if we have more time to build up the history of our entertainment [system]? We might have the same situation [...] as what Japan is facing now. [They] look very weird to other countries.

According to Jeong, the South Korean entertainment industry has become a prominent leader and 'one of the cores' in Asia. In order to further increase its competitiveness, he stressed the importance of having a systematic industry structure. This means that the industry leverages not only good content, but also a proper legal system to monitor its development. It was also his wish that, in the future, the South Korean industry would be strong enough to influence other countries and be studied by them.

The future: An Asian entertainment empire

Yang (2012) argued that South Korean entertainment products have indigenized western popular culture by blending modern western cultures with traditional Asian ones, through which a hybrid culture is born. Although the South Korean film industry is lacking an indigenous cinematic tradition, it has created a distinctive national mode of expression and production. Jeong believed that:

> The entertainment system goes [along] with the people who live in the [same] area, right? Their own country, their own culture, they share together [...]. We have our own system. Korea, their own. Japanese, their own. China, their own. Even Hong Kong. So since the entertainment circumstances gets better, we have our own [unique characteristics].

Although Jeong reckoned that every Asian country has its 'own system' and its own unique style of management/production, he was optimistic about overcoming the cultural and language barriers to unite these Asian countries under an Asian entertainment empire, with the hopes of catching up with Hollywood.

Hollywood has the biggest entertainment market in the whole world because they use the same language – English, right? In Asia, we use different languages, but in the future the language barrier is gonna be demolished. They already demolished it, right? We share similar cultures [in] Asia [...]. We can catch up with Hollywood pretty soon.

In fact, co-financing among various Asian nations nowadays has become commonplace, and it is not rare for artists from different East Asian countries to be featured in the same television programmes or movies (Chua, 2004). Moreover, it has been proposed that the consumption of cross-cultural productions may ultimately lead to the emergence of an 'East Asian identity' (Chua, 2004). Therefore, the emergence of an Asian entertainment industry might not be entirely impossible.

Creation of celebrities in South Korea

Qualities of potential celebrities

Jeong was very much aware of audiences' expectations of celebrities in South Korea, pointing out that the audience demands that celebrities be well-behaved and adhere to 'a very high level of morality. [Celebrities] deserve to be respected'. In contrast to the situation in other countries, celebrities are respectable figures in South Korea; those who cannot live up to the high moral standards set by the public are immediately abandoned. Jeong explained that, as not many people are tall, handsome or beautiful, people in the entertainment industry who demonstrate strong passion will have a good chance of succeeding. A good example is PSY, a South Korean singer, songwriter, record producer and rapper whose single '강남스타일' 'Gangnam Style' (2012) became a worldwide hit.

Roles of celebrity managers/management firms in creating celebrities in South Korea

Most celebrities in South Korea are not discovered by chance; rather, they are systematically selected and have to undergo training organized by entertainment management firms over a long period of time (Yang, 2012). As a celebrity manager and the CEO of a celebrity management company, Jeong revealed that he played a significant role in selecting and arranging training for potential talents. When selecting potential talent, Jeong is clear in terms of what he is looking for and the qualities a potential celebrity should possess:

I don't find a new one I never knew [about]; I find somebody I have already known in my head. I planned [...]. I have a thousand people in my head. Thousands [of] actors and actresses in my head. [The] only thing I need is to find [the one who is suitable].

Most of the time, the qualities Jeong seeks are based on successful examples of celebrities in other countries:

I want to make a Korean Jackie Chan. I just imagine someone who looks like or possesses the charisma like Jackie Chan in Korea [...] and then I look for them. It's like I have somebody in my mind who looks like Leonardo DiCaprio and I can make this person a Korean Leonardo DiCaprio.

As such, Jeong has adopted a market fulfilment approach in the celebrity manufacturing process (Rein et al., 1997). According to Rein et al. (1997), there are three marketing styles for launching aspirants: (1) the pure selling approach; (2) the product improvement approach; and (3) the market fulfilment approach. In the pure selling approach, the agent sees the aspirant as a fixed product and attempts to sell directly to the best market that they can find. In the product improvement approach, the agent tries to improve the abilities of the aspirants in order to attract the market's interest (Rein et al., 1997). The market fulfilment approach, however, stands in stark contrast to the previous two styles: in this approach, the agent chooses to produce celebrities in response to the needs of the market. More specifically, an agent will look for the most promotable candidate among thousands of minimally qualified aspirants and systematically develop the chosen aspirant into a product that the market needs (Rein et al., 1997). In the case described by Jeong, he would develop the aspirant's character according to his idea of a designated celebrity and then arrange specific training for them.

Final insights

Andy Warhol (1968) famously said: 'In the future, everyone will be world-famous for fifteen minutes'. The historical evolution of the entertainment business clearly underlies the path to fame, even for ordinary people. Due to their different historical, political and sociocultural backgrounds, the celebrity co-creation system is undoubtedly very different in western and Asian societies. Moreover, given that the system of celebrity creation has only been in place since the birth of mass commercial culture, it has at times been less systematic in both regions. As stated by Gamson (1992), 'changes both in the concrete organization of publicity and in the technology and media through which recognition is disseminated have had a profound impact on the operation of celebrity' (p. 2). In this chapter, we described the major parties involved in the co-creation process in both western society and Asia, and explained the reasons why they were put in place at certain times. Even today, publicity is powerful and manipulative. Turner (2004) observed that publicity is so powerful in the entertainment industry that it might 'compromise the independence of the news media and its capacity to simply tell the truth as it sees it' (p. 45). As the media continues to rely on publicists or managers to gain access to A-list celebrities in order to boost its sales or ratings, publicity is able to infiltrate into news production (Turner, 2004). As such, it is obvious that there exists a tug of war in the relationships between the representatives of celebrities, publicists, the media, studio firms, entertainment corporations and celebrities themselves – sometimes they are in conflict, whereas at other times they are co-dependent and inseparable from each other.

According to the cultural discount thesis, the appeal of an entertainment product from a particular country/culture diminishes in other geographical regions because foreign consumers find it difficult to identify with the home nation's values, beliefs and styles (Hoskins & Mirus, 1988). It is undeniable that each market will have its own unique entertainment culture, yet a distinctive entertainment culture would also hinder the expansion of the entertainment industry into foreign markets. Hong Kong and South Korean domestic markets were too small to economically support the local entertainment industries and celebrities. As a result, the two regions needed to expand into neighbouring/foreign markets, meaning an exchange of efforts and cooperation is unavoidable.

Based on the celebrity interviews, we identified five major characteristics in the co-creation process of celebrities in Greater China and South Korea:

1. The political situation of a country has an immense impact on the development of the entertainment industry. Both mainland China and South Korea experienced decades of political upheaval; this led to the stagnation of their entertainment industries, which only started to develop once the political struggles within these nations ended.
2. The process of creating celebrities in Greater China involved multiple parties, including the celebrities themselves, managers, record labels/management companies and the media. None of them had complete control over the process.

   In South Korea, although different parties are involved, entertainment groups usually have a greater extent of control over the creation of a star thanks to an intensive training system and image management.
3. In Greater China, particularly in Hong Kong, celebrities normally possess some degree of charisma and talent. These gifted selves have usually been discovered by chance, and have come to prominence because of some special talent or some 'magical' innate quality. Although incompetent 'celebrities' have sometimes been thrust into the limelight as well, ultimately only the talented are able to survive.

   In South Korea, the barrier of entry for aspirants seemed much lower. Although there is a very rigorous process in selecting celebrities from among thousands of potential candidates, South Korean aspirants did not need to embody any inborn charisma or talent in order to become a star in the first place. Theoretically, anyone could become a celebrity. According to Jeong, people can be turned into a celebrity through intensive training and image management. In contrast to other East Asian countries, such as Hong Kong, celebrities in South Korea are seen as highly respectable figures in society and are expected to behave themselves.
4. As most of the surviving celebrities in Greater China are talented, skilled people, managers in Greater China have largely been portrayed as mere facilitators, whose major role is to amplify celebrities' inherent gifts by securing media exposure and negotiating work deals for them. In the process of launching an aspirant toward high visibility,

managers have not been the ultimate decision-makers, but may have worked together in partnership with celebrities. Both Cheng and Kwok shared how they showed respect for their artists and tried their best to accommodate their wishes, which sometimes clashed with the interests of the record labels/management firms.

In South Korea, the managers/management firms seemed to be in charge of the entire celebrity-making mechanism. The managers/management firms selected the potential celebrities before systematically developing and training them into profitable products. Celebrities seemed to be at the mercy of the managers/management firms, and those who failed to comply with the images designed by them would be abandoned immediately. Jeong explained that he would devote a lot of time to building and managing celebrities' images by 'recreating their biography' (i.e. teaching them what to reveal and what not to reveal about their personal history and private lives) while making sure they have the 'correct understandings' of their lives.

5. In Greater China and South Korea, although the qualities of the celebrities have occupied a central position, they have not been the only determinant of their success or failure: the media have also played an indispensable role in creating celebrities as well. The media have served as a bridge between celebrities and audiences while maintaining a complex relationship with managers/management firms. Sometimes the media have played a subsidiary role and cooperated with the representatives of the celebrities in order to make news more favourable for the celebrities.

In sum, the development and subsequent rise of the South Korean entertainment industry has frequently been discussed in relation to the concepts of globalization, regionalization and localization (cf. Chua, 2004; D. Kim et al., 2009; Park, 2004; Yang, 2012). Furthermore, the Korean wave of international cultural expansion has been perceived as a case of alternative globalization (Yang, 2012), and a counter-example of both media imperialism and west-centred globalization (D. Kim et al., 2009). Asia has been a potential cultural force against the west, and Jeong believes that it would be beneficial to unite Asian countries in order to develop an Asian entertainment industry that could catch up with Hollywood.

However, the formation of such a union has not been without difficulties, as various Asian countries speak different languages, and have their own distinctive entertainment cultures and system of production/management. Nevertheless, the cooperation among various Asian countries in the area of entertainment productions has become increasingly common. For example, the film 赤壁/*Red Cliff* (Woo, 2008) gathered a production team consisting of members from Hong Kong, mainland China, Taiwan and Japan; and the film 赤道/*Helios* (Luk & Leung, 2015) featured actors and actresses from Hong Kong, Taiwan and South Korea. The reality television show 奔跑吧兄弟/*Hurry Up, Brother* (Im, 2014) (a Chinese variety show based on a South Korean variety show called *Running Man*) was also a collaborative effort, with a mix of celebrities from China, Hong Kong and South Korea. It is clear that entertainment corporations in both mainland China and South Korea are very competitive for the leadership in Asia. Although it is hard to foresee which market will become the leader of 'Asian Hollywood' in the near future, both language and cultural barriers need to be overcome for an Asian entertainment empire to become as influential as Hollywood.

Notes

1 The stage name of Kwon Ji-yong (權志龍), a South Korean rapper and a key member of the famous Korean band Big Bang.
2 A reality television singing competition in mainland China.
3 A local band.
4 Both SM and YG are South Korean entertainment companies that operate as a record label, talent agency, music production company, event management and concert production company.

Chapter 3

Celebrities in marketing communications

Introduction

Celebrities sell. Celebrity marketing is a tactic aligning a product or service with celebrities, used by many marketers who believe that celebrities have the ability to influence brand affinity and consumer purchase intent.

As consumers, our minds are often bombarded with information and stimulation; as such, using celebrities in marketing communication initiatives might be a way to stand out from the crowd. Indeed, a company can generate huge profits and an immediate change in its public perception by matching the right celebrity with the right product/service and placing them in the right marketing communications campaign. However, if it is done poorly, it can ruin a brand as well as the celebrity him/herself overnight.

This chapter attempts to delineate the background of using celebrities in marketing communications, identifying both the benefits and risks of this strategy. In addition, this chapter unveils some possible factors that affect the effectiveness of the use of celebrities in marketing communications. For this chapter, we interviewed two marketing communication professionals in Hong Kong to share their experiences in using celebrities in their marketing communications campaigns, namely Anson Shum, marketing and communication director (Greater China) of the Bluebell Group, and June Lee, communication director (Asia-Pacific) of a well-known western cosmetics brand.

Use of celebrities in marketing communications

Marketing communications are used to facilitate the exchange process and the development of relationships between consumers and firms by creating awareness and interest in the companies' products/services (Belch & Belch, 2014). In order to communicate a consistent image of a firm to its target consumers, integrated marketing communications are applied which coordinate a wide range of marketing and promotional tools, including advertising, direct marketing, interactive/Internet marketing, sales promotion, publicity/PR and personal selling (Belch & Belch, 2014). In general, celebrities are perceived to be influential tools in marketing communications (cf. Elberse, 2013a; O'Mahony & Meenaghan, 1997; Pringle, 2004). One common usage of celebrity in marketing communications is celebrity endorsement, which is a form of brand or advertising campaign involving a relationship between a firm and a celebrity that occurs for an agreed-upon duration of time. In such an arrangement, the fame of the celebrity is used to help promote a product or service. In common practices, celebrities are usually paid for the effort and time they devote to a given form of marketing communications. Celebrities can be involved in the communication processes in various ways, for example, as a customer, being sponsored, or even as an owner. It is suggested that the higher the degree of intimacy between the celebrity and the brand/product, the more effective the communication (Pringle, 2004).

Celebrities have great commercial potential (Turner, 2004), and their use in marketing communication strategies is widespread around the world (Chan, Ng, & Luk, 2013; Hung, Chan, & Tse, 2011). It is estimated that in the United States, one in four advertisements use celebrities (Stephens & Rice, 1998). Similarly, in Asia, celebrities are commonly used, especially in advertisements. Advertising endorsement has been used for one basic purpose: to gain a communicative advantage over competitors. The endorser is used to arouse attention, create awareness and needs, generate favourable attitudes, and facilitate purchase intention and action (Percy & Rossiter, 1997). Belch and Belch (2004) explained that endorsement is used on the presumption that an endorser has the 'stopping power' to attract attention in a cluttered media environment, and that the positive aspects of the endorser's fame and image will transfer to responses such as brand attitude and purchase intention.

In Hong Kong, celebrity is the most frequently used strategy in television commercials for youth products, and the second most frequently used strategy in youth magazine advertisements (Chan, 2010). According to K. Chan (2010), media celebrities are employed in 40% of television commercials in Hong Kong. Nearly half of public service announcements (PSAs) in Hong Kong feature celebrities. In China, celebrity endorsement is used in 30% of all Chinese TV advertisements (Jiang, Huang, Wu, Choy, & Lin, 2015). Sun (2010) suggested that a slight imbalance exists between the number of male and female celebrities featured in Chinese TV adverts (54.7% and 45.3%, respectively). The three major categories with celebrity endorsements in China include medicines and nutritional supplements, apparel and accessories, and food and snacks. In South Korea, more than half (57%) of television advertisements are celebrity endorsed (Choi, Lee, & Kim, 2005). Similarly to China, South Korea also uses more male celebrities than female celebrities (56% and 44%, respectively). In addition, 75% of Korean commercials feature celebrities in their thirties or younger. Celebrities are normally perceived as more credible than non-celebrities in South Korea (Ferle & Choi, 2005). In both China and South Korea, only a few exceptions feature foreign celebrities; thus, local relevancy appears to be a crucial factor that contributes to the effectiveness of a brand campaign.

Benefits and risks of using celebrities in marketing communications

In general, celebrities are perceived as an influential tool in market communications (cf. Agrawal & Kamakura, 1995; O'Mahony & Meenaghan, 1997; Pringle, 2004). This is because of their ability to attract customers' attention, which might then lead to an increase in product/brand awareness (Chan et al., 2013; O'Mahony & Meenaghan, 1997; Pringle, 2004). Van Krieken (2012b) explained that celebrities are able to attract attention because they embody attention capital – an abstract and self-reproducing form of capital. Attention capital allows celebrities to act as attention traps, drawing attention not only to themselves, but also to the networks surrounding them (van Krieken, 2012b). Therefore, celebrities are effective in diverting media and public attention to the products/brands they are affiliated with to achieve a 'cut-through' effect, helping advertisements stand out from the surrounding clutter (Erdogan, 1999).

Moreover, the use of celebrities can boost the sales of a product and improve a firm's stock market valuation (Agrawal & Kamakura, 1995; Chung, Derdenger, & Srinivasan, 2013; Elberse & Verleun, 2012; Mathur, Mathur, & Rangan, 1997), and its use in marketing communications can lead to greater purchase confidence and intentions (Atkin & Block, 1983; Chan et al., 2013; Petty, Cacioppo, & Schuman, 1983). More importantly, celebrity endorsements are a business-stealing strategy, as the increase in market value for a firm brought about by celebrity endorsements may lead to a decrease in the market value of competing firms (Garthwaite, 2014; Knittel & Stango, 2011; Mathur et al., 1997). In other words, celebrity endorsements are able to increase sales in both an absolute sense and relative to competing brands (Elberse & Verleun, 2012), giving firms a market edge over their competitors.

In addition to benefiting firms, celebrity endorsements garner free publicity for the celebrity spokespersons and help enhance their popularity (Cashmore, 2014; Pringle, 2004). Conversely, the product image may transfer back to the endorser image, while perceived attitudes toward the brand may also be transferred back to the celebrity endorser. Thus, although a positive product image may benefit the endorser, a negative product image may damage the endorser's image, affecting its credibility and reputation (Charbonneau & Garland, 2010; Doss, 2011).

Notwithstanding that the use of celebrity offers many positive, constructive influences on brand image, there are some inherent risks of using celebrities in marketing communications. For instance, the celebrity spokesperson may overshadow the brand/product, causing consumers and the media to focus solely on the celebrity endorsers, and neglect the brand being promoted in the process (Cashmore, 2014; Erdogan, 1999). In addition, celebrities are still humans: they display variability and inconsistency, and might unexpectedly change their behaviour, views and perceived personality (Pringle, 2004; Rein et al., 1997). If a celebrity spokesperson suddenly changes their image – or worse, becomes embroiled in a controversy or scandal – they might negatively affect the firm's reputation as a result, potentially even initiating a decrease in the firm's market value (Knittel & Stango, 2011; Pringle, 2004). Therefore, using celebrities in marketing communications does not necessarily guarantee success.

In fact, some scholars have already cast doubt on the effectiveness of using celebrities in marketing communications, especially in the area of influencing consumers' purchase intention (Agrawal & Kamakura, 1995; Ibrahim, 2010; O'Mahony & Meenaghan, 1997;

Ohanian, 1991). Previous academic research has presented mixed results related to celebrities' influence on consumers' purchase intention, and it has been suggested that celebrity has an insignificant impact on consumers' buying behaviour (Erdogan, 1999; Ibrahim, 2010; O'Mahony & Meenaghan, 1997; Ohanian, 1991; Temptalia, 2011). Among the criticisms regarding the disadvantages of using celebrity in marketing communications, overexposure and/or multiple endorsements was the most prevalent. A celebrity endorsing multiple products/brands is a common practice in Hong Kong. For instance, famous Hong Kong actor Moses Chan (陳豪) endorses telecoms, food and beverages, housewares and a financial institution. Famed female singer Joey Yung (容祖兒) endorses electrical appliances, skin care products, and food and beverages. Previous studies have suggested that consumers give less credibility to a celebrity who endorses many products, and may lead to a weakening of the brand association (cf. Hsu & McDonald, 2002). Market practitioners should carefully consider the use of celebrity in integrated campaign planning, and strive for a balance between the frequency of celebrity exposure and the effectiveness of campaign outcomes. New and upcoming talents (e.g. bloggers, independent singers, sport stars and former news reporters) are potential options, as are mainstream celebrities such as renowned singers and actors/actresses.

Factors affecting the effectiveness of the use of celebrities in marketing communications

Celebrity is not a panacea; nevertheless, some factors might enhance the effectiveness of their use in marketing communications. To begin with, the credibility of a celebrity may affect the advertisement's effectiveness (Cashmore, 2014; Lafferty, Goldsmith, & Newell, 2002; Ohanian, 1991). According to the source credibility model, the expertise and trustworthiness of a source may affect message effectiveness (Hovland, Janis, & Kelley, 1953). Expertise – also known as 'competence', 'expertness', 'authoritativeness' and 'qualification' (O'Keefe, 1990) – is commonly represented along scales such as trained–untrained and qualified–unqualified. Trustworthiness – also known as 'character', 'safety' or 'personal integrity' (O'Keefe, 1990) – refers to the listener's degree of confidence in the speaker and message, as well as their level of acceptance towards it. In other words, it is the listener's trust in a speaker. Numerous studies have supported the notion that trustworthiness affects attitude change: it is the extent to which the source is perceived to know the 'correct' position on the issue, and the extent to which they will be motivated to communicate that position (Petty, Ostrom, & Brock, 1981). Therefore, a celebrity perceived to be trustworthy and knowledgeable about a product category is more effective in spreading the advertising message (Lafferty et al., 2002; Ohanian, 1991).

Source attractiveness is another theoretical framework for explaining endorser effects in advertising. The components of source attractiveness include likability, familiarity and similarity: the more attractive a source, the more effective the communication (Hovland et al.,

1953; Kelman, 1961; McGuire, 1985). Similarly, a more attractive celebrity spokesperson is more effective in communicating brand messages and consumers will be more likely to endorse the attitudes that these spokespersons endorse (Chan et al., 2013; Erdogan, 1999; Gilovich, Keltner, & Nisbett, 2010).

However, credibility and attractiveness alone are not enough. In order to enhance the effectiveness of advertising, the image of a celebrity spokesperson should be congruent with that of the product/brand: the higher the degree of perceived fit between the brand image and the celebrity image, the more effective the communication (Chan et al., 2013; Erdogan, 1999; Kahle & Homer, 1985; O'Mahony & Meenaghan, 1997). Moreover, the nationality of the endorsers should also match the image of the products/brands. For example, in the context of China, foreign celebrities are perceived to be a more effective messenger in promoting products with foreign symbols, but they are deemed less trustworthy and knowledgeable than Chinese celebrities when promoting products with Chinese symbols (Sun, 2010; Zhang & Zhang, 2010).

The methods for using celebrities in marketing communications and consumers' involvement level might also affect the advertising effectiveness. The effect of synergy between a firm and a celebrity endorser does not arise automatically. Simply juxtaposing a celebrity with a product/brand is not enough; the celebrity spokesperson needs to be integrated with the brand and the message for it to be effective (Pringle, 2004). According to the elaboration likelihood model (ELM; Petty et al., 1983), consumers will vary in the degree to which they are likely to engage in the elaboration of information relevant to the persuasive issue. 'Elaboration' here refers to (roughly) engaging in issue-relevant thinking (O'Keefe, 1990). The degree of elaboration forms a continuum, from extremely high to extremely low or no elaboration. The ELM suggests that persuasion can take place at any point along this continuum; it distinguishes the extent of high and low elaboration according to two routes of persuasion: central and peripheral. The central route represents the persuasion processes involved when elaboration likelihood is relatively high. People involved in the central route may extensively examine information contained in the message, and closely scrutinize the message/argument and other issue-relevant material. The peripheral route represents the persuasion processes involved when elaboration likelihood is relatively low. People involved in the peripheral route may employ a simple decision rule to evaluate the advocated position. For instance, people might be guided by whether they like the communicator or whether the communicator is attractive. The use of a celebrity is most effective when consumers are more concentrated in peripheral elaboration.

In sum, using celebrities in marketing communications benefits both the firms/brands and the celebrities involved. In order to enhance the effectiveness of using celebrities in marketing communications, one should consider the factors that might affect their use in marketing communications, including the degree of image congruence, budget and the geographical locations/target audience of the marketing campaigns. Marketers should make sure to choose an affordable celebrity who can appeal to the target audience, and whose image is consistent with the brand/product image. For this chapter, we interviewed two marketing communication professionals in Hong Kong, namely Anson Shum, marketing and communication director (Greater China) of the Bluebell Group, and June Lee, communication director (Asia-Pacific) of a well-known western cosmetics brand. They will share their real-life experiences in working with celebrities for their brands and companies, and their concerns surrounding working with celebrities in this digital age.

Marketing communication professionals' interviews

Anson Shum

Shum is the marketing and communication director (Greater China) of the Bluebell Group. Affiliated brands of the group include Moschino, Carven and Ladurée. Before working for the Bluebell Group, Shum was the head of PR and marketing at Jimmy Choo Asia and Hugo Boss Asia. Shum is a skilled professional in fashion and marketing communications.

What is celebrity?

In marketing communications, celebrities are usually characterized by their high presence and familiarity among the public, who serve as objects of respect because of their 'outstanding skill in their chosen field of endeavor' (Pringle, 2004, p. xxiv). They are effective at arousing attention, creating awareness, generating favourable attitudes, and facilitating purchase intention and action (Rossiter & Smidts, 2012). As a professional marketing communication practitioner, Shum also believes that celebrities are effective at leveraging their fame to draw attention. However, there is no absolute definition for the term 'celebrity'. Shum describes celebrities as 'influencers' who have contributed to or received recognition in their own sectors: 'If you are the head or founder of an advertising agency, you are a celebrity. A celebrity model is also a celebrity, meaning anyone can be a celebrity in many different sectors in a society'.

Does celebrity work in marketing communications?

Shum acknowledged that the use of celebrities is a common practice for many brand campaigns in Hong Kong. As mentioned above, the effectiveness of using celebrities in marketing communications can be explained by the concept of source attractiveness. The components of source attractiveness include likability, familiarity and similarity, and it has been suggested that the more attractive a source, the more effective the message (Kelman, 1961; McGuire, 1985). Therefore, it is suggested that celebrities – as a source with which the public is familiar and whom consumers know – are effective endorsers of a brand (Chan et al., 2013). Echoing previous studies, Shum also reckoned that an attractive source with whom a public is familiar can enhance awareness and purchase intention toward a brand. He shared one of his experiences on a successful marketing campaign for a brand called Ladurée (a world-famous macaron shop), in which he employed different famous celebrities

Figure 13: Anson Shum, marketing and communication director (greater China) of the Bluebell Group, is sharing his views about the use of celebrity in Greater China.

Figure 14: Anson Shum, skilled professional in fashion and marketing communications.

Figure 15: Anson Shum is interviewing ShuQi, the international Chinese movie actress, at the Jimmy Choo event.

on various social media for product promotion. In 2012, Ladurée opened its first retail store in Hong Kong. In order to promote its grand opening in the city, Shum decided to send free samples of the company's macarons to 'influencers' in various sectors, such as stars, writers, DJs and athletes, and invited them to upload a Weibo post about the products. The viral campaign was a huge success, with more than 600 people lined up outside the retail store on the day of its grand opening.

According to Shum, a famous celebrity is useful for generating a positive influence on brand promotion. A celebrity's frequent media exposure might increase consumers' perceived familiarity with that person despite the fact that they might not personally know each other. The perceived familiarity may then lead to an increase in consumers' emotional attachment with the celebrity and their perceived trustworthiness. Therefore, when compared to a complete stranger, celebrities stand a better chance of attracting consumers' attention and arousing their interests in the advertised products. According to the source attractiveness model, people tend to believe someone who is attractive and with whom they are familiar (McGuire, 1985). Shum illustrated his views using an imaginary situation:

> Imagine you were on the street and someone handed out a flyer to you. If you did not know that person, […] you could just easily ignore him/her without a second thought. But if he/she was your relative and told you there was a sale nearby, you would probably listen to him/her, thinking that someone you knew would not lie to you, and you might thus go to the sale. No matter whether you bought something or not, at least you were motivated to go to the sale.

In addition to benefiting the brands, the use of celebrities in marketing communications might also enhance the reputation and popularity of the celebrities involved (Cashmore, 2014; Pringle, 2004). Ideally, a brand and a celebrity help each other to grow together, which means that the celebrity might help attract attention to the brand, while the brand might also bring publicity to the celebrity (Pringle, 2004). Similarly, Shum also regarded the use of celebrities in marketing communications as an act of reciprocity, and he explained this win–win situation through his experience working with the Taiwanese artist Godfrey Gao (高以翔). Shum recalled an experience while working as the head of PR and marketing at Hugo Boss Asia. He invited Gao – a then unremarkable Taiwanese actor – to work as a presentation model at a PR event. He subsequently invited Gao to his PR events from time to time, and even brought him to Europe to participate in a fashion show, where Gao made his first international appearance.

Shum noticed that the fashion show served as a turning point in Gao's career, as Gao was then invited to participate in Louis Vuitton's global marketing campaign after the show. Similar to Cashmore's (2014) observation of the existence of a feedback loop between a brand and a celebrity, in which credibility might transfer from one medium to another and then back again, Shum also noted that, while a brand might enhance the credibility and popularity of a celebrity, the celebrity – once they become a superstar – might benefit the

Figure 16: A thank you note by Godfrey Gao, Chinese model and artist, to Anson Shum.

brand through their association with it. Therefore, Shum was willing to nurture a long-term relationship with celebrities, in which the brand and the celebrity could grow together and benefit one another. He explained: 'If I can help someone and make him/her more popular among the public, why not? Maybe he/she will then come to my PR events more often, and I think it's a very good relationship'.

Although celebrities might bring benefits to the firms, there are also some potential risks when using celebrities in marketing communications. Pringle (2004) explained that some people inherently hate celebrities and that their negative feelings might affect the effectiveness of the communications. Shum also noted the potential risk in using celebrities after communicating with staff in retail stores. He realized that celebrities might negatively affect sales: 'Some customers might be unwilling to purchase certain items just because those items were worn by some particular celebrities'.

In order to reduce the risk, Shum rarely chose a controversial celebrity, as he shared Cashmore's (2014) and Erdogan's (1999) concerns that the presence of a celebrity might overshadow the brand. He believed that a controversial celebrity might bring extra media publicity, yet consumers might ultimately focus their attention on the celebrity instead of the brand being promoted. He gave Sire Ma (馬賽), who was involved in a sex scandal in 2014, as an example to explain his views: 'If I invited her to come to the event, [...] her presence might attract many paparazzi, but would the attention be diverted to the brand or focused only on her? That's why I rarely invite controversial celebrities'.

In addition, Shum perceived the decreasing impact of stars as another potential risk in using celebrities in marketing communications. Continuity and consistency are important determinants for achieving success when using celebrities in marketing communications (Pringle, 2004). However, celebrities are characterized by their short life cycle of fame (Elberse, 2013a), meaning firms might not be able to use a particular celebrity continually, as they might fade out of the limelight after a couple of years. Shum believed that a successful marketing campaign relies on long-term planning. However, he noted that the life cycle of celebrities today has become shorter and shorter, and there is rarely a representative superstar. Thus, the brands cannot rely on one particular celebrity for marketing communications, meaning brands have a limited number of superstars from which to choose from for long-term promotions. Shum commented that these situations are not good for long-term business planning and might negatively affect the effectiveness of using celebrities in marketing communications.

Furthermore, according to Shum, the value of a celebrity is limited. Although the use of a celebrity might temporarily attract attention or increase media exposure, it might not help increase sales significantly or benefit the brand in the long run. He noted that, although fans still worship celebrities, they are now more selective in purchasing what the stars choose or endorse: 'It's not like if a star eats a mooncake, then his/her fans follow and buy those mooncakes'. Such an observation resonated with previous academic research, where mixed results were found in terms of celebrities' influence on consumers' purchase intention (Erdogan, 1999). Whereas some acknowledged that the use of celebrities in marketing communications has led to greater purchase confidence and intentions (cf. Atkin & Block, 1983; K. Chan et al., 2013; Petty et al., 1983), some have concluded that celebrity has an insignificant impact on consumers' buying behaviour (cf. Ibrahim, 2010; O'Mahony & Meenaghan, 1997; Ohanian, 1991). In sum, using celebrities in marketing communications did not necessarily guarantee success compared with many other factors affecting its effectiveness.

Factors affecting the use of celebrity in Greater China

Image congruence

It is generally believed that the celebrity image and the brand/product image should be congruent for effective marketing communications (cf. Erdogan, 1999; Kahle & Homer, 1985; Kamins, 1990). Shum also noted the importance of image congruence. Every brand has its own unique DNA and an established brand identity, and the image of the celebrity has to match up with that: 'It is not necessary to look for the top celebrities for every brand; the choice of celebrities depends more on the nature of the brand and the brand DNA'.

Shum explained this concept using the example of the French brand Carven, which is an affiliated brand of the Bluebell Group. In Shum's words, Carven is an affordable designer label, and the brand's style is pure and fresh. Because of its brand nature, instead of hiring established superstars, the brand prefers up-and-coming artists: 'Carven adopts a different approach from that of Louis Vuitton [LV]. Usually LV looks for the top celebrities, like Li Bing Bing [李冰冰], but Carven prefers relatively new faces, like Bai Baihe [白百何] or Janice Man [文詠珊]'. Although neither Bai nor Man are A-list celebrities, their images are coherent with Carven's brand image. Therefore, Shum reiterated that top celebrities are not always the right choice.

Budget

Pringle (2004) stated that one of the guiding principles in the use of celebrities in marketing communications is finance, and marketers have to be aware of the amount of money the firm can afford before choosing a celebrity. Shum also listed the budget as a determinant of his choice of celebrity in marketing communications. He acknowledged that his collaboration with celebrities is intrinsically a business. Unlike situations in the past, when celebrities were more loyal to a specific brand and people could easily identify who endorsed which brand, Shum needs to negotiate with the celebrities for a mutually agreeable price/package every time:

> It was relatively easy to associate a certain brand with a particular star, like associating Audrey Hepburn with Givenchy. Nowadays, stars are not loyal [to a specific brand]. Most of the time, they look for monetary rewards, and fewer and fewer celebrities are willing to come to and support an event without being paid just because they truly like the brand.

In light of this trend, Shum emphasized that it is wrong to think that a larger budget guarantees a more successful marketing campaign. He personally expressed that 'it is the most challenging and most fun to achieve a good advertising effect with a limited budget'. He presented Ladurée's viral campaign (mentioned above as an example) and conveyed that the campaign was launched with almost no budget. In return, the celebrities' online posts brought great media exposure and attracted much attention to the brand, and they were '100 times more effective than putting an advertisement in traditional media'. Therefore, the budget is a significant factor affecting the use of celebrities, but it is not the most important one.

Regional preferences

Pringle (2004) suggested that celebrities used in marketing communications should be chosen to appeal to a very specific target audience. According to the source attractiveness model (McGuire, 1985), a source known and liked by the consumers is a more effective messenger than an unfamiliar source or somebody disliked by consumers (Kelman, 1961;

McGuire, 1985). However, an attractive source might not be equally liked by or familiar among consumers in various geographical regions. As Shum noted:

> [E]very region has its particular preference for celebrities. For example, mainland Chinese is not very interested in and is not emotionally attached to Hollywood stars; Taiwanese are not interested in celebrities who are only popular in mainland China; Hong Kong people tend to choose local stars or foreign celebrities, and sometimes they might choose not to favour the mainland Chinese ones.

Therefore, Shum confessed that it is quite difficult to decide on a celebrity who could appeal to consumers in every region of Greater China (including Hong Kong, Taiwan and mainland China). In his opinion, Angelababy (楊穎), a famous Chinese model/actress in Greater China, is a relatively popular choice for regional marketing campaigns.

> Angelababy is quite well known and isn't negatively perceived by consumers in Taiwan, Hong Kong or mainland China […]. Also, because she happens to be dating a mainland Chinese actor, and she started her career in Hong Kong, Hong Kong people feel a special attachment to her, and if Hong Kongers like a particular artist, usually the Taiwanese will not have a negative impression of him/her.

Shum recalled that, in the past, Hong Kong celebrities could serve as representatives of the Greater Chinese region because they were very popular in the region, as well as among the Chinese diaspora. Moreover, Hong Kong has historically been the only gateway to China. According to Shum, before China's economic reforms, Hong Kong had great advantages over other Chinese cities that were not open to foreign investment: 'Most people would first think of Hong Kong when they talked about China'. As foreign countries could not reach other Chinese cities like Shanghai and Beijing directly, they chose to come to Hong Kong. Shum pointed out that this was also the reason why 'many international stars would come to Hong Kong to make an international appearance […]. They could not go to Shanghai or Beijing, so they chose Hong Kong'. However, after China opened up, foreign corporations could reach other Chinese cities directly. Thus, Hong Kong lost its significance and was no longer the sole representative of the country.

Due to the changes in the economic and social environment, Shum noticed the decreasing significance of Hong Kong celebrities and its entertainment products in Greater China. In the last two decades, Chinese cities have developed their own local productions and nurtured their own local celebrities. Moreover, with increasingly advanced technology, mainland Chinese consumers have been able to directly access a greater variety of foreign programmes. Therefore, they no longer need to rely solely on Hong Kong for entertainment products or have to 'watch TV programmes produced in Hong Kong, or pay attention to the Hong Kong celebrities'. In the face of these changes, Shum remarked, more and more celebrities returned to mainland China to develop their careers. He believed that integrating into the mainland Chinese market was the way out, and in the future, 'the differences between Hong Kong celebrities and mainland Chinese celebrities will disappear, and they will be identified as Chinese celebrities only'.

Because of the decreasing significance of previously representative Hong Kong superstars, it has become increasingly difficult for marketers to come up with celebrities who can appeal to every region in Greater China. Shum revealed that, given the difficulty in locating one ideally suited candidate, sometimes more than one celebrity might be chosen for regional events so as to cater to the tastes of consumers in different cities.

June Lee

June Lee is the communication director (Asia-Pacific) of a well-known western cosmetics brand. Before working for the cosmetic company, she worked as the e-commerce sales director, global marketing director, and regional PR and AD manager for various European brands.

Economic value of using celebrities in brand strategy

Brand names are used to communicate the attributes and meanings of the products, and, if put to good use, are able to bring substantial financial value for the companies (Arvidsson, 2006; Belch & Belch, 2014; Vaid, 2003). In order to maximize sales volume and maintain a competitive advantage over others, companies develop various branding strategies to create and maintain brand equity[1] (Belch & Belch, 2014). Celebrities are generally believed to be an effective tool in branding (cf. Elberse, 2013a; Pringle, 2004). These popular figures in society are able to grab public attention and generate interest in

Figure 17: June Lee is sharing her views about the use of celebrities in brand strategy.

Figure 18: June Lee, the communication director (Asia-Pacific) of a worldwide leading professional makeup company in Hong Kong.

the brand, thereby increasing or maintaining the brand's competitiveness in the market (Elberse, 2013a; Pringle, 2004). Moreover, celebrities can be used as a 'brand cue' (i.e. by closely associating familiar faces with a brand), and can help in generating recognition and communication (Pringle, 2004).

During the interview, Lee delineated the benefits of using celebrities in branding. She noted that, in Asia, the term 'celebrities' is generally used to refer to well-known people in the entertainment business, such as actresses/actors, TV stars and models. She explained that celebrities are characterized by their 'charm' and the ability to attract people:

> No matter if you knew this person before or not, [...] the moment you are facing this person, you suddenly become a big fan of this person even though you never really listened to his [or her] song or never watched his [or her] movie before.

According to Lee, celebrities' ability to attract people is a huge benefit for brands, as they can instantly draw public attention to the brand with which they are associated. She further illustrated her point with her experience working with the famous American singer Lily (pseudonym). In 2014, Lily was invited to be the spokesperson of a new cosmetic brand campaign and attended an event in a cosmetic retail store in Hong Kong. Lee was surprised by the instant attention Lily brought to the brand when she noticed that '[Lily] was posting three photos through her Instagram, I think immediately we won a million likes or followers'. The products Lily endorsed sold out and Lee was told by the staff in the retail store that 'in the store where [Lily] did her autographs, [...] there were people just coming and taking photographs in front of these light boxes'.

In fact, celebrities are not only effective in drawing public attention to the brands. McCracken (1989) observed that celebrities are exemplary and inspirational figures to the public, and their cultural meanings can be transferred to the brand/product for consumers' appropriation. Similarly, Lee stated that celebrities in Asia serve as public role models whom people look up to in terms of appearance and lifestyle, and people love to fantasize about the celebrities' glamorous existence. She was aware that these positive and glamorous images of celebrities could be transferred to the brand through mere association. She demonstrated her views with an imaginary situation: '[If] we saw that somebody living cool was carrying the Starbucks tumbler and walking around with it, suddenly [the brand] would become a symbol of the coolness, right?'

In order to quantify the economic benefits brought about by celebrities, researchers have adopted methods such as the event study methodology (Agrawal & Kamakura, 1995; Ding, Molchanov, & Stork, 2011) and the intervention model (Elberse & Verleun, 2012). The former is used to measure the magnitude of the effect of an announcement of a celebrity endorsement contract on stock return, while the latter is employed to evaluate the impact of celebrity endorsements on sales.

Lee does not use either of these methods to assess the economic value of celebrities. She revealed that professional agents were hired to quantify the economic effect of using celebrities in branding in order to justify the budget spent on a campaign. When evaluating the economic effect, instead of stock return (Agrawal & Kamakura, 1995; Ding et al., 2011) and sales (Elberse & Verleun, 2012), the amount of coverage of the events, the number of Facebook likes, etc. were calculated. Lee admitted that they did not have a precise formula for assessing the effect; however, a benchmark was set for evaluation.

> If we spend, I don't know, US$100K, what makes us feel it is worthy? We don't have that mathematics yet, but what we can do at best is grading all the accumulative data and then believing that this is something that definitely contributed to the brand, our news and then the buzz around it.

Although celebrities might tend to bring a positive economic impact, celebrity endorsement fees have continued to rise and might lead to decreasing returns (Agrawal & Kamakura, 1995; Ding et al., 2011). Lee expressed similar concern about the large sum of money paid to celebrities. She noted that, although celebrities could make noise and attract publicity for the brands, the celebrities' services were 'getting a little bit overpriced':

> For the big brands, like a fashion brand, when they do the party, the money that they're paying for [the celebrities] to just be there for, let's say, 30 minutes, it's really become a little bit crazy. We are now really thinking, like logically, what kind of value they actually return to the client side.

However, the persistent use of celebrities suggests that it is a profitable and worthwhile advertising strategy (Agrawal & Kamakura, 1995). Lee also noted that, due to the intense competition among brands, a lot of clients were willing to pay the high price, especially in the present digital age, when the attention brought by celebrities always has a chance of being amplified in social media rather than being just a one-time headline in the newspapers.

Factors affecting the choice of celebrities in brand strategy

Image congruence
Rein et al. (1997) identified 'cultural trends' as one of the factors affecting the choice of celebrity endorsers. In the past, typically 'nice' and conventional celebrities were preferred, yet nowadays more and more unconventional or even controversial celebrities are hired to accommodate the increasingly diversified markets (Rein et al., 1997).

Lee was also aware of a gradual change in the choice of celebrities in the fashion and cosmetics sectors. Pringle (2004) noted that the use of celebrities was well established in the cosmetics and fashion industries, and the choice of celebrities was one of the determining factors for the success of its brands. Therefore, fashion and cosmetics brands were careful when choosing celebrity spokespeople. Similarly, Lee observed that, around five years ago, big fashion brand names such as Prada, Louis Vuitton and Chanel were very picky and strict when choosing celebrities for their brands, selecting only the *crème de la crème* of celebrities.

In those days, according to Lee, a celebrity spokesperson was chosen chiefly based on the principle of image congruence (cf. Erdogan, 1999; Kahle & Homer, 1985; Kamins, 1990), which means the image of the chosen celebrity and the brand image should be congruent to achieving a more effective communication effect. Lee explained that the chosen celebrities were usually elegant and glamorous, and their image was a perfect fit for the brands: 'At that time, we were very strict. Our own stance [is] whether this person is really fit for the images that our brands are, you know, speaking to the general public'. In contrast, Lee noted that elegant and glamorous celebrities are no longer as trendy nowadays:

> Even though it's still, like, you know, a US$10,000 Agnès b. bag that you want to be seen [with]; like some young kids with cool stuff – I don't know, like a pair of jeans – carrying the Agnès b. bag. We are living in an era that consider, like, something cool.

Attention capital

According to Lee, brands now value the attention capital (van Krieken, 2012b) of celebrities more and are relatively less picky in selecting a spokesperson. In her experience, a celebrity who is currently in vogue would usually be chosen as they could instantly bring public and media attention to the brands. She further shared her recent experiences working with Lily. She confessed that she was not very familiar with the American singer before inviting her to be the spokesperson, and thus 'didn't really feel what kind of impact she has on the young people'. To her surprise, the campaign proved to be a huge success and Lily's online posts about her brand were 'liked' by more than 1.3 million netizens:

> I think the impact is sometimes really beyond what you experience, because maybe I never really lived in that generation, so I didn't expect that the impact would be […] huge at the instant level. So yeah, it was a big awakening for me.

Product category

A product category can serve as an important factor affecting the choice/use of celebrities in branding. As Kamins (1990) argued, a physically attractive celebrity might be an effective endorser for an attractiveness-related product category, but it might have an insignificant effect on a product category unrelated to appearances. Therefore, because of the varied nature of products, celebrities who are effective spokespeople in product category X might not achieve the same results in product category Y.

Alternatively, instead of the choice of celebrities, Lee reiterated that brands of different product categories might adopt separate merchandising strategies because consumer target groups might approach the products in different ways. She observed that consumers cared more about the style of a fashion brand. Instead of insisting on buying the same products featured in advertisements, consumers were willing to purchase other similar items as long as they were of the same style:

> It isn't necessarily the exact white skirt that [a celebrity] was wearing […]. The thought of setting the images that this brand is leading the style is not like this brand selling the one particular bag [or] particular outfit. I mean, of course, people are talking about it, but it's not really related to a certain product.

As Lee mentioned, the main focus of branding in fashion is brand style; therefore, fashion brands usually do not focus on a particular product in promotions and can select a celebrity endorser from a relatively wider range of candidates. She offered Prada as an example and explained the process of constructing the brand's history:

> We wouldn't really mention, like, this is the dress that Charlize Theron was wearing at the Oscars in the year 2000. We wouldn't do that. We kind of have a collection of those, you know, of this big collage, a collage of the images where Nicole Kidman, Charlize Theron and Uma Thurman were all wearing Prada dresses to the party.

However, Lee noted that, when buying cosmetic products, consumers usually look for one particular product or colour, and do not settle for another one. She gave an example of buying a lipstick to explain her point:

> Pink lipsticks – how many shades can you think of? But the customers want that particular pink lipstick. That's what I think is also pretty amazing. They don't [go with a similar] one, which maybe even suits [their] skin colour better […]. But somehow they still want that [particular] one, so the stress is bigger to us actually.

Lee revealed that cosmetics brands usually hire a particular celebrity to promote and be associated with a distinctive product. For instance, Lee recently invited Susan (pseudonym), a popular New Zealand singer, to promote a dark purple lipstick – a colour closely connected with the singer:

> We had just one lipstick colour for her because that's kind of her signature, which is a very dark purple kind of colour. So when we are approaching the celebrity, depending on the industry you are in, I think it's very, very different. So we became very specific about it.

Final insights

Using celebrities in marketing communication is not something new. Celebrity endorsement dates as far back as the 1760s, when Josiah Wedgwood, the founder of the Wedgwood brand of pottery and chinaware, used royal endorsements and various marketing devices to create an aura around the company name that gave the brand a value far beyond the attributes of the product itself (Almquist & Roberts, 2000). As we all now live in a celebrity-fixated world, celebrity endorsement has become a common marketing communication strategy for advertisers, marketers and PR professionals (Turtle, 2013). If executed correctly and effectively, matching up the equity of a celebrity's image with a brand will create a win–win situation (Keller, 2008): the celebrity enjoys the positive impact on their fame and gains publicity (Cashmore, 2014), while the company experiences a boost in product sales (Chung et al., 2013), and product or brand awareness (Chan et al., 2013).

However, as shared by the two renowned marketing communication specialists, celebrity endorsement seems to be undergoing a transformation. The following list details a few challenges faced by both interviewees, as well as their concerns in using celebrities in today's marketing communication in Asia.

1. Having a celebrity endorse multiple products or brands has become a conventional practice in the current complex marketing environment. For example, the international actress Carina Lau (劉嘉玲) has had endorsement contracts with Bulgari, Longines and SK-II, to name just a few. Shum mentioned during the interview that using a celebrity familiar to the public can enhance awareness or even purchase intention, yet overuse or overexposure of a celebrity might generate the opposite result. As delineated in the chapter's introduction, many scholars perceive multiple endorsements to be a disadvantage for a company or a brand (cf. Ilicic & Webster, 2011). In the 1980s, Mowen and Brown (1981) employed attribution theory (Kelley, 1967) to study multiple product endorsements. Their findings showed that, when a celebrity endorses only one product, those advertisements are perceived more favourably and as being more interesting (Mowen & Brown, 1981). Tripp, Jensen and Carlson (1994), on the other hand, utilized the source credibility model to investigate the impact of multiple product endorsements, finding that a celebrity is perceived as more trustworthy and more of an expert when only endorsing one brand. In addition, trustworthiness, expertise and the liking of a celebrity significantly decrease when the celebrity endorses multiple products. More recently, Hsu and McDonald (2002) found that consumers give less credibility to a celebrity endorsing various products, which weaken consumers' process of brand association. Hence, the implication here is that advertisers, marketers and PR professionals should carefully consider using the same celebrity for multiple products or brands. In the long run, multiple endorsements might erode a celebrity's credibility and image, while also making it impossible to evoke the expected response from the

target audience. Using different yet less exposed celebrities might be an option for continuously employing an already popular celebrity.

2. The relationship between the celebrity and the company or brand is relatively weak nowadays for various reasons, which might include the greater number of endorsement opportunities from which celebrities can choose. They might prefer not being tied up by a long-term endorsement contract so as to allow them to look for more monetary rewards. Second, as Shum discovered, today's celebrities have less influential power in marketing communication. Companies or brands might find it difficult to employ a particular celebrity continually, as today's celebrities are characterized by their short life cycle of fame (Elberse, 2013a; Pringle, 2004). Third, according to Shum, the value of a celebrity is limited. Using celebrities might temporarily enhance the products' or brands' visibility, but it does not guarantee an increase in sales (Ibrahim, 2010) or the brand's value in the long run. Therefore, in response, today's companies are willing to sign multiple celebrities to maximize the impact in the market and promote their products or brands. However, this leads to another challenge for advertisers, marketers and PR professionals.

3. Celebrity endorsement is hitting an all-time high, with big companies and brands being willing to pay big to take multiple celebrities on board. For example, SK-II signed Tang Wei (湯唯), Ni Ni (倪妮), Ayase Haruka (綾瀬遥), Momoi Kaori (桃井薫) and Godfrey Gao (高以翔) to promote its brand, using celebrities with different nationalities to appeal to different regions in Asia. According to Lee, celebrities can charge extremely high fees nowadays. As there are more endorsement opportunities and stiff competition among brands, companies – especially the big ones – are willing to invest in celebrity endorsement, thereby inflating the costs. At the same time, including celebrities with more endorsements would put them in higher demand and allow them to charge a higher fee than celebrities with fewer endorsements. During the interview, Lee noted that although celebrities could draw attention and publicity for the brands, their services are 'getting a little bit overpriced'. If celebrity endorsement fees continue to rise, this might lead to decreasing returns for companies (Ding et al., 2011). As Shum expressed, it is critical to negotiate with the chosen celebrities carefully to find a mutually agreeable price and package each time. As suggested by Pringle (2004), finances are one of the guiding principles in the use of celebrities in marketing communications, and marketers need to be aware of the amount of money the company can afford before approaching a celebrity. After all, celebrities can make a product or brand, but they can also break the bank of a company by flushing away millions of dollars.

Given the aforementioned concerns, the process of celebrity endorsement has become more complicated and challenging. Change in practice is inevitable. In this digital age, advertisers, marketers and PR professionals have started transforming their traditional model for applying celebrity endorsement. One of the major shifts is that companies and brands are able to market themselves across online and offline platforms (Salup, 2014).

Marketing has become much more transparent and more prevalent today thanks to the Internet and social media. As Lee noted, many companies are still willing to pay the high price for celebrity endorsements because, given that they face intense competition among brands in the present digital age, the endorsing celebrity can help amplify the impact via their social media platforms and create a bigger noise. Similarly, together with creativity, Shum expressed that the Internet and social media help a lot in the practice of celebrity endorsement nowadays. As he stated, while adhering to a limited budget, celebrities' online posts about a product or a brand can almost guarantee bringing high visibility and exposure to the market. With the ability to disseminate messages instantly and widely, incorporating celebrity endorsements in social media is a wise tactic today.

In addition, in order to strengthen the relationship between celebrities and brands, companies are now turning to partnerships with celebrities rather than having a one-and-done deal. For example, Popchips, a brand of processed potato and corn products in the United States, invited Katy Perry to create her own flavour of popcorn and become one of the company's investors. Lady Gaga was also invited to be a creative director and inventor for Polaroid. In Hong Kong, Maggie Cheung (張曼玉) was once the brand image creative director of Izzue (a fashion brand), and Michelle Reis (李嘉欣) and Jennifer Tse (謝婷婷) were invited to collaborate with Venilla Suite (a local shoe chain store) to design a collection of shoes:

> [The partnership] does not limit the celebrity's endorsement to what is contracted in an agreement, but provides the celebrity with the freedom and hopefully the desire to get behind a brand [and company] and fervently promote it to his or her fan base, ultimately the brand's target consumer.
>
> (Turtle, 2013, n.p.)

After all, matching up a celebrity with a brand or a company is just as tricky as a marriage. It takes time to understand one another and compromise to meet one another's needs. If the 'marriage' of a celebrity and a brand has a sustainable commitment between them and can stand the test of time, they can both live happily ever after.

Note

1 Brand equity refers to 'an intangible asset of added value or goodwill that results from the favorable image, impressions of differentiation, and/or the strength of consumer attachment to a company name, brand name, or trademark' (Belch & Belch, 2014, p. 59).

Chapter 4

Celebrity in media

Introduction

As Heidi Klum says on *Project Runway* (2004), a reality series where aspiring designers compete for a chance to break into the industry, 'As you know in fashion, one day you're in, and the next day you're out!' Indeed, this saying applies not only to fashion, but to the entertainment business as well. The rise and fall of a celebrity can be quite unpredictable and sometimes uncontrollable.

All modern media have become flooded with celebrity (Pringle, 2004). Celebrity is an important part of the mass media; some people might even say that media builds celebrities. The public would not be exposed to celebrities without the media as the media shows celebrities via television, newspapers, magazines, movies, different forms of advertising channels, etc. to reach the audience. Celebrities and the mass media have a complicated, entangled relationship: celebrities gain fame and publicity from the media, while the media earn massive public attention and profit by dishing out celebrity hype. Thus, one might see a mutually beneficial relationship between them. However, such a tension-filled relationship cannot always be tamed. For example, some celebrities find the close supervision coming from the media distasteful; similarly, the media dislike some celebrities' arrogance. Hence, a kind of indivisible and hostile tension gradually and accumulatively develops between them, which may possibly develop into a destructive relationship. Indeed, the relationship between celebrities and the media are interdependent yet asymmetrical. To media, the celebrities they use to create substantial commercial return is always changeable, while celebrities only have the mass media as a society-wide system to help accomplish their self-propaganda (Gamson, 1992). It comes as no surprise that partial celebrities realize that the media can build them up as well as, in the future, tear them down.

This section starts with an overview of the prevalence of celebrity in media to serve as the backbone of this chapter. This chapter examines the love–hate relationship between celebrities and the mass media. It also reviews how celebrities lived before and after the birth of the Internet and social media, as we believe that the emergence of these tools have triggered ripples in celebrity culture. We interviewed three renowned media practitioners in Hong Kong to discuss the relationship between celebrity and media in the entertainment industry in Asia, particularly in Hong Kong and South Korea. Interviewees include Francis Mak (麥潤壽), a well-known radio host in Hong Kong; Patrick Suen (宣柏健), a seasoned columnist and film critic in Hong Kong who is keen on Asian films and Korean pop culture; and Kam Kwok-leung (甘國亮), an experienced practitioner in the Hong Kong entertainment industry. We hope that their insights will shed some light on explaining the inextricable relationship between celebrities and media, both traditional and social.

The prevalence of celebrity in the media

The mainstream print media has been dominated by market-driven journalism, which appeals to the public through sensationalism and showbiz news (Chan, Ma, & So, 1997). Indeed, in the face of increasingly intense competition, media industries – not just print media – have moved toward an entertainment-driven economy, and are often using the spectacle of celebrities to maximize profits and expand their audience base (Galbraith & Karlin, 2012). Galbraith and Karlin (2012) adopted the word 'spectacle' to specifically point out that celebrities are now becoming the focus of media attention simply because they are the focus of media attention, and that bringing about a media spectacle is 'a self-generating system of media promotion' (p. 13). In a similar vein, Driessens (2012) used the concept of 'democratization' to denote the changing nature of celebrity. Increasingly, individuals are not achieving the status of celebrity because of exceptional innate qualities or outstanding achievement (Gamson, 1992; Marshall, 1997); instead, being the centre of media attention and being famous are already enough (Driessens, 2012). In other words, fame is no longer achieved, but attributed and driven by the media (Cashmore, 2006). Therefore, the extent of influence and the capacity of media corporations may greatly affect the visibility, and thus popularity, of a celebrity. For example, transnational media corporations based in the United States are 'at the top of the world media hierarchy', and dominate the finances, production, distribution, exhibition and marketing of entertainment contents around the world (Mirrlees, 2013, p. 241). As a result, involved celebrities can achieve global visibility and popularity more easily than celebrities participating only in local television programmes.

All of these observations point to a tight relationship between the media and celebrities. In fact, celebrities have always been highly dependent on the media for visibility (Braudy, 1997; Burke, 1992; Dyer, 2004; Evans, 2005). The media have always been an indispensable channel for the circulations of celebrities' texts and images. Evans (2005) called these images 'mediated persona' to emphasize celebrities' absolute dependence on the media to create and disseminate their personae to the public, concluding that it is the only means for an individual to attain the status of a celebrity.

However, it was not until the present age that the prevalence of celebrities' presence in the media reached its highest level. Nowadays, celebrities have become almost ubiquitous in various media outlets, and their images are systematically utilized by media industries to market their media and entertainment commodities (Evans, 2005; Galbraith & Karlin, 2012; Pringle, 2004; Turner, 2004). Turner (2004) noted that today's transnational companies strive to produce global commodities, so the media and entertainment industries are also increasingly globalized. At the same time, technologies used as systems of delivery have begun to converge, which allows these companies to deliver the same content via different media outlets. Consequently, these companies have started to expand their bases across various media platforms in order to maximize profits. In the realm of media production, Hong Kong has a long tradition of broadcasting foreign content on English-language channels (Fung, 2004). With the emergence and rising popularity of cable TV, the practice of 'borrowing' television formats, content or even entire programmes becomes essential (Fung, 2004). Such a practice not only satisfies the globalized desires of the audience, but also reinforce Hong Kong's status as an international city. In the face of these social and technological changes, Turner (2004) concluded that celebrities have become increasingly important for the media and entertainment industries because they are very useful agents in connecting these cross-media processes, assisting media commodities to move smoothly across different media formats and systems of delivery.

Turner (2004) is not alone with his observation. Speaking within the context of Japan, Galbraith and Karlin (2012) used the concept of 'intertextuality of celebrities' to explain their ability to move across various media platforms and act as an 'axis around which the media revolve', while positioning Japanese idols as multimedia performers who '[operate] within a system of meanings and codes that are referencing other texts' (p. 10). The intertextuality of celebrities is evidenced by the fact that Japanese celebrities are constantly cross-referenced among various media texts, including different TV programmes, newspapers and magazines. Similar to Turner's (2004) observation, Galbraith and Karlin (2012) determined that this kind of intertextuality is economically beneficial for the media industries as it can help the media nurture a closer relationship with its audience, allowing it to promote and sell other media by connecting previously disparate media texts.

Symbiotic relationship between celebrity and the media

The media and celebrities are in fact engaging in an interdependent and symbiotic relationship: although the celebrities need the assistance of the media to attain fame, media companies can benefit economically from featuring celebrities. However, this does not necessarily mean that they are equal partners: the power relations between these two parties vary not only in different geographical regions (Turner, 2004), but also in different times (Gamson, 1992). Before elaborating on the power relations between the media and celebrities, it should first be clarified that the media–celebrity relationship often refers to the relationship between media corporations and the celebrities' representatives/management companies, rather than between media corporations and the individual celebrities. The media corporations and celebrities' representatives/management companies engage in a tug of war over commercial interests and market power (Gamson, 1994; Turner, 2004). Sometimes these corporations cooperate and sometimes they are in conflict; however, they are ultimately in sync in the sense that they are all following the capitalist logic and capitalizing on the individual celebrities' images to maximize profits.

Many researchers and critics have concluded that people live in a 'culture of celebrity' (Schickel, 1985). According to Rojek (2001), mass media representation is the key ingredient in the formation of celebrity culture. Indeed, celebrities will not be prominent without the mass media. As Drake and Miah (2010) concluded, 'media exposure is the oxygen that sustains the contemporary celebrity' (p. 55). Once a celebrity gets soil to root, they will then rely on the mass media to grow. The visibility of celebrities is highly determined by the media (Hollander, 2010); in the same vein, Hellmueller and Aeschbacher (2010) commented that the media play a vital role in creating the notion of celebrities, as they provide visibility and a distribution channel for celebrities to market themselves, thereby contributing to their renown in society. Celebrities thus utilize the platforms provided by various media to create 'para-social' interactions (Horton & Wohl, 2010) when they, for example, speak directly from the television or movie screen to the audience (Alperstein & Vann, 1997). According to Horton and Wohl (2010), this 'para-social relationship' refers to the illusion of a face-to-face relationship between the performer and the audience via the mass media (such as radio, television and movies). Such interaction is always one-sided, non-dialectical, controlled by the performer and not susceptible to mutual development (Horton & Wohl, 2010). Yet, as Hollander (2010) added, without the media's help in supplying the public with information about celebrities, or without the channel of media in creating the illusion of the 'para-social interaction/relationship', audiences would have no awareness of their existence.

Any celebrity is in fact irresistible to the strong influence of the mass media in the process of celebrification (C. Bell, 2009). 'Celebrification' can be defined as a process of crowning an ordinary person or public figure as a celebrity (Driessens, 2013). In distancing an individual from ordinary people, mass media can be perceived as one of the major players in such a transformation process (Couldry, 2003). Celebrities rely on the repetition of media exposure to gain massive attention from the audience, thereby establishing and maintaining their 'big names'. To maximize one's exposure rate, many celebrities try to be active in different spheres of entertainment, such as TV dramas, movies and music productions. In Hong Kong and many other Asian countries, the usual practice is for celebrities to engage in multiple entertainment spheres. Such a multimedia mix is commonly known as 'ge-ying-shi' (歌-影-視), or 'Music-Film-TV' (Bordwell, 2000). Examples include Raymond Lam (林峯) of Hong Kong, Rain (鄭智薰) of Korea, Jay Chou (周杰倫) of Taiwan and Adam Levine of the United States. These celebrities are not only eager to bring pleasure to the audience, but they are also, by actively participating in multiple entertainment spheres, grabbing for a diverse and massive audience's attention. With the right image – it is irrelevant whether it is a good or bad one – projected to the audience (as well as the attention gained from them), celebrities will become famous, get consistent and repetitive media exposure, and attract more and more fans and followers. Hence, they can maximize their income and gain (hopefully) desirable attention from entertainment producers and the general public to develop and escalate their career in the entertainment industry (Hellmueller & Aeschbacher, 2010).

However, as previously mentioned, celebrities are well aware of the mass media's power in constructing and deconstructing their status in the industry. They realize that both their status and popularity lie in the hands of the mass media. Indeed, the mass media have their own agenda when deciding whether someone is newsworthy or worth putting on-screen or in headlines. After all, mass media outlets are ultimately profit-driven. Media not only constantly create an overwhelming amount of celebrity-based stimuli for the public, but they also use information about newsworthy celebrities to stimulate and sustain the audience's attention and desire, consequently generating and maintaining their own economic benefits. It is common to find repetitive reporting on such newsworthy celebrities across media. Some social scientists have found that human beings are 'hardwired to be fascinated with celebrity, and that human beings' brains receive pleasurable chemical stimuli when they see familiar faces' (Altman, 2005, p. 1). The media therefore help generate renown to promote celebrities. However, this is not their dominant goal: it is, in fact, more like a strategy to ensure that they financially benefit from the entertainment business (Hellmueller & Aeschbacher, 2010).

Traditionally, media corporations have had a strong commitment to society and a relatively low commitment to profits. However, many present-day media companies are gobbled up by mega corporations with a predominant obligation to profits (Altman, 2005). From the media's point of view, celebrity has become an economic good because the demand for such content has gradually but consistently increased (Schierl, 2007). Although today's media conglomerates concentrate on economic benefits, they diffuse moral responsibility. When covering a celebrity's (personal) life becomes the audience's source of entertainment, there is an increasing amount of non-legitimate news and/or eye-catching stories about celebrities reported by the mass media. Obviously, a soft story that contains a harsh criticism of celebrities will sell. As indicated by Hermes (2006), by reading and watching such news stories, the audience can engage in the fun of speculation and the pleasure of gaining 'forbidden' knowledge, although they might have some degree of reservations about their truthfulness (p. 305). On the one hand, the increased opportunity to glimpse into celebrities' 'private lives via (intrusive) media means that people can get closer to their idols and spend considerable sums of money' (Pringle, 2004, p. 1). On the other hand, as 'our expectations of privacy decrease, our expectations for receiving more information – our expectations of what are public – increase' (Calvert, 2000, p. 78). This is why covering the scandals and the private lives of celebrities is prevalent nowadays.

It is true that such reporting will enhance a celebrity's visibility (which is vital to their career), yet there are always drawbacks. According to Rein et al. (1997), 'becoming visible means that the media will not only glorify acts abut also magnify sins' (p. 31). Similarly, Johansson (2006) added that witnessing the celebrity's misbehaviours and misfortunes is the audience's biggest pleasure. Therefore, to create the 'talk of the town' and sell stories, the media sometimes go beyond a celebrity's limitations and/or privacy. Dismissing a celebrity's humanity has become a trend in the media. In fact, celebrities are still human beings with emotions and personal opinions, yet these qualities are generally disregarded in the media. The media only care about hunting for the next big headline, disregarding the possible negative impact imposed on celebrities and/or society. It is no surprise then that some celebrities dislike the media, especially the paparazzi.

However, for some celebrities, 'no publicity is bad publicity'. This group of celebrities do not care if their stories are 'magnifying [their] sins' or 'glorifying their acts' (Rein et al., 1997) – as long as they are visible in the market, they are willing to cooperate or collaborate with the media. Some celebrities even use and/or sell information about their private lives to the media to market themselves. As Gamson (1992) said, 'many people are trying to manipulate image' just to attain fame and status (p. 78).

Needless to say, the public, media and celebrities are interdependent on one another. Each party has its own motives and agenda. Although the mass media dish out celebrities' images and stories for money, attention, subscribers or followers, celebrities forfeit, to some extent, their visibility and privacy for fame, money and fans. Meanwhile, the public focuses their attention (and sometimes money as well) on accessing a celebrity's information in order to satisfy their need for voyeurism (Hellmueller & Aeschbacher, 2010). Such a vicious yet realistic cycle will continuously exist in the celebrity industry, which has become a battlefield of control and constant visibility (Hellmueller & Aeschbacher, 2010) between celebrities and the mass media.

Celebrities before and after the emergence of the Internet age

As previously mentioned, the celebrity–media relationship actually refers to the relationship between media corporations and celebrities' representatives/management companies. In the tug of war between these two parties over commercial interests and market power, the rights and autonomy of the celebrity individuals are often neglected. However, the situation has begun to change with the emergence of the Internet and social media. The advancement of technology has sparked profuse growth in the number of media platforms available to celebrities and the ever-changing entertainment industry, thus altering the traditional symbiotic relationship between celebrities and media. In this section, we will look into how the emergence of the Internet and social media have changed celebrities in media.

The before: Fostering the asymmetrical relationship between celebrities and the mass media

Before 1990, which marked the advent and widespread use of the Internet, celebrities only had the use of traditional mass media as a huge platform from which to market themselves. Platforms generally considered to be part of traditional media include television (both broadcast and cable), radio, movie studios, music studios, newspapers and magazines. Needless to say, the media act as a bridge between the audience and celebrities. As Horton and Wohl (2010) noted, one of the characteristics of the mass media is that they give the audience the illusion of a face-to-face relationship with the performer. Such an illusion has been called a 'para-social relationship' (Horton & Wohl, 2010, p. 35). Horton and Wohl

(2010) suggested that such a relationship is characterized as one-sided, non-dialectical, controlled by the performer and not susceptible to mutual development. Having said that, how much control a performer or a celebrity has in building and maintaining the para-social relationship with the audience is questionable. After all, the media's role as a gatekeeper always determines who, what and when the audience should receive.

The television industry altered the entire celebrity landscape by providing every household with celebrity news that created a new world of fame, where people became 'famous for being famous' (Boorstin, 1971). Television broadcasters usually provide dramas, comedies, game shows or reality shows (in which celebrities are now heavily involved) to audiences during prime time hours. In the same line of thinking, David Blake, a professor of English at the College of New Jersey in Ewing, said that 'television, more than any other cultural development, has radically changed our experience of celebrity. Television has made celebrities both prevalent and ubiquitous' (Altman, 2005, p. 2). Due to the repetitiveness and extensive amount of celebrity coverage, the public feels closer to celebrities, who they consider their 'imaginary friends'. This could be explained by Langer's (2006) speculation of the emergence of a 'personality system' in celebrity culture via the advent of television, which is contrary to the classical paradigm of the star system that is usually manifest in the film industry.

According to Langer (2006), television celebrities in the personality system are portrayed as part of ordinary life; they try to construct and/or foreground intimacy and immediacy with the audience by 'playing' themselves, instead of playing 'parts' that emphasize their identity as 'stars' (p. 185). To make themselves more well-known, celebrities establish a continuing relationship with their audience by regularly appearing at dependable events (i.e. events that are positively reinforcing their images) and integrating themselves into the routines of the audience's daily lives (Horton & Wohl, 2010, p. 37). It is not hard to locate examples of television celebrities playing a character and becoming part of the public's life. In Hong Kong, television dramas are the most important source of entertainment for most citizens (Fung, 2004). In 1977, Hong Kong's TVB produced a 110-epidsode television drama entitled 家變/*A House is Not a Home* (Hing, 1977). The character Lok-lam (洛琳), played by Liza Wang (汪明荃), gained a great deal of popularity in society. Not only did the drama become the talk of the town, but many females even mimicked Lok-lam by having the same haircut as the character, and presenting themselves as independent and successful. Another example of a character that resonated with society was Carrie Bradshaw. In 1998, Home Box Office (HBO) produced an American television romantic sitcom called *Sex and the City* (Star, 1998). The public adored Carrie Bradshaw, played by Sarah Jessica Parker, the romantic heroine of the show. People not only talked about and discussed the show itself, but also followed her lifestyle and her wardrobe. In 2009, *The Guardian* even named Carrie Bradshaw an icon of the decade, stating that 'Carrie Bradshaw did so much to shift the culture around certain women's issues as real-life female groundbreakers' (Wolf, 2009) Looking at these two examples, Langer's (2006) contention that television produces 'personalities' rather than 'stars' is worth revisiting. According to Jermyn (2006), 'a television performance/performer now has the capacity to inspire and maintain the breadth of speculation and fascination that only a star, and not a mere "personality," can occupy' (p. 80).

Many believe that television celebrity is more accessible than film celebrity (Hesmondhalgh, 2005). According to Marshall (1997), 'film celebrity draws on lofty aspirations to serious, legitimate culture, whereas television tends to aspire to the everyday' (p. 126). When comparing television with film celebrities, the television celebrity is structured to reinforce the feeling of close proximity to the real and the familial (Hesmondhalgh, 2005). Similar to Hesmondhalgh (2005), Marshall (1997) suggested that television constructs a discourse of sympathetic familiarity around its stars. In contrast, film celebrities keep trying to distance themselves from their audience, remaining just beyond their audience's reach while reinforcing their identity as stars (Langer, 2006; Marshall, 1997), thereby maintaining an imaginary relationship with the audience. For example, in Hong Kong, Aaron Kwok (郭富城), Tony Leung (梁朝偉) and Maggie Cheung (張曼玉), to name just a few, carry out tremendous work to create an aura that the audience can only admire from afar. As indicated by Marshall (1997), film stars consistently project an image of inaccessibility and extraordinary quality to ordinary people.

Publicity is a crucial ingredient for leading a film actor/actress into the world of celebrity (Marshall, 1997). To gain the audience's attention and identification, an emerging film star exhibits his or her ordinariness 'as a marked entrance point' in the film industry (Marshall, 1997, p. 91). Hence, the physical characteristics of film performers are important to their entrance ticket. Film actors/actresses whose physical characteristics are identified by the audience and the film industry are called 'physical performer(s)' (Marshall, 1997, p. 95), and the uniqueness of their physical characteristics plays an important role in maintaining an edge in the industry. However, as Marshall (1997) suggested, if the characteristic is replicable and/or replaceable by other actors/actresses, then the inherent value of the emerging film star in the industry is limited. Once the industry and the audience have identified a physical performer's characteristic as their representation, they will begin to be constructed as a 'public personality' (Marshall, 1997, p. 100). With the recognition of the industry and the public, film stars will then focus on linking up their screen presence and their personal lives, which would not challenge their characteristics that are suggested in their films. Establishing a public personality, together with the film star's accomplishment in the industry, would then escalate their career to another level. According to Marshall (1997), the ultimate film star or celebrity should have 'individually transgressed the constructions of public personality that have been placed by the film apparatus and the public' (p. 100). For instance, Chow Yun-Fat (周潤發), a Hong Kong actor who turned himself into a world-famous superstar, likes 'de-celebrifying' himself from time to time by taking public transport, shopping in local markets, or even taking selfies with fans in public areas. Thus, Chow has achieved independence from the ways in which his films have painted him (Marshall, 1997). Indeed, there is no single formula for becoming an ultimate film celebrity. By looking at Andy Lau (劉德華) as an example, 'humble beginnings, hard work, and honesty' seem to be the characteristics a successful film celebrity should possess (Marshall, 1997).

Both television and film celebrities' images are not just about their shows and films, but also the promotion of those shows and films – and the stars themselves – through public appearances, media interviews, biographies and coverage in the press of the stars' doings and private life (Dyer, 2004). Celebrity journalism began with the advent of the copper engraving and printing press at the beginning of the nineteenth century, which allowed the extensive dissemination of images of individual faces, as well as promoted the concept of fame (C. Bell, 2009). Alongside the visual revolution (Boorstin, 1962) and the wider accessibility of images (Hellmueller & Aeschbacher, 2010), the emergence of photography in post-Civil War America led to a tremendous growth in the mass publication of newspapers and magazines (Hellmueller & Aeschbacher, 2010). Markets for entertainment were then developed and further reinforced by the press, who realized the value in creating and maintaining famous individuals to sell their newspapers and magazines (Marshall, 2006a). Unlike celebrities in the film industry, who emphasize their distance from the audience and embellish their aura, celebrity journalism works to make famous celebrities more real and works to provide a greater intimacy with their everyday lives (similar to the celebrities on television) (Marshall, 2006a, pp. 317–318). A celebrity's status and level of fame decide their newsworthiness, thereby determining who gets the headline or cover story (Drake & Miah, 2010; Marshall, 2006a).

Celebrity journalism originated from the introduction of yellow journalism, a type of journalism that offers limited or no legitimate well-researched news, but instead uses eye-catching headlines or cover stories to sell more newspapers or magazines (Campbell, 2001). Techniques like exaggeration, scandal-mongering and sensationalism are commonly employed in yellow journalism to create stories about people. Thus, some people consider such journalism unprofessional or even unethical (Biagi, 2012). By extension, tabloid journalism has in itself become a brand of celebrity journalism. As Johansson (2006) mentioned, supermarket tabloids (i.e. gossip magazines) focus on exposing a celebrity's hidden secrets by adopting invasive journalism methods, such as chequebook journalism and paparazzi coverage. Specifically, popular tabloids present not only celebrities' world of glitter and glamour, but also their misfortunes (Hermes, 2006; Johansson, 2006). The public certainly might experience some kind of guilt for enjoying such a narrative, yet, as Johansson (2006) discovered, such guilty feelings do not hinder the public from consuming the tabloid celebrity stories.

Due to the rise of tabloid journalism, the paparazzi have become one of the biggest occupational groups contributing to celebrities' visibility (Hellmueller & Aeschbacher, 2010). According to Gold (2001), the paparazzi refers to those 'photographers who aggressively pursue celebrities in order to take candid, often compromising photographs of them for publication' (p. 111). Paparazzi are an important agent for enabling celebrities to become famous, get published and involve their audience; however, celebrities' privacy is often infringed upon by the unethical practice of these photojournalists. An excellent example of this is Princess Diana, whom many people believe died as a result of the paparazzi's manoeuvres while tracking her in cars. Thus, as Hellmueller and Aeschbacher

(2010) suggested, the term 'paparazzi' became (in)famous as an impingement on the right of privacy. Indeed, both the general public and journalists consistently and increasingly recognize paparazzi as deviant from other kinds of photographers, denigrating them as the 'worst of the worst' (Mendelson, 2007, p. 169). Paparazzi not only take pictures of celebrities with glamorous appearances, but also pursue images that display celebrities' deviant behaviours (Hellmueller & Aeschbacher, 2010). They are often criticized for their overaggressive search for an unexpected picture of a celebrity, which often leads them to legal complexities. In 2009, Sienna Miller, Amy Winehouse and Lily Allen won injunctions in the United Kingdom that prevented the paparazzi from following them and gathering outside their houses (Saner, 2009). More recently, in the United States, celebrities have successfully persuaded California law-makers to pass an anti-paparazzi law, which took effect in January 2014 (Puente, 2014). The regulation means anyone who harasses a celebrity's child by taking their picture, including in a public area, is punished with a year in jail and a fine of US$10,000. However, even with the risk of possible legal implications, the number of paparazzi has not dropped, but rather increased; needless to say, money plays a central role in this (Hellmueller & Aeschbacher, 2010). Mel Bouzad, one of the top paparazzi in Los Angeles, claimed to have made US$150,000 for a picture of Ben Affleck and Jennifer Lopez in Georgia after their break-up (McCarthy, 2009). It seems that the paparazzi's financial gain wins over their sense of social responsibility and integrity. After all, paparazzi are a pretty significant reason why a celebrity becomes and continues to be famous. Celebrities also realize that disappearing from the pages of newspapers and magazines, including tabloids, will consequently lead to a decrease in celebrated fame, glorious adoration and significant pay cheques. As Jennifer Buhl, a former paparazzo, shared with *USA Today*:

> I get that it's annoying. I felt guilty when I photographed Jodie Foster once with her son – it felt a little invasive. But after that, I started to understand more about the symbiotic relationship, and how (celebrities) use us and need us and want us most of the time.
>
> (Puente, 2014, n.p.)

The after: Balancing the imbalance between celebrities and the mass media

With the spread of the Internet and social media, celebrities no longer rely on the power of the traditional mass media to suffuse their faces to the public. To attract people's attention, the Internet, using Web 2.0 technology, offers social media as a platform for celebrities to market and promote themselves. Celebrity individuals are now able to achieve fame without the help of traditional mass media outlets and management companies. The Internet and social media have given part of the power and autonomy back to the individuals by lowering the barriers of entry to the entertainment markets. Moreover, increasingly sophisticated technology greatly reduces the cost of selling, producing and reproducing entertainment goods; the mediation of representatives, such as agents, producers and retailers, is no longer needed, and individuals can now produce and disseminate their creations directly to the consumers through the Internet at an affordable price (Elberse, 2013a). The rise of social media has led contemporary celebrity culture into a highly heterogeneous experience (Hellmueller & Aeschbacher, 2010).

Some of the aspirants entering the entertainment markets through social media have successfully attained popularity on their own, and ultimately achieved a celebrated status. For example, Justin Bieber first caught the public's attention and subsequently became famous after his mother uploaded videos of him singing covers of various songs on YouTube. This kind of 'do-it-yourself (DIY) celebrity' (Turner, 2004) is also evident in Asia. In Japan, the music cover section of the Internet video-sharing site Nico Nico Douga (ニコニコ動画) provides a space for individuals to upload their song covers, and some aspirants, such as Piko, Clear and 96Neko, have become popular among netizens through the website. Similarly, in China, the Internet has democratized the process of celebrity-making to a certain extent. Roberts (2010) asserted that digital media signifies 'a "victory of the common people" over the narrow interests of traditional media' (p. 235) because it provides an alternative channel to established media for aspirants to attain fame by themselves. For instance, the female blogger Sister Furong Haa (芙蓉姐姐) became nationally famous after posting her life stories and pictures on the Internet bulletin boards of Tsinghua University and Peking University (Roberts, 2010; H. Zhang, 2013).

At first glance, digital technology seems to be giving individuals greater leveraging power against the large-scale media and entertainment corporations; however, most successful aspirants in the digital media will ultimately sign contracts with established content producers and be incorporated into the industry (Elberse, 2013a; Turner, 2004). For example, Justin Bieber was signed to RBMG, a record label based in Atlanta, and Piko was signed to Ki/oon Music, a sub-label of the Sony Music Entertainment. In this way, instead of going against traditional media, digital media may actually serve as a testing ground where established media and entertainment corporations can choose talents.

Likewise, most celebrities are aware of the rising importance of social media for themselves and their audience; now they (and/or their team) actively use these networks to create their own profiles, and make their own faces and content available to the social media community (Marshall, 2010). As Drake and Miah (2010) indicated, the Internet, including social networks and blogs, has downsized the gatekeeping processes that exist on traditional mass media platforms. Thus, celebrities have started to present themselves in more realistic, unfiltered ways to the audience (Marshall, 2010). Furthermore, the online media platforms provide 24/7 accessibility, dynamic content and immediacy that are unavailable in print and television (Hellmueller & Aeschbacher, 2010). These online media channels pose the possibility for people – typically fans and followers – to have 'direct' contact with a celebrity, as celebrities (and their teams) publish their own stories and post their images to allow the audience to get closer to their very reality (Marshall, 2010). For Murray (2009), celebrities self-publishing stories indicates their efforts to try to gain back the power they lost to the fast-paced gossip industry (p. 39). At the same time, Muntean and Petersen (2009) asserted that celebrities' messages on social media platforms have an advantage in the flood of information sources because the audience perceives these as the authentic celebrity voice and a privileged channel to the star themselves. Théberge (2005) thus concluded that the Internet and social media have enabled the relationship between celebrities and their audience to become increasingly reciprocal.

As observed by Hellmueller and Aeschbacher (2010), today's audience is increasingly and actively participating in producing celebrities' visibility, as high-tech devices make it easy and convenient to take pictures and videos. According to Lerman (2007), the evolution of the Internet and social media has fostered users' participation: 'Users are actively creating, evaluating, and distributing information' (p. 1). For example, *Apple Daily*, a Hong Kong-based tabloid-style newspaper, encourages people to provide photos or videos to its outlet, offering them at least HKD 500 and HKD 1,000, respectively, for publication. Although the reward might not be significant, such an offer does attract ordinary citizens to become one of the news feeders. Due to the availability of smartphones and other technologies, citizens can often report breaking hard and soft news faster than traditional media reporters. Through this, the concept of citizen journalism has emerged. Turner (2007) characterized such participation as a shift 'from elite to ordinary' (p. 154), which has especially taken place in today's print, television and Internet content production. Correspondingly, Marshall (2006b) argued that such user-generated media is a further example of the breakdown in control of mediated culture by the major players or elites in the entertainment industry.

As the number of mass media platforms has increased, so too has the competition for audiences and advert dollars (Altman, 2005). Currently, an overwhelming amount of information related to celebrities is available, especially with the emergence of the Internet and, consequently, citizen journalism. In fact, media saturation has led to rapid competition to provide information, which creates the potential for media outlets to report information prematurely, inaccurately or partially (Schmitz, 2012). With the aid of the pervasive Internet and social media, today's celebrities can themselves clarify, explain and delineate any misrepresentations, false rumours and/or scandals instantly, without any manipulation and/or screening from the traditional media outlets. Through this, celebrities are gaining back some control of their representation in the industry. However, one cannot rely exclusively on the use of the Internet and social media; according to Daschmann (2007), the masses of (aspiring) celebrities have to compete for the public's (limited) attention (p. 186). In such a competitive environment, a celebrity must therefore remain present on all accessible media channels (Seifert, 2010, p. 60).

Growing up in a celebrity-saturated culture helps turn one into an expert on how the media works. Everyone – especially Gen Xers and beyond – has some degree of ability to deconstruct the media, understand the ingredients added and unmask the tricks created (Altman, 2005). These people are no longer taking celebrity news at face value. Dan Kennedy, media critic at the *Boston Phoenix*, thinks that today's media consumers are more sophisticated than in the past and thus less obsessed with celebrity. The overwhelming content from celebrities and the media has made the public more and more aware of its authenticity, and even fostered 'detective work' for investigating which news and/or images are 'real' and which are not (Burgess & Green, 2009, p. 29). Having said that, both scholars and practitioners consider the audience to be an influential factor on media routines (Shoemaker & Vos, 2009). A non-virtuous circle exists: as the media cover celebrities (because that is what the public wants), the media then, in response to the demand, end up covering celebrities even more (Altman, 2005). As long as the mass media still believe audiences value dramatic stories of celebrities, they will continue to feed that need in various ways. As Annenberg School's Martin Kaplan says, 'celebrity news attracts eyeballs. We can't help it. Fame is mesmerizing' (cited in Altman, 2005, p. 7).

Although digital media does not radically subvert the power hierarchy in media and entertainment industries, it does have substantial influence on the production models of these industries (as previously mentioned) and celebrity culture. In the past, celebrities, especially film stars, led a larger-than-life existence. As encounters with these stars were often irregular and sporadic, the distance between them and the audiences was great (Langer, 2006). However, with the emergence of digital media, celebrities can now disseminate their mediated personae and daily stories without the filtering of the traditional mass media outlets; at the same time, the audience can also have 'direct' access to celebrities by commenting on posts or interacting with celebrities through social media platforms (Hellmueller & Aeschbacher, 2010; Marshall, 2010). Therefore, encounters with celebrities are now easier and possibly more regular, and the seemingly closer celebrity–audience relationship could thus challenge the perception of celebrities as a larger-than-life existence.

To conclude, the relationship between celebrity and media is non-static, with fluid dynamics between them that depend on interrelationships in terms of context, the celebrity and the types of media. We interviewed three renowned media practitioners in Hong Kong, representing different media channels, to discuss the relationship between celebrity and media in the entertainment industry in Asia, particularly Hong Kong and South Korea. Interviewees include Francis Mak (麥潤壽), a well-known radio host in Hong Kong; Patrick Suen (宣柏健), a seasoned columnist and film critic in Hong Kong, who is keen on Asian films and Korean pop culture; and Kam Kwok-leung (甘國亮), an experienced practitioner of the Hong Kong entertainment industry.

Media practitioners interviews

Francis Mak (麥潤壽)

Francis Mak (麥潤壽) is a well-known radio host in Hong Kong, who has extensive work experience in the radio industry. He has worked for the public broadcaster Radio Television Hong Kong (RTHK) for more than 25 years, and later became the head of an independent

Figure 19: Interviewing with Francis Mak, a well-known radio host in Hong Kong.

Figure 20: Francis Mak at Hong Kong Baptist University, School of Communication.

digital broadcaster, Digital Broadcasting Corporation Hong Kong Limited (DBC). In 2002, he established the Never Give Up Association, which organizes a range of activities and training for teenagers during the summer vacation, which aims to teach teenagers how to manage their emotions, develop interpersonal skills and become good leaders.

Celebrity industry in Hong Kong

Rein et al. (1997) suggested that the celebrity industry evolved through four stages: (1) the cottage industry stage; (2) the early industrialization stage; (3) the late industrialization stage; and (4) the decentralization stage. In the late industrialization stage, specialists, rather than aspirants/celebrities, were in control of the celebrity-production process, and master organizations were responsible for coordinating the services provided by the increasingly sophisticated industry specialists (Rein et al., 1997). Mak observed that the celebrity industry in Hong Kong entered a similar stage in the 1980s, when the entertainment sector began to operate like an industry in which celebrities were artificially manufactured.

According to Mak, the entertainment industry in Asia (e.g. Hong Kong, Taiwan, Japan) during that period was dedicated to producing high-quality celebrities using a meticulously planned production process. He offered Jimmy Lin (林志穎) as an example, explaining that his instant rise to popularity upon initial exposure was due to thoughtful planning and intensive training. Indeed, 'his looks, his clothes and his dance – everything was made perfect before he was presented in front of the public'. As Horton and Wohl (2010) argued, the image of personality and performance resulted from a form of standardization worked out by the celebrity and their managers while relying on a certain formula. This suggests that a pattern of images can be recognized by an audience over time. Celebrity image is therefore largely subject to the control of celebrity industry specialists.

Distinctiveness of radio hosts in Hong Kong's entertainment industry

Although the public image of pop stars may be highly dependent on their managers and companies, radio hosts present a rather different case. According to Mak, the celebrity-making process in the radio sector seemed to be less developed in comparison to other entertainment sectors, such as television and the movies. Rein et al. (1997) observed that, in the earliest stage of the evolution of the industry, which they called the 'cottage industry stage', aspirants were largely on their own, as support from industry specialists was not available, and so they had to depend heavily on self-training, self-initiative and perseverance. Similarly, Mak noted that aspiring radio hosts in Hong Kong lacked support from specialists, and had to rely on their own efforts to achieve success and fame. He believed that the differences could be partly attributed to the dissimilar natures of their work.

In Mak's opinion, celebrity radio hosts were to a large extent distinct from celebrities in other entertainment sectors, such as singers and actors/actresses. He observed that singers or actors/actresses often had to try many times before achieving the perfect results when they recorded albums or acted in films; most of the time, they had a script to follow and 'only needed to focus on delivering the speech with the appropriate emotions'.

In contrast, most radio programmes nowadays are broadcast live (Rudin, 2011). Voice training, which is usually done by senior staff or specialists, is essential for aspirants (Fleming, 2010). Such training, accompanied by intensive practice, is useful in improving the competence of the radio hosts, and can help realize the full potential of their voices so that they can talk in a clear, natural, relaxed and confident manner (Fleming, 2010). Mak reiterated that training is necessary for radio hosts because a detailed script cannot be prepared beforehand:

> You cannot call 'cut' in radio. You can do that in film-making. You can reshoot the scene and change a single word which is not delivered well, and even if you have already called 'cut' 29 times, you can still go for a thirtieth reshoot, but we cannot do that in radio.

Live broadcasting thus requires radio hosts to be really good at their job and puts great pressure on them to be perfect every time. Therefore, in Mak's opinion, celebrity and radio hosts are distinct from celebrities in other sectors because they have to be well-trained. Yet it is difficult to teach a person how to speak appropriately or manage the voice of a radio host in the same way that the looks of a singer or actor/actress are managed. He explained that 'even surround sound will not help. You cannot change the voice of a person, right? And it is impossible to remould every single word one uses in oral communication'.

On the other hand, Mak explained that Hong Kong's celebrities in other entertainment sectors differ from radio hosts because they depend extensively on appearances. He argued that their good looks were already enough to instantly grab public attention. In contrast to radio hosts, who have to work hard on their own to become a fluent speaker, the appearances of a singer or actor/actress can be easily changed and manipulated by an entourage of cosmeticians, hairstylists, costume designers, etc. As he put it, 'This group of people is standing behind an artist, and they can help the artist plan everything. But radio hosts have no one'.

For radio hosts, having a distinctive style – which Mak called 'character' – in hosting radio programmes is the main determinant of success. Trewin (2003) indicated that it is important for radio hosts to create a unique sound or form a special style, as this becomes a selling point and can make a host stand out from the competition. In a similar vein, Mak explained that a unique character could help a radio host stand out and be distinguishable from others:

> [R]adio hosts must develop their own unique character, and they should not be talking about a certain topic simply because others are all talking about it. Even if they really want to talk about it, they should do it from a different angle or in a different style.

By maintaining a unique and consistent character, Mak's earlier radio programmes with RTHK brought him career success in the radio industry. He described his own style as 'sharp' when he interviewed his guests on-air. For him, adopting such a style was 'challenging', but his radio shows attracted huge media attention that has made him a celebrity radio host in Hong Kong. At that time, the content of his interviews was often covered in newspaper headlines, and such coverage, as he put it, 'made his name widely known to the general public'. Mak further noted that, unlike celebrities in other sectors who can be turned into an instant hit with just one song or one movie, radio hosts cannot easily attain fame or become famous overnight: '[They] will not come to prominence because of only one radio programme or by hosting a programme for just one year [...]. It is not possible. They have to build their fame and audience year after year'.

In terms of celebrities' life cycles, Mak observed a contrast between radio presenters and other forms of public figures in the entertainment industry. According to him, the life cycle of celebrities in the popular music industry is much shorter nowadays because celebrities are highly dependent on their good looks and are not well-trained in the area of performance skills:

> Many of our singers do not have a thorough training in basic skills. A producer may even think, 'well, since she has become the winner of Miss Hong Kong Pageant, maybe we can immediately produce her music album'. And the songs will be made perfect in the recording studio. That's why she can never perform well live because she does not have the basic skills, right?

In Mak's opinion, radio hosts usually enjoy a relatively longer career than pop singers and actors/actresses not only because the successful radio host is equipped with solid professional skills, but also because their image is always considered 'authentic', and they are perceived as one of the public. Therefore, radio hosts' careers can circulate in society for a relatively longer period. Meanwhile, the on-screen image of an actor/actress is often perceived as a fake. Mak demonstrated his point with the example of well-known film character Mark Gor (Mark 哥), played by Chow Yun-Fat (周潤發) in 英雄本色/A Better Tomorrow (Woo, 1986):

> A group of people is standing behind to help build the image, but if you are made into Mark Gor [Mark 哥], you can only be Mark Gor, and every time I see you, you are Mark Gor. But that image is only a fake [...]. And if the popularity of the film or the song dwindles, that false appearance will also be gone.

Mak's arguments over the notion of an authentic image provide insights into how the perceived authenticity of a celebrity's public image is favourable to the celebrity–audience relationship. His emphasis on radio hosts having an authentic character was echoed in Langer's study (2006) on television personalities. According to Langer (2006), the decoding process necessary for television to win audience consent 'is fixed principally in terms of questions about personal authenticity: how "real" and "genuine" are these personalities performing in the public arena' (p. 193). In the same way, for radio stations, gaining the

Figure 21: Francis Mak – the renowned radio host in Hong Kong.

audience's trust and consent also requires the radio hosts' construction of 'authentic' personalities to some extent. In contrast to film stars, television and radio personalities become intimate and familiar to the audience over time as they are embedded in 'cycles of repetition' (Langer, 2006). Radio hosts, like other television personalities, are likely to be appreciated by the audience as a 'real' person, not only because they have regular contact with their audience, but also because their personas presented on-air are believed to resemble their private character (Horton & Wohl, 2010).

Current radio industry developments in Hong Kong and its celebrity production

Nowadays, radio is a secondary or background medium that accompanies other activities (Rudin, 2011). It is inexpensive and can be listened to almost everywhere; because of its accessibility and mobility, radio serves as a constant and intimate companion in people's lives (Gazi, Starkey, & Jedrzejewski, 2011; Rudin, 2011). However, intense competition from other media outlets has led to a gradual decline of the significance of the medium, and the public – especially the younger generation – is not listening to the radio as much as in the past (Fisher, 2007; Rudin, 2011). Still, researchers remain optimistic about the future of the radio industry, and believe that the medium is capable of reinventing itself and adapting to the new media environment (cf. Fisher, 2007; Fleming, 2010).

In Hong Kong, radio listening seems to remain robust. At present, there are five licensed terrestrial radio stations (including one public broadcaster) and numerous other Internet radio stations in the city. Radio is a common medium in society and almost half of the population in Hong Kong listens to the radio regularly (Centre for Communication and Public Opinion Survey, 2005; Consumer Search Group, 2010). However, in Mak's opinion, the radio industry in Hong Kong has experienced a gradual decline in the last decade.

Mak was pessimistic about the prospects of the industry. He observed that radio was not as popular as it was in the past and had since become 'a sunset industry'. According to him, one of the factors contributing to the downfall of the radio industry in Hong Kong has been the onset of deindustrialization over the past two decades. He pointed out that the radio industry was most vibrant in the 1980s, when there were a lot of factories in Hong Kong; indeed, factory workers constituted a large proportion of the industry's audience. The later relocation of the factories to mainland China thus led to a significant decrease in radio ratings.

On the other hand, he noted that the industry was no longer able to produce its own celebrities, and nowadays most of the radio hosts can only achieve fame through other media outlets, such as television. He mentioned two popular celebrity radio hosts, Sammy Leung (森美) and Kitty Yuen (小儀), as examples:

> In recent years, the public has not gotten to know about the radio hosts from their radio programmes. Like Sammy and Kitty, they are using television to increase their popularity, as it is not enough to do it only with the radio.

Mak's remark resonates with Langer's (2006) analysis of personality system: 'The personality system, crucially embedded within television's cyclical rituals, can much more readily facilitate a sense of familiarity and accessibility' (p. 187). In other words, television allows for the repeated appearances of its personalities that often coexist in our everyday lives. Because of the merits of different mass media platforms, it appears beneficial for radio hosts to rely on, and make use of, multiple media platforms to develop and sustain their careers, as well as in reaching out to different audiences.

Mak identified a widespread lack of talent as another reason for the downfall of the industry. As previously indicated, he believed that it is very difficult to train a person to become a good radio host, and the success of a radio host depends much on personal effort. However, he observed that aspiring youngsters nowadays only want to attain instant fame and are not willing to tolerate the hardship in order to become truly competent:

> [Many aspiring youths] are very different from people in my generation. What we want to do is to produce a radio programme of high quality, but what they want is only to achieve fame. They are not really passionate about the job and that's why I can't see into the future of the industry.

Furthermore, unlike what is observed in the west (Fleming, 2010), Mak believes that there are not many good radio hosts for newcomers to learn from or emulate in Hong Kong,

Figure 22: Francis Mak with his Never Give Up Association's students at Digital Broadcasting Corporation Limited (DBC).

and few of the experienced radio hosts have time to teach the younger ones. Therefore, he reiterated that the newcomers could only depend on themselves, and only achieve success and fame through hard work. He suggested that, for example, '[they] have to learn not to say too much "er, hmm, uh" etc. And you can only practice by yourself, no one can help you with that, right?' As a result, aspiring radio hosts tend to strive for success and fame on their own, which also reflects the distinctiveness of the celebrity-making process in the radio sector.

In terms of the functions of radio hosts, Mak noted that radio was previously able to provide the latest information to the audience: 'Music radio hosts like Blanche Tang [鄧藹琳] would be the first person in Hong Kong to get hold of a copy of *Billboard*', and were first to access information about the latest popular songs and albums. However, Mak was aware that, with increasingly advanced technology, audiences were able to obtain information or listen to artists' latest songs through other media channels, like the Internet. Thus, radio hosts could no longer play the role of a leader or a trendsetter; radio lost its advantages and its role of disseminating the latest information became less significant, especially in the area of music.

Yet, interestingly, music programmes are still the most listened to radio programmes in Hong Kong (Centre for Communication and Public Opinion Survey, 2005). Fleming (2010)

Figure 23: Francis Mak with his Never Give Up Association's students at Radio Television Hong Kong (RTHK).

explained that radio is not only a jukebox; for young people, music is a way to establish an identity, which at the same time, also tends to determine their speech, behaviour and style of clothing. Consequently, the conversation around music could be as important as the music itself, and music radio programmes potentially stand out among other music providers and content suppliers due to its ability to provide a conversation around music, as well as in facilitating a dialogue between the audience and the hosts (Fleming, 2010). Therefore, the importance of radio in the consumption of music may not be necessarily declining.

Patrick Suen (宣柏健)

Patrick Suen (宣柏健) is a seasoned columnist and film critic based in Hong Kong who writes about Asian films and Korean pop culture. After completing his MPhil degree at the University of Hong Kong in 2000, he began to work as an editor at various magazines, such as *Men's Uno*, *JET*, *Mr* and *Ming Pao Weekly*, where he has had numerous opportunities to collaborate with different stars and celebrities. His personal enthusiasm for South Korea (he started to learn Korean in 2001) unexpectedly enabled him to work as a freelance translator at various events for many famed Korean stars, such as Lee Young-ae (李英愛), Kim Soo-hyun (金秀賢), and idol groups such as G-Dragon and Girls Generation.

Figure 24: Patrick Suen with Ji Jin-hee, a renowned South Korean actor.

Celebrity in media

As mentioned by Turner (2004), celebrity is a product of the representational process employed by the media in their treatment of prominent individuals. Suen claimed that celebrities actually function in certain ways to satisfy the needs of the media. For example, the media can invite celebrities to pose for editorial photographs or to partake in other commercial collaborative projects organized by media organizations. If the celebrities promise to participate accordingly, the media will feature them in its editorial coverage in return, thereby accelerating their fame through extensive publicity. Suen asserted:

> All the famed celebrities are created by the media. Without the propagation of magazine, television, radio or the newly emerged digital media, such as Facebook and YouTube, our world would not have the so-called celebrity. Being a celebrity means being famous. The only way to achieve this status is to be promoted by the media.

Some scholars have asserted that this relationship is reciprocal and the media need celebrity as well. Schierl (2007) attributed this phenomenon to the gradual and consistent demand for 'celebrity content' from a public that turns celebrities into a valuable economic good.

According to Boorstin (1971), the word 'fan' is etymologically derived from 'fanatic', which characterizes relationships based on an intimate knowledge of a personality generated and supported by the mass media industry, and maintained by the personality's capacity to control media attention. Suen elucidated that this might be due to the strong persuasiveness and attractiveness of the celebrity in increasing readership and driving sales, thereby enhancing media outlets' economic benefits. As noted by Suen:

> Fans are crazy. I mean they are extremely crazy. […]. They do not mind doing anything that can be measured in dollar signs. Therefore, by simply showing the celebrities' faces on the media, it could attract a lot of people to consume not only the media, but also the products portrayed in it. After all, society needs celebrities as people – no matter in which generation they were born – to have a strong desire to admire someone.

However, from Suen's perspective, today's celebrities are not as distinctive and valuable as previous ones. This can be attributed to the creation of social media such as Facebook and Twitter, which have turned many celebrities into an ordinary, too-approachable person: 'Through social media, celebrities have become so down-to-earth nowadays. They may tell you that they have eaten a bowl of Korean noodles […] or have been to a café and enjoyed a waffle'. On the other hand, in the 1970s and 1980s, 'fans might have needed to stand at the entrance of the radio station for so long in order to take a twenty-second glance at the celebrity'.

Suen said that, with the propagation of media, nowadays everyone has the opportunity to become a celebrity. According to Elberse (2013b), the rise of digital technology has reduced the cost of production and distribution, thereby allowing entertainment industries' amateurs and other industry outsiders to generate and disseminate their own creations. Unlike the traditional media, which operate in a linear, one-way model, social media (e.g. blogs, Facebook, Twitter) are in fact interactive in nature. Therefore, people can make good use of the digital channel to spread their creations to their target audiences.

> [They gradually] build up sizable fan bases by themselves. For example, Lady Gaga has over 61,000,000 followers in her Facebook account by updating her status occasionally; while in Hong Kong, a lot of celebrities are using Weibo to build their fan bases. These channels give them power in negotiations with [traditional] media producers, which in turn enables [them] to secure higher compensation [as if a celebrity].
>
> (Elberse, 2013b, p. 197)

Such power through digital media is not limited to celebrities. Suen explained that 'in many cases, someone just uploaded a clip online, and out of nowhere he/she could enjoy an instant fame, hence becoming the so-called "celebrity"'. Given that an ordinary person can turn themselves into a celebrity out of nowhere, Suen regarded media as the most important agent to create celebrity, in accordance with the argument proposed by Elberse (2013b). The scholar asserted that the rise of digital technology and social media has further reinforced media's power not only in propagandizing celebrity culture, but also in creating and/or upholding a star's popularity. Such power, previously wielded only by the gatekeepers within the traditional media organizations, has been shifted to the hands of individuals. Individuals can now bypass the media gatekeepers, directly and freely disseminating their messages to the public via digital medial platforms.

According to Marwick and Boyd (2011), 'networked media is changing celebrity culture, the ways that people relate to celebrity images, how celebrities are produced, and how celebrity is practiced'. Celebrities use social media nowadays to develop and maintain their audience (Senft, 2008). Although this might lead some critics to comment about the declining social and economic value of celebrity, others advocate that this provides opportunities for the celebrities to simultaneously construct and craft their intended identities, in addition to controlling and maintaining their fan base (Marwick & Boyd, 2011; Turner, 2004).

Changing media and entertainment landscapes in Hong Kong

As an experienced media practitioner, Suen commented that the media in Hong Kong has developed into a very sophisticated business:

> Starting from the 1970s to 1980s, arrays of magazines have been published in Hong Kong. Even when I was in my tender age, a newspaper called *Television Daily*[1] was issued, dedicated to reporting television programmes, stars and entertainment news on a daily basis, which was very rare in other countries.

However, Suen expressed the opinion that Hong Kong's media development has recently encountered obstacles, prompting it to lose its sheen. First, it lacks a clear direction, much like the whole entertainment business in Hong Kong:

> We do not know what to do next [...]. The paparazzi reporting style used to be very entertaining to the audience, yet people started to feel bored. In many aspects, there is nothing special to shed light on [in Hong Kong].

Second, the entertainment industry in Hong Kong was not tactical. The term 'guerrilla' was used as a metaphor to describe how the practice of the Hong Kong entertainment industry tried to create as many new stars as possible with limited foresight:

> If the new stars become famous, that's great! If not, just let it be. For instance, in a local music company established by a renowned Hong Kong male singer, many artists failed to become notable and popular in the long run, because I think the entrepreneur did not have a thorough plan.

As such, whether it is based on his sarcastic or pessimistic perspective, Suen perceived Hong Kong celebrities as no longer being persuasive and marketable.

Third, the lack of communication between media and entertainment industries in Hong Kong has also contributed to the cessation of their development:

> Reporters still think that they are privileged to reveal the scandals of the artists [and entertainment companies]. They are immersed in a very traditional mode of thinking, leading the whole media industry to be stagnant, with a rather old-fashioned mentality or media logic.

Suen mentioned the 'excommunication incident' of a Korean female star from a regionally celebrated Korean girl group to illustrate his point:

> Kelly [pseudonym], a member of a famed Korean girl group, was rumoured to be kicked out [...]. While many people were afraid that this might pose a negative image on the entertainment company, the reality was that the company collaborated with a tabloid and tried to disclose some bad news about Kelly from time to time, making people think, 'Oh, the company is not that bad… Kelly herself is so weird that she is obsessed with her lover and own fashion brand [without putting much effort into the group]'. The timing was perfect.

In contrast, media business development in mainland China and South Korea has recently enjoyed a meteoric rise, arguably due to closer collaboration between the media and entertainment companies. Instead of taking a defensive role when dealing with the aggressive media, these entertainment companies have cherished the power of the media and diplomatically used them to meet their own ends.

Escalation of the South Korean entertainment industry and its celebrity

The Korean wave became a global sensation in the mid-1990s, and caused rapid development in both the media and entertainment industries. *The Economist* (2012, n.p.) wrote that 'Korean pop is turning into an export success. Groups such as Super Junior and 2NE1 now sell millions of CDs and concert tickets in other parts of Asia'. This phenomenon was also noted by Suen: 'To me, they are created by standardized formulas'. He explained that, to make these idol groups successful, the group members should initially be endowed or 'equip' themselves with an alluring face and body shape so as to become the epitome of charm and object of admiration: '[Korean] girl groups usually sell their sexiness and their long legs, whereas the boy groups sell their fit bodies and handsome faces'.

Suen admitted that South Korea's influence on Hong Kong's media landscape is so strong and prevalent that it is not only limited to the media industry itself, but also the daily life of citizens:

From 2010 onwards, more and more media outlets and publishers started inviting me to write columns related to South Korea, and it was truly sporadic! Everyone started talking about this country, and the topic was not only confined to entertainment, but also lifestyle […]. Just taking Korean food culture as an example, it in fact has not changed a lot since twenty years ago, yet many people suddenly became so fascinated with Korean fried chicken simply because of one extremely popular television drama [*My Love from the Star (별에서 온 그대)* (Chang, 2013)] in which Jeon Ji-hyeon [全智賢] frequently eats fried chicken.

The proliferation of the Korean wave immediately triggered the Hong Kong media's interest in reporting any Korean news, subsequently overshadowing the influence of Japanese and other cultures.

Many lifestyle magazines targeting adolescents no longer report Japanese fashion nowadays. In the past, Japanese fashion was categorized as chic and youthful. It is now superseded by Korean fashion, and information about Korean street style and cosmetics has flourished and is coveted by the young audience.

Figure 25: Patrick Suen with Jun Ji-hyun, a renowned South Korean actress.

Figure 26: Patrick Suen with Choi Si-won, a renowned South Korean singer (a member of the South Korean boy band Super Junior) and actor.

However, when discussing the future development of the Korean entertainment industry, Suen expressed concern since the 'Korean Wave' market has almost saturated:

[The Korean pop music industry] is now situated in an embarrassing juncture. Members of many famed Korean groups are gradually entering their thirties, and many people are getting tired of seeing them in the media [...]. [For the new generation], it's very hard to loyally worship a single group for more than ten years. Famed groups such as Super Junior and Girls Generation have been established for nearly ten years and many of their fans have turned from teenage girls to married housewives.

This also explains why the management companies of these K-pop stars gradually devoted much more effort toward refashioning them as movie or television stars to suit the evolving needs and conditions of the audience or fans.

Media collaboration with Korean celebrities

When Suen talked about the experience of collaborating with different Korean stars, he asserted that the work mode of the Korean star industry is in many ways similar to the Japanese one in that they both heavily emphasized protecting the image of the celebrities:

They [Korean entertainment companies] required us to prepare the work to a meticulous level. For example, they may require us to send all the interview questions for their perusal and revision in advance [...]. They are inclined to manage the image of their celebrities seriously.

Suen shared one incident to demonstrate how Korean artist management personnel generally overprotect stars:

I met an up-and-coming Korean girl group before [...]. Everyone thought that they are quite adorable and amiable. The fact is that, however, they are respectively kept at a distance from everyone by a curtain set between each seat while travelling. That means I could not have any conversation with them even though they were sitting right next to me.

In comparison, the work mode of Hong Kong's and mainland China's entertainment industries is different. As portrayed by Suen, 'Comparatively, we can have a more direct conversation with the stars in Hong Kong, Taiwan, or mainland China, and we do not need to prepare too much. We just need to inform the artists about the clothing style'.

According to Suen, the overprotective practice of those in the Korean entertainment industry has scared off many Hong Kong media and entertainment industry personnel. In many cases, individuals have hesitations in working with Korean stars after the first collaboration as 'they could be very troublesome':

> They, on the one hand, have the compulsive 'seek after truth' mentality, resembling the Japanese style that requires you to prepare everything at the outset. Yet, on the other hand, they would become very 'flexible' [and chaotic] right before or during the event by altering everything planned.

Suen elucidated that not all Korean stars are difficult to work with. It would be easier to work with actors or actresses as most of them are more mature, and their artist managers would not protect them like spoiled kids:

> To me, making a movie is an act of teamwork. If you are not performing well, other people may put the blame on you. Yet, when you are a singer, you are a superstar that you just need to stand on the stage and the fans will scream accordingly. This may create an illusion.

In recent years, numerous established Korean celebrities have successfully started their own entertainment business or artist management companies. Suen attributed this to the fruitful experience they faced in the entertainment industry, as well as to their foresight:

> To me, legendary celebrities such as Lee Byung-hun [李秉憲] and Bae Yong-joon [裴勇俊] are really smart. They foresaw that their fame could never last into their seventies and therefore, by utilizing their personal experience and connections in the showbiz, they set up their own entertainment companies in order to perpetuate their legacy by creating new stars. One notable example is Kim Soo-hyun [金秀賢], who was in fact reared by Bae Yong-joon.

Kam Kwok-leung (甘國亮)

Kam Kwok-leung (甘國亮) is an experienced practitioner in the entertainment industry, and has achieved great success in television, film, radio, stage and writing. He has served in senior posts at various media outlets, including Hong Kong Video Publishing Company, TVB, Asia Television (ATV), Star TV, Phoenix TV, Metro Radio and Commercial Radio. Because of his active engagement, he has been hailed as a dignitary in Hong Kong's creative and entertainment industry.

In 1970, he made his debut on TVB after joining the artist training programme; in 1974, he played the main role in the classic Shaw Brothers horror film 蛇殺手/*Killer Snake* (Kuei,

Figure 27: Interviewing with Kam Kwok-leung, an experienced practitioner of the entertainment industry in Asia.

1974). Two years later, he was promoted to director and worked on numerous shows before his further promotion to producer in 1978. The films and television series' he produced and/or directed include 孖生姊妹/*Between the Twins* (P. Chan, 1978), 神奇兩女俠/*Wonder Women* (Kam, 1987), 秦俑/*A Terracotta Warrior* (Ching, 1989) and 熱愛島/*Passion Island* (Kam, 2012). In addition to his achievements in the entertainment industry, Kam is also a fashionista who participates in various fashion events.

Celebrity in Hong Kong's television industry

According to Altman (2005), 'television has made celebrities both prevalent and ubiquitous' (p. 2). As indicated by Kam, the television industry in Hong Kong contributes a great deal to creating celebrities. Due to its popularity, people are able to receive news stories about television artists, increasing their visibility and subsequently transforming them into celebrities.

Because of the development of media, we can gather news from everywhere. We can watch news, witness the Americans land on the moon, as well as listen to the most popular music group Lotus simply by pressing a button at home [...]. [In the old days,] you would never imagine that you could watch a movie from your own TV screen.

Television dramas have been one of the most important sources of entertainment for Hong Kong as it developed into a global city (Fung, 2004). Most citizens in Hong Kong gather news about celebrities from the television. As a result, the relationship between television and celebrities has become complementary and inseparable.

Kam believes that the establishment of artist training programmes by television broadcasters is beneficial to the formation of celebrities. Starting with the issue of cable television licenses in the 1950s, Rediffusion Television Limited (RTV) established an artist training programme to provide professional training to create talents interested in acting and/or performing. In 1971, four years after the launch of TVB, the broadcaster formed another programme to produce artists and Kam was one of the first candidates to participate:

The idea [of establishing a professional artist training programme] comes from Sir Run Run Shaw, a Hong Kong entertainment mogul. He thought that every industry needs teenagers to sustain its development. In fact, nothing is better than starting a training programme as it can gather a group of teenagers with enthusiasm in planning their future, as well as [gathering those] with great aspiration. The qualities of these candidates should be better than those found by a talent agent.

Figure 28: Together with Andy Lau, a famous actor and singer in Asia, Kam Kowk-leung was one of the award presenters at the 7th Hong Kong Asian Film Festival.

Figure 29: As the graduates of the TVB artist-training program, Kam Kwok-leung and Chow Yun-fat were planning a TV program to pay tribute to their former teacher, Chung King-fai (SBS), a Hong Kong actor, director, TV producer, program host and performing arts educator.

Figure 30: Kam Kwok-leung and Coco Lee, a famous international singer, at the Ming Pao Weekly Annual Dinner in 2013.

Figure 31: Kam Kwok-leung and Michelle Yeoh, a renowned international actress, at the 7th Hong Kong Asian Film Festival in 2013.

Figure 32: Kam Kwok-leung and Tony Leung, a famous international actor, at the premiere of Leung's movie – *The Silent War.*

TVB's artist training programme was not the first one in Hong Kong, but it was the most sustainable and successful one. According to an online article (Sina News, 2012), the TVB artist training programme initially lasted for one year, when candidates had to learn knowledge about movie editing, dramaturgical approach and acting skills, among other skills. From 1984, the programme was restructured into three specific programmes, specifically targeting the development of artists, dancers and hosts. The training duration was also shortened to six months. The first three months mainly focused on theoretical concepts, while the last three months involved practical experiences. Several famous celebrities graduated from this artist programme, including Chow Yun-fat (周潤發), Andy Lau (劉德華), Tony Leung (梁朝偉), Stephen Chow (周星馳) and Carina Lau (劉嘉玲). These celebrities are not only well-known in that territory, but also throughout Asia and worldwide.

Media and celebrity: The good and the bad

Many scholars have argued that the media are the determinants of celebrity, yet Kam questioned its effectiveness. From his perspective, the effect of the media is mainly confined to a small, local level. Therefore, the notion of so-called celebrity is also limited to a particular territory:

> The celebrities [produced by Hong Kong media] are just well-known for our citizens of 7 million [...]. How about people in other countries? Mexico? Yugoslavia? Argentina? [...]. A TV station is normally just a local station so that its effect is bounded [by] its own borders.

From Kam's point of view, the importance of local media in creating celebrities is overvalued.

As mentioned by Marshall (1997), today's film industry works closely with famous celebrities because of their independence and close connection with their audiences, which can stimulate the box office. According to Mazdon (2006), major gatherings such as the Cannes Film Festival are extremely important events in the filmic calendar, both nationally and globally. Given that these events receive extensive media coverage, celebrities are eager to participate in them in order to increase their visibility worldwide. However, as an experienced practitioner of the media and entertainment industry, Kam claimed that these award ceremonies are not representative at all, as they are often held by several countries. Consequently, their effects are limited to these countries:

> For a prize presentation ceremony receiving attention from more than 80 countries across the world, it is in fact only produced by approximately 400 people in America. Therefore, many names shown on the results look extremely unfamiliar to many of us living in Hong Kong [...]. So how do we calculate whether a person can be regarded as a celebrity or not?

If he/she does not have influence in a particular market that he/she could not receive any return from there, then how can we regard him/her as a celebrity?

As further pointed out by Kam, two types of media influence the visibility of celebrities. Good media cover the positive aspects of celebrities; they help celebrities develop a more positive image and increase their visibility. However, 'there are some degrading and despicable media in countries such as the United Kingdom, the United States and Japan. The practitioners working there all fool around'. The *National Enquirer* is an American supermarket tabloid published by American Media Inc. (AMI). It publicly promotes the idea of paying sources for 'unvarnished' stories and photos of celebrities. Given how mainstream media pride themselves on their professionalism and ethical standard, they are generally disgusted by these practices and believe sometimes the *National Enquirer*'s coverage has gone too far. For example, in February 2012, it posted an article showing Whitney Houston having collapsed from a cocaine and alcohol binge during her world tour, claiming that she only had five years left to live. Two days later, she was actually found dead in her room (TMZ staff, 2012). In the week following Houston's death, the *National Enquirer* published a photo of her body in an open casket on its front page (Ravitz, 2012). Similar examples exist in Hong Kong as well, such as the gossip tabloids *Oriental Sunday* and *Next Magazine*, which initiated the Edison Chen (陳冠希) photo scandal in 2008 by printing intimate and explicit photographs of Chen and various female celebrities, including Gillian Chung[2] (鍾欣桐), Cecilia Cheng (張柏芝), Bobo Chan (陳文媛) and Rachel Ngan (顏穎思) from the Hong Kong Discuss Forum (Frater, 2008). This scandal dominated the front covers of gossip magazines in Hong Kong for a while. As Kam expressed, celebrities in these media are often poorly represented, while stories are often exaggerated or even fabricated, making them 'notoriously visible'. For instance, 'from time to time, there is news about the private sexual life of the celebrities, as well as their misbehaviour. In no way is such news beneficial [to either celebrities or society]'.

Interestingly, when asked to comment on the paparazzi, Kam provided a unique perspective for explaining the practice, which he sees as an equal exchange between the media and celebrity. To him, some celebrities intentionally choose to trade their own privacy to sustain their visibility. Without the paparazzi, celebrities do not know how to expose themselves to the public.

How could you show your 'unintentional' sexiness to the public? Everybody loves seeing these photos. Without this platform, how could you publish these photos? Are you going to post them on the wall? Nothing is better than having the paparazzi [take photos of your private life].

Erica Yuen (袁彌明) (2007), a Miss Hong Kong contestant in 2005, used her *Apple Daily* column (originally published on her personal blog) to discuss the popularity of particular 'scandals' published in tabloid magazines in Hong Kong. She identified three categories in her interpretation: (1) 'true material' (真料); (2) 'collaborative material' (夾料); and (3) 'leaked material' (放料) (Yuen, 2007). 'True material' involves the paparazzi obtaining stories by patiently and relentlessly following a target around or through accidental encounters. An example of this is when the media followed and investigated Andy Lau (劉德華) to uncover his marriage with Carol Chu (朱麗倩). To Yuen (2007), this is a fair game. 'Collaborative material' refers to stories in which the subjects script everything with the reporters, including the theme and all the details. According to Yuen (2007), collaborative stories are usually completely favourable to the subject. For example, in March 2015, producer Tiffany Chan (陳明英) (also known as 'Mrs. Heung' [向太]) did an interview with *Apple Daily* in which she delineated the behind-the-scene details of dismissing Cecilia Cheung (張栢芝) from the movie *3D 封神榜/Legend of the Gods* (Hui & Yeung, 2016). The report seemed to accuse Cheung of unprofessionalism, which served Chan's purposes.

'Leaked materials' include stories in which the subjects tipped off the reporters or photojournalists about where and when to show up, as well as what to expect when they got there. For example, after Heidi Chan (陳慧玲), the official wife of casino tycoon Alvin Chau (周焯華), gave birth to daughter Damiana on 30 May 2015, rumours were rife that Mandy Lieu (劉碧麗), Chau's extramarital girlfriend, leaked the news of her childbirth in London to the media herself in an attempt to provoke the then pregnant Chan (Hsia, 2015). Photos were taken to show Lieu with her newborn daughter. Such a move was a two-tiered achievement for Lieu, who accomplished her personal goal in provoking Chan while satisfying her need to gain publicity.

To Kam, although paparazzi do infringe on the privacy of many celebrities to a certain extent, they in fact satisfy the public's strong need for celebrity news. At the same time, to enhance one's visibility, some celebrities 'do not attend to their professionalism properly' while also selling their own privacy to the media for publicity. As indicated by Pringle (2004), the extensive opportunities for a glimpse into the private lives of celebrities via intrusive media means that people can get ever closer to their idols, which can in turn sustain the visibility of those celebrities.

Social media: A boost or a drug

Finally, Kam criticized the overuse of social media that diminishes the value of celebrities:

> Just think about where the values [of the celebrities] go. From a more positive point of view, it is convenient. For example, 'Bus Uncle' from Hong Kong[3], DJ Soda from Korea[4], Guo Mei-mei (郭美美) from China[5], etc. However, when celebrities become extremely reachable, […] I leave you to judge their own values.

Kam's criticism of digital media concurs with Marshall (2006), who claimed that the presentation of the self via blogs and webcams has generated an implausible surplus of sources of the self that consequently undermines the value of the many celebrity discourses that now circulate.

While the emergence of social media has provided numerous opportunities for ordinary people to popularize themselves, more and more 'microcelebrities' have emerged for whom fame is relatively narrow in scope and likely to be transient. Kam explicitly stated, 'I encouraged them to think twice before taking action. If [those interested in entering the entertainment industry] perform poorly in analysis, they would probably fend for themselves […]. It's not a joke'. Indeed, Kam believes it is easy nowadays for someone to become famous through the support of traditional, digital and social media, although sustaining such social influence is another story.

Final insights

Due to its extensive reach, the media are an influential vehicle in people's everyday lives (Biagi, 2012), shaping how the masses think and behave. As Couldry (2012) explained, our 'ways of making sense of the world work primarily through, or in reliance on, media' (p. 160). Indeed, it is almost impossible to consume media without seeing a celebrity nowadays, especially as we are all living in a celebrity-fixated world.

Media is a business and the general public is its target audience. Like any other business, the media must generate profits to operate and keep its business running. To do so, the media feed its target audience with what they want to see, read and listen to via various channels, such as television, print and radio. As the general public is living in a celebrity-obsessed society (Esch, 2013), and has a strong interest in and appetite for the affairs of celebrities, the media make celebrities the main focus on their different channels. For example, magazines feature celebrities on their covers and within their pages; newspapers have a special section that focuses exclusively on celebrity news; and there are channels such as E! in the United States and programmes such as 娛樂頭條/*Entertainment Headline* (2009) in Hong Kong whose sole purpose is reporting on celebrities. After all, as a business, the media must strive financially: they must market what is appealing to its audience, which often seems to be stories about celebrities.

Without question, the media coverage of celebrities is a money-spinning exploit for the media organizations (Gregory, 2008). The public enjoys hearing and seeing about the lives of the rich and famous. People are now more captivated by the personal and private realms of celebrities (Gorin & Dubied, 2011), rather than their work and achievement. Notwithstanding this, people have a certain amount of *schadenfreude*[6] when it comes to the lives of celebrities (van Dijk, Ouwerkerk, van Koningsbruggen, & Wesseling, 2012). People truly enjoy the pitfalls that celebrities experience. Due to such substantial demand and lucrative economic benefits, the media crave exclusive stories about the private lives and/or misdeeds of celebrities to attract its target audience and so they buy their stories. As a result of this intensive desire for exclusivity, some celebrities even sell their privacy to the media to gain public attention and publicity. As Johnson (2004), a reporter for the popular British celebrity publication *Closer*, observed, 'celebrity gossip is a national obsession and a unifying experience across all social groups' (p. 55).

As previously mentioned, celebrity and media have a symbiotic yet asymmetrical relationship. Media can create a celebrity; in turn, celebrities can feed the media with stories that sell. However, its strong, prominent position in today's society gives the media the inordinate power to establish, maintain or even destroy a celebrity, as they can choose to downplay certain celebrities while sensationalizing others (Gregory, 2008). For example, if the media do not believe that someone is newsworthy, as gatekeepers, they will not report on that person. And if the media opt not to report on that person, that person will not gain public exposure. And without public exposure, that person will remain 'unknown' or become 'de-celebrified'. Yet, with the emergence of the Internet and social media, celebrities finally have a platform to voice their own stories, develop their own fame and gain publicity. As such, some scholars and practitioners have asserted that the media still hold the substantial and ultimate power to make or break a celebrity (cf. Evans, 2005).

Based on our interviews with three renowned media practitioners, we identified four major insights about how celebrities relate to the media.

1. Although some scholars (e.g. Van den Bulck & Tambuyzer, 2008) have a similar view as Suen – i.e. that celebrity is created and driven by the media – Mak and Kam believe that an aspirant's talent and professionalism are important in the process of celebrification and keeping one's celebrity status. Stars such as Tom Hanks, Meryl Streep and Chow Yun-fat (周潤發) have few soap-operatic elements in their lives, but their successful careers have continued unimpeded, and their celebrity statuses have flourished as a result (Gabler, n.d.). As Mak stated, an aspirant, especially in the radio industry, must establish a sense of uniqueness and professionalism to develop a long life cycle in the industry. Such uniqueness and professionalism always come from the aspirant's hard work in developing their own character and polishing their talents. Kam added that, if one's talents and character are replicable and replaceable, they will have very limited value in the entertainment industry.

2. Today's celebrities can be divided into two major categories: (1) exceptionally talented 'self-made' stars (i.e. those who gained their status through their superior talents and abilities); and (2) relatively unexceptional 'manufactured' celebrities (i.e. those who are famous through media publicity) (Furedi, 2010). Kam indicated that society is filled with the second category of celebrities. He asserted that today's celebrities, especially those in Hong Kong, lack talent and accomplishments. Similarly, Turner (2006) asserted that these individuals have no particular talents and no specific career objectives beyond the achievement of media visibility. Rojek (2001) called these celebrities 'celetoids'. These celetoids, in Kam's eyes, rely merely on unsavory appearances and behaviour to steal the spotlight and gain public attention. As many scholars have observed (e.g. Furedi, 2010; Rojek, 2001; Turner, 2006), such celebrities often disappear as fast as they are

constructed. According to Boorstin (1971), genuine fame should be earned via 'the slow, the "natural" way' rather than the 'manufactured' or 'artificial way'. In addition, Kam pessimistically considered that such a phenomenon negatively affects celebrity culture as a whole.

3. Rojek (2012) once said that 'today celebrity culture is global and ecumenical. National traditions are not necessarily privileged. Recognition of glamour and achievement is drawn from around the world' (p. 173). As a result of globalization, celebrity culture has become a worldwide phenomenon, where people from across the globe can consume celebrities from any location (Penfold, 2004) via different media channels. For example, contemporary Hong Kong teenagers are frantic about American, Korean and Japanese stars. When Kam critically defined celebrity, he emphasized the context sensitivity and reach that a celebrity could establish and maintain. In this globalized society, together with state-of-the-art (media) technologies, Kam asserted that a true celebrity today should possess an ability to create global influence. Similarly, L. Wong and Trumper (2002) explained that celebrities no longer merely belong to a particular territory. Suen also highlighted the trend of creating famous celebrities on a global level. Instead of limiting celebrities' development within local markets, many entertainment management companies have started to create celebrities who appeal to international landscapes. This is evident in the Asian market, where many Korean idol groups consist of members of various nationalities who can speak multiple languages. Holmes and Redmond (2010) concluded that today 'celebrity is recognized to be a global, international, yet also often culturally "local" phenomenon which produces modes of representation that can be felt as empowering, disingenuous and impossible to attain' (p. 7). Yet being a global celebrity is not easy. Driessens (2012) stated that there is an 'abundance of celebrities whose fame does not extend further than the limits of their particular local media-scapes' and there is a 'fairly limited number of celebrities who might be famous on a truly global scale' (p. 110).

4. In their interviews, Kam and Suen both indicated reservations and concerns regarding the development of celebrity culture in Hong Kong. Driessens (2012) observed that different media cultures crossing different contexts will generate their own celebrities; these will then shape particular celebrity cultures correspondingly. Kam blamed certain media outlets and celebrities in Hong Kong for shifting the conventional ideology behind media and celebrity cultures from an emphasis on one's talents and achievements to simply focusing on one's appearance and private life. Given the huge demand among the general public for celebrities' personal affairs, the media persist in locating the private stories of celebrities. In addition, celebrities understand that the circulation of media representations of themselves can render them famous and provide publicity (Driessens, 2012); accordingly, some celebrities collaborate and/or sell their own stories so as to become recognizable in society. With such increasingly prevalent practices, more and more upcoming celebrities – as well as more established ones – focus on working with the media rather than developing and polishing their talents. Ultimately,

according to Kam, celebrity culture in Hong Kong will gradually collapse. For Suen, he emphasized a more macro level, concluding that Hong Kong's entertainment industry has no forward direction, no well-developed strategy and no effective communication with the involved industries, especially when compared to what mainland China and South Korea are currently doing. These contributed to his assertion that Hong Kong's entertainment industry, as well as its celebrity culture, is losing its edge in Asia.

Notes

1 The newspaper was first published in 1969 and eventually dissolved in 1995 due to rampant competition from another local paper in Hong Kong, *Apple Daily*.
2 One of the singers in the popular Cantopop idol group Twins.
3 One of the 'characters' in a viral YouTube video of a quarrel on a bus between 'Bus Uncle' and a teenager in 2006. The video was widely circulated and known in Hong Kong for its profanity. https://www.youtube.com/watch?v=EsYRQkmVifg
4 A young and attractive South Korean female DJ. After appearing in an American music video, she was suspected of having undergone plastic surgery.
5 In 2001, she claimed on Weibo to be a manager for the Red Cross Society of China. Her wealthy lifestyle shown on the Internet led to suspicions of her using donations for personal enjoyment. Donations to the organization subsequently reduced, yet there was no evidence that she works or has worked with the Red Cross.
6 A German word which means the pleasure one derives from witnessing the misfortune of others.

Chapter 5

Celebrity and identity

Introduction

The complex and contested relationships between celebrity and identity have given rise to a sociological study of celebrity culture in the west (cf. Kapoor, 2013; Marshall, 1997; Rojek, 2001; Shils, 2010; Turner; 2010; van Krieken, 2012a). As the material reality of celebrity disappears into a cultural formation of meaning, it morphs into an ever-changing and intertextual sign, being discursively yet differently constructed. As such, celebrity can never be completely determined, but is subject to negotiation in the process of signification (Marshall, 1997). This is why, in Marshall's (1997) view, celebrity is 'an embodiment of a discursive battleground on the norms of individuality and personality within a culture' (p. 65). Given this, there exists a wide range of celebrity signs in society to which different audiences and social groups may hold very polarized viewpoints.

In recent years, Hong Kong and mainland Chinese cultural critics have also paid attention to the proliferation of celebrity culture in urban China, discussed the phenomena of 'ordinary' stardom of Cantopop singers, and debated the fame of young Hong Kong female models and Chinese female celebrities, as well as their significance in empowering fans to form subversive social, cultural and gender identities (Kengo [Ip], 2010; On-Tou [Law], 2012; H. Zhang, 2013). Moving away from China, we have seen new studies on *jimusho* (the entertainment industry system) in Japan, offering us a better understanding of the systematic and meticulous mode of production of Japanese idols and celebrity in the context of Asia (Marx, 2012).

Social and historical contexts are of crucial importance when linking celebrity culture to identity politics (Dunn, 1998). In this chapter, we will first define the distinction between the terms 'identity' and 'identification', followed by a discussion of how socio-technology changes identity. In this chapter, we have four in-depth interviews with Denise Ho (何韻詩), Hilary Tsui (徐濠縈), Pakho Chau (周柏豪) and Bob Lam (林盛斌). These four leading celebrities in Hong Kong's entertainment industry will further explore the issues around identity and celebrity culture.

Identity and identification

In his book *The Making of Political Identities* (1994), Laclau differentiated between 'identity' and 'identification'. Laclau considers the term 'identity' to be an original object of recognition – the essence that defines a person. This belief suggests that identity is determined by intrinsic qualities, such as birth, biology and life experience. Meanwhile, 'identification' is regarded as a process of identity formation, in which identity is not inherent, but constructed by the external forces of the individual (Laclau, 1994). Similarly, Hall (1990) suggested that the term 'identification' can be used to characterize the work involved in constructing identities, including its processes, contradictions and complexities.

This notion of identification raises questions about the identity-formation process. Is identity self-constructed, and thus an essentialist conception of identity; or externally imposed, suggesting a constructivist conception of identity (Dunn, 1998)? In response to this, 'identity politics' – whether negotiating for a single identity or multiple identities – has arisen as a result of people's resistance to the oppression of institutions linked to the subjectivity of identity (Lind, 2013).

The idea of identity can be discussed in light of what Gergen (1996) coined the tradition of 'psychological essentialism', which suggests that the mind and self are separate from the external material world. This essentialist notion of identity can be traced back to the western tradition of classical philosophers, such as Aristotle and Plato, who emphasized the ideals of pure forms and mentality over the material world. Another view of identity, which also challenged the essentialist notion of identity, comes from the postmodern and post-structuralist theorists of the 1980s and 1990s (Miller, 2011). In postmodern accounts, identity is considered to be discursively constructed (Fuss, 1989), which is derived from the claim that identity and social life are constituted in texts or representation (Dunn, 1998). Derrida (1984) argued that identity is constructed through marking differences; to him, 'the identity of a mark is also its difference and differential relation' (p. 16). For example, in this post-structuralist analysis, establishing the identity of 'man' entails the creation of the opposite identity of 'woman' (Hall, 1990). In a similar vein, Foucault suggested that identity is constructed within discourses created by specific institutions, as well as in and through specific sociohistorical contexts. Identity 'places its own point at the origin of all historicity' and is 'not a theory of the knowing subject but rather a theory of discursive practice' (Foucault, 1970, p. xiv). Along this line of thought, identity is intrinsically fluid: it is not fixed and has a shifting character over time (Dunn, 1998).

Identities are therefore tied to domination and exclusion, and are contingent on time and place (Miller, 2011). They originate externally in language, and are maintained through discursive practices, discourses, application of power, and the labelling of otherness or difference. As such, identities are often contradictory and changeable (Miller, 2011). Such a post-structuralist claim is grounded in actual developments in social and cultural realms. Scholars of this tradition have argued that society is 'fragmented' by processes of signification, consumption and power, and has therefore faced a 'decline of reason and unitary identity' (Dunn, 1998). This theoretical account considers the instability of culture as a reflection of the identity crisis in a material sociohistorical context. In particular, the changes in an advanced capitalist society have 'generated strains' on personal and social identity (Dunn, 1998).

Socio-technological changes and identity

The advent of advanced technology in the 1990s added further complexity to the post-structuralists' forms of identity. Studies on online culture have found that online interactions demonstrate a high degree of identity play (cf. Poster, 1995; Rheingold, 1993; Stone, 1995; Turkle, 1995). According to Miller (2011), the following major characteristics of the online environment enable such a transformation: access to anonymity that frees people from constraints; identity performance based on self-descriptive texts; multiple parallel identities; and the possibility to create identities that are impossible offline. These fluid and shifting characteristics have led to the Internet offering a condition in which the notion of a centred and stable self is increasingly indefensible (Gergen, 1996). At the same time, they illustrate that identity is not seen as an essential equality, but is instead seen as performed. Therefore, as the Internet has become a mass medium, different forms of online self-representation have rendered identities 'recentred' rather than 'decentred' (Miller, 2011).

In this respect, these studies of online identity emphasized the 'liberation from meat [i.e. the body]' (D. Bell, 2001), as cyberspace allows a disembodied identity construction that is free of typical markers (e.g. gender and race). This liberation from the body contributes to an online self that is decentred and fragmented, and could be seen as 'inherently transgendered' (Stone, 1995), thereby having 'the potential for the demise of patriarchal (as well as other) forms of oppression' (Miller, 2011, p. 164).

In the twenty-first century, a body of literature examining online communication technologies and the use of the Internet has pointed out that images and self-representation through images on social networking sites, rather than textual descriptions, are the dominant content in the online world. According to Miller (2011), the popular online environment has become more 'anonymous' and people tend to use social networking profiles to represent their offline 'selves'. Thus, in contrast to the findings from early Internet studies of the 1990s, contemporary studies examining the online world have indicated that the 'offline' and 'online' worlds have become more integrated, leaving little room for decentred identities and identity play.

One of the major phenomena of the Internet age has been blogging. Blogs became popular in 1999 and peaked around 2004–05, especially in developed countries. In particular, personal journal blogs became a popular topic of investigation among academic researchers in the 2000s (cf. Rak, 2005; Schmidt, 2007). Blogging exemplifies a type of online behaviour that characterizes what Giddens (1991) called the 'late modern age'. In a late modern society, individuals have relatively more freedom and capacity to reshape their identities because they can be free from the traditions and history of the globalized world. In this context of disembeddedness, social relationships are considered voluntary, and people therefore gravitate toward intimacy and relationships based on trust and mutual self-disclosure. Because of the possibilities inherent in allowing anonymity, 'the internet in general and blogging in particular is seen as the ideal environment [...] for pervasive self-disclosure and relationship building' (Miller, 2011, p. 170).

Such an attempt at constructing online identity can be further understood by drawing on the concept of the network society. In his books *The Rise of Network Society* (1996) and *The Power of Identity* (1997), Manuel Castells argued that identity is a response to the threats brought about by globalization, counteracting the homogeneity, lack of uniqueness and placelessness associated with globalization. According to Castells (1996), 'our societies are increasingly structured around a bipolar opposition between the net and the self' (p.3). According to Castells, identity can be instrumental in resistance and political mobilization as it becomes increasingly embedded in a network society. Set against this backdrop, identity is closely linked to personal resistance against external forces in a network society; identity politics could therefore be seen as a characteristic of the digital information age.

Another more popular form of online culture has been social networking websites (SNWs), such as Facebook. SNWs tend to promote a recentring of online identity within the offline, embodied self (Miller, 2011). Scholars have demonstrated that a self-representation profile on a social networking site is embedded within the context of offline contacts and friends (Boyd & Heer, 2006; S. Zhao, Grasmuck, & Martin, 2008). According to S. Zhao et al. (2008), identity construction on Facebook involves three modes in particular: first, the 'visual self' is displayed to create desired impressions; second, the 'cultural self' is constructed in the form of showing preferences, consumption and tastes; and third, 'self-description' is included in the profile sections. Mobile networking technology, the requests of 'distributed presence' (van den Berg, 2009), and hence the mixing of one's different social contexts (e.g. family, friends, other business contacts, etc.) and identities on a social networking site (e.g. Facebook or a microblog) have arguably led to a more centred and situated self. In these cases, individuals might tend to maintain consistent identities under the social media panopticon.

An example of identity construction could be the Twitter profile of celebrities. Marwick and Boyd (2011) argued that a celebrity's image on Twitter is constructed as a part of people's everyday lives and thus is culturally persuasive. In this respect, celebrity culture generates cultural meanings in people's everyday lives by creating a self that can be consumed by the online audience. Online media offers a platform for celebrities to disclose their 'backstage' to their fans, communicating with them directly and making conversations visible to the public. Like Facebook, Twitter produces 'context collapse' (Boyd, 2008), in which 'multiple audiences, usually thought of as separate, co-exist in a single social context' (Marwick & Boyd, 2011). A celebrity will therefore need to maintain self-image through 'impression management' strategies, which involves an ongoing adjustment to the perceptions of audience judgement (Goffman, 1959). For example, a celebrity can acknowledge fans publicly and create affiliations with followers using language. Moreover, instead of maintaining a distance from their fans through formal middlepersons, such as artist managers or agents, celebrities can use social media to project a shortened distance between themselves and their fans, create a sense of intimacy, and gain status and attention.

Meanwhile, fans can directly engage in a dialogue with and gain a response from celebrities. In this sense, the power relationship between the celebrity and their fans is seen as less polarized. Celebrity identity is therefore shaped in a bottom-up manner by the public, who are able to interact with the celebrity directly through microblogging sites. Yet the opening up of communication does not equalize their status. Rather, the power differentials between 'celebrities' and 'non-celebrities' still exist (Marwick & Boyd, 2011). According to Marwick and Boyd (2011), 'new media not only provides new outlets for the exploration of celebrity, but complicates the dynamics between celebrity practitioners, their audiences, and those who occupy spaces in-between' (p. 156).

Thus far, the important social and cultural theories and debates surrounding the nature of identity and identification processes have been broadly presented. Although some scholars consider identities to be fixed objects, other argue that identities are subject to alteration, representation and signification over time, and are contingent on place, particularly through texts, discursive practices and images. Previous studies have demonstrated that technology has been increasingly powerful in shaping the development of self-identity construction. In the twenty-first century, new media and digital culture are becoming more crucial in terms of a celebrity's identity construction, as they bring complexity to 'star qualities', celebrity culture, fan–star relationships and the celebrity production industry. The subsequent four case studies, based on in-depth interviews with Denise Ho (何韻詩), Hilary Tsui (徐濠縈), Pakho Chau (周柏豪) and Bob Lam (林盛斌) – leading celebrities in Hong Kong's entertainment industry – will further explore the issues around identity and celebrity culture, as well as their relationship to Hong Kong society. In doing so, they debunk the essentialist notion of 'star qualities' and celebrity identity as intrinsic, endowed and fixed, comprehend the discursive construction process, and link the meanings of celebrity (as a symbolic and mediated sign) and their identity formation to Hong Kong's specific environment.

Celebrity interviews

Denise Ho (何韻詩)

Denise Ho (何韻詩) (nicknamed HOCC) is a renowned Cantopop singer and film actress. As a newcomer to showbiz, she first won the 15th New Talent Singing Award in 1996. Since then, she has released more than twenty Cantonese records and received an array of significant music awards, including the Best Cantonese Female Singer at the Chinese Music Media Awards and the Female Singer Award (Bronze Award in 2002, Silver Award in 2005 and Gold Award in 2006) at Commercial Radio Hong Kong's Ultimate Song Chart Awards. In 2011, she was nominated for the Best Mandarin Female Singer at the 25th Annual Taiwan Golden Melody Awards. Ho has frequently venerated her musical master, the late legendary pop singer Anita Mui (梅艷芳), as her most important muse and an inspiration for her musical career.

Committed to supporting people in need – ranging from the elderly to the sick, the poor, the young and the disabled – Ho established her own charitable foundation in May 2007, entitled the HOCC Charity Fund. She is one of the founding members of the BigLove

Figure 33: Interview with Denise Ho at the Department of Sociology, The University of Hong Kong.

Alliance, a non-governmental organization established in January 2013 advocating equal rights for LGBT communities in Hong Kong. Ho is also one of the few local singers who openly supported the Occupy Movement in September 2014 (also called the Umbrella Movement and Civil Disobedience Movement) by both advocating for full universal suffrage in Hong Kong and participating in the protest. In the same year, Ho became a columnist for *Apple Daily* (one of Hong Kong's most widely circulated newspapers). In March 2015, Ho officially announced that she was no longer represented by mainstream record company East Asia Music (Holdings) Ltd. (with whom she had signed a contract in 2004) and was now an independent artist/singer.

Manifesting celebrity identity amid the global upsurge of ICT

In the digital age, the ubiquity of information and communications technology (ICT) seems to offer an opportunity for everyone across the globe to 'liberate from the meat' (D. Bell, 2001) so as to construct, present and manage their self-identity autonomously in cyberspace. According to Roberts (2010), the advent of the Internet made 'the process of celebrity formation more "democratic"' (p. 235). Apparently, ICT enables individuals to exert their bottom-up power so as to influence and control the process of celebrity formation; one may even be able to determine their own aspirations, which in the past was mostly determined and monitored by established media organizations and entertainment corporations. However, this may also reinforce one's powerlessness in the process of celebrity formation amid the digital panopticon and multi-faceted power relationships between celebrities, other entertainment industry participants and faceless yet hypercritical netizens. Overall, technological advancements have altered, broadened and even problematized the very notion of celebrity in society, making it a socioculturally contingent concept that complicates identification processes.

As indicated by Ho, some notable differences exist between how celebrity was defined in the past and how it is defined in today's digitized world. In the past, people who were regularly featured in the mass media could be considered as celebrities. In the age of traditional media, Ho claimed, one had to possess talents or have some exceptional abilities to be named a celebrity. The celebrity–audience relationship was characterized by the passive audience who aspired to the glitzy lives of celebrities, identified with the stories portrayed by their song lyrics, and so forth. Prior to the 1990s, the general public considered celebrities to be a distant social group, like the stars in the sky. This group was utterly unreachable, and personified certain ideal qualities and personalities within local cultures. Ho explained:

> When I was small, […] as a fan, you could never critique your idol's image from head to toe. Or, even not talking about your own idols, […] if I saw Chow Yun-fat [周潤發] eating egg waffles, for instance, I would never be able to stand aside and immediately comment on his act [and] perhaps be a very passive audience only.

Yet, according to Ho, nowadays the meaning of celebrity has transformed and become increasingly inclusive, especially since the emergence of the Internet culture and its permeation into our everyday lives. The rise of reality television shows and the Internet has blurred the boundary between celebrity and non-celebrity, making it more difficult to define the concept. People can now become famous overnight because of just one highly mediatized video or blog post. Although such a change in celebrity culture signifies a loosening of social hierarchies, exclusive status systems and the restricted definition of celebrity, Ho hesitated to categorize these celetoids (Rojek, 2001) as celebrities because of their short-lived life cycles as public figures (Turner, 2010), as well as the media industries' further manipulation of the symbolic economy in the service of their own interests (Turner, 2010). She recalled an example of such a phenomenon:

> Particularly in Taiwan, it is common that when there is a fad, a person becomes a topic and […] attends some variety shows [and] becomes a talking point over a certain period of time. Shall we consider this type of people celebrity? The person has made his/her name well-known. But his/her [fame's] lifespan might be very short. Perhaps he/she would disappear after two weeks. That's why I feel that it is difficult to talk about the word 'celebrity' […]. It's difficult to define.

Ho's example resonates with what Turner (2010) referred to as the 'demotic turn' whereby 'ordinary people' have become increasingly visible within celebrity culture on websites, television, radio, etc. Psychologically, the general public can easily identify and associate themselves with the 'ordinariness' of these celebrities because they provide them with hope (an imaginary sensation) and excitement about becoming famous and successful out of their dreary everydayness. In reality, it is uncertain whether or not this form of celebrity can manifest a sustainable fame and identity. Problematically, the digital democratization of celebrity culture discursively produces a compulsion for ordinary people to become famous, exposing them to an immense level of competition for attention and scrutiny that will last until the day these 'instant celebrities' lose their lustre. Yet the unwanted criticisms and unfulfilled dreams remain.

Celebrity culture and digital surveillance

Although television has already allowed the public to evaluate and adjudicate on the conduct of public figures and celebrities, essentially placing these people under surveillance (van Krieken, 2012a), the widespread use of the Internet and ICT has further reinforced the interactive mode of communication between celebrities and audiences, empowering viewers in scrutinizing celebrities second by second.

From Ho's viewpoint as a celebrity, although the Internet has enabled more interaction and closer relationships between celebrities and audiences, celebrities pay a price for their popularity, namely the loss of their freedom and privacy:

> You lose your freedom and privacy [as a celebrity]. [And its] even more extreme, especially in this age. In the past few days – as you might have seen – who is dating whom, and who are back on […] – it seems like everyone in the whole world is their mother. It seems [as though] all things [related to celebrities] are the public's business.

One positive aspect of the Internet is that it makes celebrity admirers feel psychologically more connected with their idols, enabling them to conveniently garner the celebrity news that they crave. Fans eventually become more enthusiastic in various ways, and the formation of an individual star's fame in particular and celebrity culture in general is accelerated (Ferris & Harris, 2011). The Internet is a platform of 'context collapse' (Boyd, 2008) on which different social contexts are mixed. The public, consisting of multiple audiences – from family, personal friends, fans and business contacts to the anonymous netizens around the world – can radically magnify ideological values, directly and openly criticizing a celebrity (from very polarized and subjective perspectives) on their official and personal Facebook or Weibo accounts for their public image or personal lifestyle, with no responsibility. Such damaging comments usually 'go viral' online very quickly. Based on Ho's observations, such a development has triggered an unhealthy celebrity–public relationship, trapping today's celebrities under an ideological scrutiny that limits not only the symbolic signs they represent, but also their physical actions and behaviours:

Now we are, like, lying on the chopping board. People who dislike us can randomly 'shoot an arrow' at us any time or slap our face [...]. I feel like today's celebrities, or maybe [those who work] in our field, have become punching bags, which is another identity for us.

Ho also conveyed how she felt about the influence of the Internet on celebrity culture, suggesting that it had impacted how celebrities behave. Indeed, celebrities tend to be more hesitant when speaking their minds or they are very careful with their words:

So that means you have to consider very carefully before you take every step: Is it safe to do this? You try to stand at the safest platform which doesn't lead you to more troubles. So this gradually turns into a type [of attitude]: I don't need to care about the things that are not related to me. This is in fact rather scary, I mean, this attitude.

She offered two reasons why celebrities have become more careful with their words. The first is linked to economic concerns, which are especially apparent when a celebrity is asked by media journalists to comment on controversial social, political and/or cultural issues.

Figure 34: Ho asserted that nowadays celebrities have become the 'punching bags' in public.

Second, they are afraid of being criticized. Regarding the latter, Ho noticed that there is the potential for online media, such as forums, to magnify and propagandize celebrities' remarks into soundbites and make them the 'target' of news headlines. As Miller (2011) noted, the supremacy of hypersurveillance is further immortalized in and through the media and entertainment industry:

> [Under the] digital panopticon [...] people limit their actions and behave differently when they feel as though they are being watched [...]. [A] sense of being oppressed [makes someone] become fearful not of doing wrong, but of being seen as wrong [...] not conducive to a free or democratic way of life.
>
> (Miller, 2001, p. 131)

Given that they are part of the larger entertainment industry system, celebrities may need to abide by and satisfy the existing rules, and follow what companies say in order to maintain their 'institutionalized' charisma (Shils, 2010). Otherwise, their career may be at risk or even jeopardized. A celebrity's power is also structured within the ideological media system, and organized around the social ideals of gendered identity, appearance, behaviour and even political outlook (van Krieken, 2012a). In March 2015, another outspoken, openly gay Cantopop singer Anthony Wong (黃耀明) admitted that he had not received any work in Hong Kong or mainland China for nearly half a year after his open support and active participation in the Occupy Movement. Although Wong thought the financial sacrifice was worth it, he worried about Hong Kong itself, as local people have become more conservative and prudent in relation to this movement (V. Chow, 2015).

For mass media, public personality is endowed with the attention capital necessary to increase viewership and be leveraged into sales (van Krieken, 2012a). Ho acknowledged the economic value of celebrity and indicated that, as in all kinds of industries and organizations, the amount of rewards varies across different roles (i.e. types of creative workers) within the entertainment industry. Although a famous celebrity might earn more than a marketing executive, an artist manager, a producer or a technician in the entertainment industry, they also need to sacrifice their freedom and privacy to a greater extent:

> The reward is related to [...] economic efficacy. If you do not have [...] the influence, [...] if your fame is incapable of generating that level of 'noise' in public, nobody will pay attention to you when you ask for a reward of several hundred thousand or several million dollars.

The concepts of privacy and anonymous identity – first brought up by the capitalist socio-economic structure in the west during the period of urban industrialization in the late nineteenth century – started to erode again amidst the boom of media celebrity in the twentieth century. However, invasion of privacy has been gradually accepted as long as it is considered in the public interest. Nowadays, the general public believe they have the right to peep into the private life of a celebrity as part of their everyday entertainment (Miller, 2011). Suddenly, the term 'celebrity' has become an oxymoron signifying quintessence and vulgarity, supremacy and subservience, all at once.

Standing at the edge of a whirlpool

Having been involved in the entertainment industry since 1996, Ho felt that the industry is a small domain disjointed from the wider world, having its own unique set of values and standards regarding what is right and what success means. Very often, celebrities have been indoctrinated to these values:

> In fact, from the time I was growing up and became a grown-up, I had been in this circle already. So everybody in this circle has been telling you that you have to be quick! You can't be slow! You can't stop! You can't…you can't be caught up by others! There are a lot of values that were instilled in us. But what is strange about me is that, although I don't agree with that, it is hard not to be pushed by the waves, which keep pushing me along the way.

Based on Ho's experience as an artist, working in the entertainment industry has required her to put aside her own beliefs and values in order to fit into the system, and this kind of adaptation weakens the connection between the celebrity and the real world. As she said, 'You have to keep going forward, even if you do not agree with them […]. It makes you feel detached from the "ground", easily disconnected from the "ground"'. According to Ho, this system personifies a typical commercial and capitalist logic of the entertainment industry: celebrities (or their mediatized image as a cultural sign) are a product to be bought and sold, gratifying the psychological needs and imaginations of audiences by being a public role model (such as a comedian to entertain the masses), or just to stimulate consumption by endorsing other commercial products. However, Ho's explication of celebrity's inevitable detachment from reality (or the 'ground') seems to expose more about her discontent with the spirit of advanced capitalism, fetishistic competition and the entertainment industry's fundamental structure (van Krieken, 2012a) than the nature of reality or whether they are exclusive traits of the entertainment industry. It also reveals her thoughts about a celebrity's ideal role in society. Ho attempted to resist mainstream 'waves' and to redefine celebrity, constantly negotiating her celebrity identity as a charismatic opinion leader of various moral and social causes, as well as being an active advocate for justice, human rights and democracy, offering spiritual support for building a better society. Interestingly, Ho seemed to eagerly bridge her public and private personae, leveraging her public visibility not for commercial sales, but for political and moral ideals. Although her mediated political identity successfully transformed many Hong Kong citizens into fans and bystanders – which undeniably promoted her own brand image – Ho seemed to heed dissenting social voices and encourage a considered examination of sociopolitical issues, rather than only creating the 'Hollywood', razzle dazzle and sensationalized 'politainment' for economic returns (Kapoor, 2013).

Ho felt that it was a challenge to strike a balance between being a celebrity and being an ordinary person because, while being able to survive or even succeed in the entertainment industry, it was not always easy to connect back to the outside world.

> I think the most challenging thing is to [...] forget your [celebrity] identity; in other words, to bear in mind that you are just an ordinary person. The whole environment made you [...] detached from the ground [...] because the mechanism is like that. This entertainment circle has its own set of value system. A standard [of] what is correct and what is considered successful to survive in such a swirl [...] because the space is so small indeed, and the world is so large. But inside that environment, everything you see has been magnified. So how can you survive and continue to survive in that environment? This is not talking about retirement. That is, in my position, how can I connect back to the ground? This is the power that I have been searching for over the years. How much should I release? How much should I control? It's like standing at the edge of a whirlpool. I think that is the position I am now standing at.

As Ho confessed, at times she was hesitant to express her true thoughts in public. Yet she sensed that the process of overcoming difficulties in making connections with and expressing her concerns about social issues in Hong Kong made her come up with a feasible strategy that, on the one hand, would not harm her career and, on the other, would allow her to stay true to herself. She was glad that she had begun to master the skills and build up her confidence in accomplishing that.

> I am fortunate that I gradually started to gain the balance. But that requires very strong faith and confidence. You have to believe that it is what suits you, not what people said. That is, you must separate yourself from the whole [media/entertainment] system before you come into contact with the outside world. The process is indeed a rather difficult one.

For Ho, listening to her own heart and vehemently defending her beliefs are of high importance. She believed that her own actions proved the fact that celebrities could walk a new path and write an alternative 'formula'. Ho seemed to hint that celebrities, particularly Cantopop singers, were being socialized in a rather one-dimensional way, only aspiring to economic success, fame and a lavish life. As she observed, many practitioners in Hong Kong's music industry were under immense pressure; they pushed themselves to the limit, worked all night and often gave up their normal social life: '[They are] not mentally and physically healthy enough, which was revealed in their creative works'. In addition, the omnipresence of 'negative energy' in Hong Kong brought about by various sociopolitical struggles made her pay more attention to leading alternative ways of life that helped her maintain her physical and mental health while, most importantly, empowering her celebrity identity.

Because in this world, no matter what, there are always some people shouting at you as a way of venting their feelings. But when you really focus on what you need to do, people see that and they will be carried away. This is what I feel over the past two years. I tried hard to realize one thing: if you believe, you do it. This goes back to the thing at the beginning: although it is difficult, you still believe it. You need to believe it. As long as you have enough faith – in fact, the time period is long, but you will start to have faith – all the pandemonium turns into a right way, gradually, that is suitable for you. Also, you can prove that in fact the way – although it might not be the most correct – is the most suitable for you. This is what I believe. It doesn't apply only to the entertainment circle; this is something everybody should bear in mind. Because there are [...] too many things that would sway your decisions and tell you that you are incorrect. Especially if you look at today's newspapers; you can find all sorts of specious reasoning. So you must trust you own instincts and listen to your heart.

Negotiating multiple identities: The social, sexual and political personae

Celebrities occupy a unique space in society. Although they do not necessarily achieve direct access to political power, their role as 'heroes' directs the behaviour and choices of others (Davisson, 2013). When asked about an artist's daily work mode, Ho mentioned that she was in the process of transformation: from doing what a celebrity/singer was supposed to do to acquiring 'a different layer in her identity' at the societal level, as she did not want to merely focus on working as a performer. Compared with the typical celebrities who often strive for a coherent and impeccable identity, portraying themselves as a born-to-be superstars and hiding their ordinary past (Davisson, 2013), Ho instead displayed a self-acceptance and desire to be able to wander between her public and personal identities, disclosing her 'backstage' identity to her fans and the public in a way that resonates with them. In a similar way to American pop singer Lady Gaga's identity construction strategy, instead of relying on mainstream media to translate her ideas, Ho has actively worked through multiple outlets to claim and craft her own identity (Davisson, 2013) – from her *Apple Daily* columns to social media platforms directly sent to her fans. She admitted that she has now become more outspoken in terms of social issues than before, although she thought it was not easy:

I dare not say [...] I am on the front line, because frankly there is always some consideration. Now everybody is [trying to find] ways to express oneself in a limited space, trying one's best to [...] influence others. This is difficult. That is, how to juggle between the two sides? This is very difficult actually.

In retrospect, Ho felt that founding the BigLove Alliance led her to be wary of contributing more to the society, despite the fact that the experience has forced her to face difficulties in striving for people's equal rights in Hong Kong, where universal suffrage for elections has not yet been implemented. She indicated:

Figure 35: As one of the founding members of the BigLove Alliance, Ho zealously advocates equal rights for LGBT communities in Hong Kong.

> I think BigLove Alliance – from coming out [of the closet] to getting involved in this matter – enabled me to be more concerned about different issues – or more. It means you have one more identity since that moment. Maybe in the past I would not express the concerns I had about some issues. That means I might not be speaking out openly. But because of that identity, having one more identity [as a celebrity social activist], you come to realize that, well, in fact I could do much more.

In November 2012, during the Hong Kong Pride Parade, Ho came out in front of her parents, the top executives of her affiliated record company and thousands of demonstrators (Fridae.asia, 2012). She became the very first Hong Kong celebrity who publicly and proudly declared her lesbian identity. Apart from being more open in discussing her sexual orientation and political stance with the mass media, she also accepted the invitation to write columns for *Apple Daily* – an empowering way to craft and claim her multiple identities. As a celebrity, Ho is strongly supported by LGBT communities and younger generations. Moreover, democrats in Hong Kong and Taiwan, who support and uphold the celebrity fantasy of humanitarianism through their beliefs, believe that, through the star, they can delegate their political beliefs to the celebrity

Figure 36: Ho writes columns for *Apple Daily*, to craft and claim her subversive sexual and political identities.

(Kapoor, 2013). For her, this was a challenge yet a cherished opportunity to make her 'true' voice heard. As Ho pointed out:

> This is a challenge to me because this is different from writing blog posts or posts on Facebook [in terms of length and depth]. The readers are different and the role is slightly different. Although my column is located in the entertainment section, I do not wish to write about gossip or something related to myself only, (which can be shared, of course). I really hope that it can be a platform for sharing our voices.

Breaking through the matrix of showbiz?

Ho argued that, despite the fact that artists often have to follow the rules of the entertainment industry, they can still have their own say:

> In fact, there are choices. I think – whether you choose to be passive or active – the power is in your own hands. Of course, many artists are like, 'OK, let's see what my agent and company have arranged for me. I won't take care of it. I will do it or... well, you have no choice. So I will do it, and earn the money'. [...] The artists of the previous

generation could be like that. They relied on them [their agents and management companies] totally. Perhaps for that generation what they really needed to care about was their performance. They relied on their assistants or companies totally. So that means they did not know how to handle something personal. But I am a bit different. I tend to need that autonomy.

In comparison to her counterparts, it appears that Ho is distinctive in her approach to managing her own identities. From her perspective, celebrities can always decide on their identities by being more independent and exercising their own power. Overall, it is difficult to say whether or not Ho has been successful in claiming autonomy as a celebrity, or in maintaining her multiple identities in and beyond the Hong Kong entertainment industry. On 24 March 2015, Ho announced through her *Apple Daily* column that she was no longer represented by East Asia Music, and had officially become an independent artist/singer without the help of any project manager or assistant. Although she did not know how her career will move forward, she had 'no fears, but unlimited hopes'. Without the support of a major record company, Ho still holds an optimistic view, believing that there are still 'plenty of possibilities' for her (Ho, 2015).

Hilary Tsui (徐濠縈)

Hilary Tsui (徐濠縈) first entered the Hong Kong entertainment industry when she was 19 years old. She is a former television and film actress who married the famous Cantopop singer Eason Chan (陳奕迅) in 2006. Since then, her marital relationship, personal life and daily (mis)behaviour have been regularly featured in the entertainment news. In 2009, she launched her first fashion boutique, Liger, with her friend Dorothy Hui, a stylist and fashion veteran. Currently a shop owner and a fashion blogger, her select fashion shops are located in prime areas in Hong Kong and Macau, and are known for carrying edgy foreign and local fashion labels. Despite being a mother, Tsui is a very active player in Hong Kong's fashion scene, being a renowned fashionista and fashion blogger (under renowned PR practitioner Francis Cheng's (鄭紹康) management) across Greater China, as well as an avid marathon runner supported by a global sportswear brand.

Tension between self-identity and public perception

According to Langer (2006), star identity embodies 'idealizations or archetypal expressions' that are 'contemplated, revered, desired and even blatantly imitated' by audiences (p. 185). In this sense, the star system is 'larger than life', involving the maintenance of distance between stars and the audience; therefore, contact with stars is 'unrelentingly sporadic and uncertain' (Langer, 2006, p. 185).

In reality, the ongoing identification process of stars throughout their career may be even more complex and dynamic, especially when they start to engage in different roles

Figure 37: Hilary Tsui, who first entered the Hong Kong entertainment industry when she was 19, is a former television and film actress.

in life apart from their public personae. Celebrities still represent an idealized and unique personality, and are no longer placed in an unapproachable position. Especially since the rise of digital media, traces of one's celebrity status will be stored online, enabling people to revisit them beyond the limitation of time and space. In this sense, a 'distant closeness' is now more commonly and tactfully maintained between celebrity and audience. Tsui stated that she resists identifying herself as a celebrity/star anymore. She did not renew her artist management contract with TVB in 2001, and since then has no longer officially worked in the entertainment industry. However, Tsui claimed that, in a small city like Hong Kong, she will be considered a celebrity forever because she was once within the entertainment circle. Indeed, she is still featured in both traditional and online media very frequently. Personally, she regarded herself as an ordinary person, 'shopping or doing something as she wishes'. In her view, a discrepancy exists between how people identify her and how she identifies herself. She feels that constantly introducing herself as a celebrity is somewhat 'embarrassing':

Maybe when I went running in foreign countries, some people would ask me how I introduce myself. I would say that I was previously an actress, but now I am a

Figure 38: Tsui still resists identifying herself as a celebrity now, but she is still frequently featured in the media, partly due to her status as the wife of famed Cantopop singer Eason Chan.

celebrity. But I myself am also opposed to that because I treat myself as an ordinary person. That is, I don't want to tell others about it, particularly when I am outside Hong Kong.

Pondering carefully, Tsui attributed the public perception of her current celebrity status largely to her having a famous husband, Eason Chan. Her celebrity status remains, and her power is further enhanced and utilized within the media system because of her association with higher-status individuals (van Krieken, 2012a), namely her husband and other married female celebrities (e.g. local singer Kay Tse [謝安琪]) or wives of male celebrities with whom Tsui has been constantly compared. According to some, being widely recognized and regarded as a celebrity is not a bad thing, yet Tsui revealed that possessing a celebrity identity also brings her unwanted attention and stress from the media industry and paparazzi – issues which do not usually bother an ordinary, unknown citizen in the crowd:

Figure 39: When Tsui was invited to participate in various luxury fashion events as an actress, a fashion blogger, a fashionista, a socialite or as a celebrity – her identities often 'touched and straddled the boundaries'.

> It must be my husband who is next to me […]. If he was nobody, and if I worked somehow in the fashion field and showed up sometimes in some events, I might be photographed by paparazzi, but I would not attract paparazzi coming to my home.

Tsui further discussed her multiple public identities, exemplified by the ways in which she is categorized during fashion events. For instance, when she has been invited to participate in various luxury fashion events, organizers have introduced her at different times as an actress, a fashion blogger, a fashionista, a socialite or a celebrity. Reflecting on the experience, she believed that her identities often 'touched and straddled the *boundaries*'. Overall, the attention capital derived from all these identifications is well utilized by the fashion brands and media in support of their own interests (Turner, 2010), although it creates inconvenience and stress for the star herself in various ways.

The boundary between public and private lives

Celebrity as defender
Horton and Wohl (2010) indicated that the public image of a celebrity can be understood as a 'persona' with which a sense of intimacy is encouraged, and where the audience appreciates

the symbolic persona as a 'real' person. This image 'is to some extent a construct – a façade – which bears little resemblance to his private character' (Horton & Wohl, 2010, p. 48). Although a celebrity's public life is constructed in and through the media system, their persona also 'creates an acceptable façade of private life [...] behind the contrived public image' (Horton & Wohl, 2010, p. 49). This implies that neither public nor private identities are intrinsic, and both involve deliberate construction and transformation under public scrutiny.

Although Tsui drew a clear distinction between her public life as a celebrity and her private life as an ordinary person, such a distinction could only be illustrated and sustained by her conscious use of social media, which gave her greater control over the extent of propagating the 'preferred' version of her private life with the public. Tsui also ambivalently confessed that she was reluctant to share her 'real' private life with the public, and that since starting her fashion business in 2009, she used social media mainly for work purposes. She intentionally made the links to her social media platforms available on the website of her fashion shop, including those to Sina Weibo (a Chinese microblog), Facebook and Instagram:

> I opened a public account [on Facebook], which is really for work. So you can see my Facebook, Instagram and Weibo, but I tend to use Instagram more often. I am quite straightforward. I don't share my private life on purpose. In other words, I don't post anything about my daughter on it. It is purely for work.

For Tsui, the posts that usually appear on her public social media platforms can be divided into several standard categories. The first category is her running experience. Second is her 'look of the day', which is also a nuanced way to promote her fashion business. Third is her endorsement of specific fashion brands and events on social media (usually requested by her commercial sponsors). She is aware of the public audiences of her online posts and thinks in-depth about the content she shares before posting it online. Yet there was also a moment when she lingered between the public and private, and when divided audience judgements of her semi-public life/identity emerged:

> I have made careful consideration before I post anything, so I am not posting randomly. The posts that I would like to share include sports, fashion. Or [...] sometimes I know they want to see whether I am with my husband [in the post]. Sometimes I take a [...] photo of the back [of my husband] [...]. I don't do it on purpose. It's really casual. For example, it is his birthday and we hope to make it happy. So I also consider that – that is, making people happy. I may post one about family or a photo of Eason's silhouette.

Meanwhile, Tsui is well aware of her influence as a celebrity, and has deliberately utilized social media to promote running and radiate 'positive energy' to the public. Here, Tsui seems to be actively and successfully engaged in a self-identification process that (either consciously or unconsciously) attempts to mediate her private self with its public counterpart,

Figure 40: As an avid marathon runner, Tsui actively uses social media platforms to promote running and to radiate 'positive energy' to the public.

and publicizing her intended star identity as an energetic, sporty and stylish figure. Apart from influencing the general public, she also realized that a number of local celebrities have followed suit and shared their own running experiences online as a strategy of image-building. When compared to promoting her own fashion style and business, sharing her own running experience gives her a greater sense of satisfaction:

This is the aspect where I gained the greatest satisfaction because I feel that I am able to share my interest. For fashion, I encountered some people who attacked me and felt that I am weird. That was not a win-win situation. Some people might say, 'The products in Tsui's shop [are] very expensive, and you have to be slim enough to go in'. So these were the voices I heard. But running is one-sided. There isn't any negative comment. So the impacts it has on other people, on me [–] I feel satisfied and happy because it doesn't just benefit me, I can also change people's habits into running. Later, I realized that, well, it's funny that people always check my time records. They know that I am okay with the speed. That became a standard: 'Tsui can make it and so can you'. So that means I have set a standard for people out there. They always challenge me. Then I will have an impetus, feeling there are so many people checking my time records. So I am quite happy about this.

Figure 41: Grace Ip Pui-Man, Josie Ho, Hilary Tsui and Dorothy Hui at the launch party of the fashion boutique Liger co-founded by Tsui and Hui in 2009.

Despite her clearly stated purpose, Tsui insisted that she was not using social media to improve her negatively mediatized public image or serve some utilitarian purpose. Rather, social media is a platform for her to express her true self, allowing her to defend her private and authentic identity from being eclipsed by the endless expansion of her socially and rigidly constructed public image under the media operation. To Tsui, it is a remedy for self-actualization and emotional fulfilment rather than a careful commercial tactic:

> In fact, I didn't make it so complicated, because I was just being myself. Perhaps ten years ago, I would pour water or soup on the paparazzi. If Instagram existed back then, I would have taken their photos and posted them there. I could be like that […]. I am not a singer or an actress, so I don't need to establish an image, a good image. What I need to establish is my personality.

Paparazzi: The intruders
Van Krieken (2012b) pointed out that audiences structure and organize their perception of celebrities 'around ideals of gendered identity, appearance and behaviour' (p. 73). The public can closely monitor and manipulate celebrities through the mass media by holding them up

against certain norms and ideological values. In this respect, celebrity identity is partly subject to the control of their portrayal by the mass media, as well as how audiences receive, interpret and respond to those messages. Such power relationships among audiences, the media and the celebrity are further complicated by the widespread paparazzi culture, whose basic interest is the attention capital of the celebrity and the rewards from circulating this (often without gaining consent from the celebrity). The invasion of celebrities' private lives and the irresponsible manipulation of celebrity signs for commercial gain raise ethical questions of where the boundaries between the public and private spheres lie (van Krieken, 2012a).

In contrast to social media, the paparazzi intrude into the private lives of celebrities, blurring the boundary between the public and the private. Tsui perceived the emergence of the paparazzi as one of the biggest challenges she faces, and the cause of certain changes in Hong Kong's entertainment industry over the past twenty years. Based on her personal experience, proper celebrity interviews conducted by print media journalists in the past were the major source of celebrity news. However, nowadays, the paparazzi's scandalous and invasive reporting style has become the major source of celebrity news:

> It still dwells in my memory that paparazzi came to be the way they are around 1995 or 1996 or 1997. The paparazzi culture has significantly occupied the entertainment industry. Today the messages that we all receive are part of the paparazzi culture.

Tsui considers the paparazzi to be intruders into her private and family life, undermining and overshadowing her power in constructing her star or even ordinary identity. She used to scold the paparazzi when she saw them following her, but now she has changed the way she reacts. As she described it, she is now mild-mannered when dealing with paparazzi:

> [Being myself] is what I always do. And because of this, some people dislike me. I scolded them whenever they [the paparazzi] followed me. Well, for a normal person, if you find that you are followed or that your family members are disturbed by them, you will scold them. I think what I was doing was absolutely normal. In contrast, now I feel I am a bit abnormal, pretending I don't see them.

No matter how hard she tried to distance her private identity from her public one, Tsui felt that it was very difficult for her to control the extent of the sharing of her private life with the public when the paparazzi only sought to collect the 'partial truth'. This might involve unexpectedly taking a picture of the celebrity or anyone closely related to them, or verbally agitating them for a controversial response, and then fabricating the remaining parts on their own. Tsui recalled a recent occurrence of this practice:

> It's always the case that, even in these few days, paparazzi waited for my daughter getting out of school. I think this is really bad. I have stated again and again in interviews and on Weibo that they should not disturb the kid [...]. I think from time to time all of us

kind of know how old my daughter is. In other words, she is not too mysterious. So I feel [why] do they need to keep following and covering this? So we three as a family, [...] sometimes it's funny that if there is a paparazzi car waiting for us, my husband will say, 'I can go distract them'. We are lucky if he doesn't care and isn't annoyed. He knows that I am irritated. So sometimes he says, 'Well, they don't follow me. They are waiting for you. The target is you'. So that means we need to look for an alternative. So my daughter was affected by such [...] paparazzi's reporting in such a way.

Paparazzi-style journalism has presented a challenge to Tsui and has made her contemplate her identity as a public figure. Tsui assumed that she always appeared on the front cover of magazines and became the target of paparazzi because of her status as the wife of Eason Chan, with the media buzz multiplied by the fact they are a celebrity couple. She admitted how she felt about this:

I don't understand indeed. Even my husband always says, 'Look! You are on the cover page of magazines more often than I am'. What he meant is that [it] is, of course, not a good thing [...]. In fact, [...] he has also asked why it was the case. That is, why I appeared on the cover page more often than he did. In fact, I don't understand why. Of course, half of the reason is that I am his wife.

On the other hand, she confessed that the paparazzi's actions are beyond her control. Today's paparazzi – an extended arm of the media system – are accustomed to fabricating news without considering its consequences to the stars and society. Tsui noticed a huge contrast between her self-image and the mediatized image, in which she is often portrayed as an ill-tempered woman – based on ideological concepts of ideal femininity and motherhood – rather than being esteemed and idolized. With this sense of losing control over the public image to the paparazzi and the trend of scandalizing celebrities for public attention, she has taught her daughter how to uphold her self-image (or conceal her personal identity and true emotions) in front of the paparazzi:

But I'd rather let it be, because it is something beyond my control and that I need to face. I can't waste my energy to denounce them [the paparazzi] every day. The major premise is to protect my child. And I need to consider my image in front of my daughter [...]. I told my daughter, 'You need to pretend that you don't see them. Just smile'. So you have to instil this message constantly. In fact, my daughter also knows that I am unhappy about it. My daughter says, 'They are so bad. Why do they need to take photos of us?' So you also need to take care of that and educate the kid.

Extended stardom in the fashion world
According to van Krieken (2012b), 'celebrities are indeed "powerless", dependent on the allocation of attention from their audience' (p. 73). In order to gain power and commercial

returns, celebrities are often trapped in a loop of upholding the public's attention. Although Tsui's quasi-celebrity status dissatisfies her in various ways, it benefits her fashion business and the fabrication of a new identity. Her active engagement in the fashion world, the business field and social media helps her craft her positive, authentic and multiple identities as a female entrepreneur, a marathon runner and a fashionista, rather than confining her public persona to merely, in her words, a 'former actress, a Cantopop singer's wife, or an irresponsible mother'. More crucially, Tsui seized her attention capital from the hands of the media (mostly newspapers and gossip magazines) for her own wilful usage. In the digital age, she was empowered to take up an active role as a media gatekeeper. During the initial period of the opening of her store, consumers followed her blogs and her 'look of the day', and identified with her fashion style; some would even purchase the same items in order to imitate her clothing style. Social media, such as Weibo and Instagram, enables her to keep her audience abreast of her latest news, which pushed her as a 'fashion citizen journalist' to 'keep updating the things that happened'. Apart from blogging, her collaborative relationship with fashion houses is also important to her status as a key player in the local fashion industry. She recognized that attending fashion events is beneficial to her fashion business, and she described her attendance as a win-win situation:

Figure 42: Tsui's active engagement in the fashion industry and social media helps her craft her positive and multiple identities as a female entrepreneur and fashionista.

For example, tonight I will go to [an event organized by the American fashion brand] Coach, doing something related to fashion. It might not be related to my store, but I think [it is useful] for self-positioning – that is, one's influence in the fashion industry and one's importance to brands. So I need to participate […]. This serves as a complement. Also, they might be promoting their products or new collections by taking advantage of me.

While Tsui helps the brands promote their merchandise, their invitations acknowledge and strengthen her status as a significant influencer/fashion blogger in the fashion industry. Moreover, it acknowledges that she is famous and identified in a professional way, but not exceedingly reliant on the legacy of her husband or her former career.

Tsui's family-oriented approach demonstrates that celebrities' image management takes into consideration both personal and family values regarding what is good and what is bad, instead of uncritically embracing the aura and symbolic status of celebrity perpetuated by the entertainment industry. Despite being put under the surveillance of the media and public scrutiny, Tsui cared more about her perceived impact on her family than the general public, fighting for her subjectivity as a half-celebrity. The image that she presents to her daughter matters more to her, as she smiled and repeated the words:

What I always say is: I need to be held responsible by my family members, not the audience outside – that is, the readers of entertainment magazines. The most important thing is my family members. That is, I know what I am doing and their opinions [and] I'd listen more to what they say. So in terms of choosing jobs – good. I am always doing something positive and healthy […]. I don't take up jobs that I am not familiar with.

Pakho Chau (周柏豪)

Pakho Chau (周柏豪), a Cantopop singer/songwriter, was previously a part-time model who officially joined the Hong Kong music industry in 2007. He has won myriad musical awards, such as the Best Male Singer Gold Award at the Ultimate Song Chart Awards , the Metro Hit Best Male Singer Award at the Metro Radio Hits Music Awards, and the Male Singer Gold Award at Commercial Radio Hong Kong's Ultimate Song Chart Awards. In addition to his active engagement in the music industry, Chau has also been the leading actor in numerous films, including 小姐誘心/*S for Sex, S for Secret* (J. Wong, 2015), 販賣．愛/*I Sell Love* (K. Chu, 2014) and 猛鬼愛情故事/*Hong Kong Ghost Stories* (Wong & Kong, 2011).

Multidimensional star identities: A singer-songwriter, spiritual leader and philanthropist
Chau defined celebrity as simply 'someone who is famous'. To him, the term 'celebrity' is not just for describing prominent figures in the entertainment business, but also for those who are in athletic, medical, financial and creative sectors. Both traditional and new

Figure 43: Interview with Pakho Chau at the Department of Communication Studies, Hong Kong Baptist University.

Figure 44: Pakho Chau has won a myriad of music awards and is a popular celebrity endorser of different international brands in Hong Kong.

media – from television and print to online – have the power to generate immense publicity and manufacture celebrities. As Chau mentioned:

> It is easy to become a celebrity nowadays […]. It is not surprising to see some Internet bloggers accumulating more than 10,000 followers. Therefore, in that particular realm, these bloggers could also be regarded as celebrities, as they are famous and influential.

Marshall (1997) suggested that the essential nature of celebrity is individuality and unique identity. Therefore, a celebrity who shares similar characteristics with others cannot sustain their popularity. As a famous singer in Hong Kong, Chau claimed that he did not intentionally force himself to develop any specific image or to fit into any archetypes of celebrity:

> Even though at the outset my company intended to portray a 'fresh, sunny boy' image for me, […] I just want to be myself […]. I never categorize myself as a particular kind of artist [–] I just do the best I can. How the audiences perceive my image is beyond my control.

Chau believes that he has taken on various roles throughout his entertainment career. As such, he should be considered a 'multidimensional singer' in many audiences' and consumers' minds, which emphasizes his conception of celebrity as a cultural product to satisfy different projected desires and to be consumed in society.

Although Chau considered his star identity to be subject to the identification of audience members, he repeatedly emphasized that his enthusiasm for music production and songwriting made 'songwriter/musician' his preferred identity, as well as the major reason for him staying in showbiz. Having composed and released more than 30 songs to date, and having received several awards as a songwriter, Chau excitedly said he enjoyed behind-the-scene jobs the most. As he put it, 'I really enjoy the process of creating music. Starting from an initial inspiration in my mind, I subsequently turn it into musical notes, and then from musical notes to a melody. I attained a sense of accomplishment in this process'. Although celebrity idolization among adolescents is largely a commercialized cultural phenomenon (Engle & Kasser, 2005), Chau was adamant that such celebrity influence over public audiences could be used in a constructive way, and he perceived writing songs and lyrics to be a particularly effective means for conveying 'positive energy' to his local fans. For instance, he brought up the lyrics of his first song, '同天空'/'Same Sky' (2007), which portrayed the importance of self-belief:

> I know many teenagers regard me as their idols [and] that they are eager to imitate me. To me, every word, every speech, every action, as well as every post of the celebrities will affect people 'following' them […]. Therefore, I must always be very positive […]. I want the listeners to believe that they could achieve whatever I had achieved […] since 'we are living under the same sky, breathing the same air' [Chau, 2007].

In addition to songwriting, Chau has also tactfully used his celebrity identity to mobilize his supporters to contribute to society, enacting their fandom into carrying out good causes and finding meaning in their social world. As an ambassador of various charity groups in Hong Kong, including the Tung Wah Group of Hospitals, the Ronald McDonald House Charities of Hong Kong and 30 Hours Famine Campaign of World Vision Hong Kong, Chau fervently advocated his own participation:

> I wish all my fans would drop their cameras, freeing their hands to do some volunteer work […]. I will continue to make a good use of my fame to promote the virtues of volunteering. Hopefully, a volunteer group can be set up so that all my fans can immerse themselves in helping the needy.

As a former representative of the Hong Kong Basketball Team Junior Squad, as well as a professional swimming coach, Chau also promoted sports among adolescents: 'I do hope I can have more opportunities to participate in the school tours with athletes in Hong Kong. We can therefore share our experiences with the students and teach them technical skills'. Indeed, Chau repeated several times, 'As a celebrity, we have the social responsibility […]

Figure 45: (Left to right) Pakho Chau, Carina Lau, Hilary Tsui, Wyman Wong and Bosco Wong at Italian high fashion label Valentino's Harbour City flagship store opening event, February 2015.

to influence more and more people'. In this sense, celebrities are somehow perceived as religious figures, and understood as sources for personal transformation and aspiration (Ward, 2011). In doing so, they become representative gods who mirror an idealized image of what it is to be human (Ward, 2011). Through celebrity idolization and identification, fans devotedly transcend their status quo and aspire to become a better person, full of love, benevolence and vigour, just like their spiritual leader.

Social media and the fan–celebrity relationship

Ferris and Harris (2011) described the fan–celebrity relationship as idiosyncratic in nature, in that it is full of complex motivations, conflicts and rewards. Thanks to the development and ubiquity of digital media, which allows fans to search for their celebrities' information easily, fan–celebrity relationships have become further complicated, intensifying the imbalances of knowledge and power between fans and the celebrity (Ferris & Harris, 2011).

With more than 900,000 followers on Instagram, Chau held the belief that the emergence of social media provides an effective platform for celebrities to communicate and directly interact with their fans at an unprecedented level: 'Most of my target audiences are between 13 and 30 years old. They are very eager to browse information on the Internet. Therefore, I can make good use of the Internet to promote myself'. According to Chau, he has developed a closer relationship with some of his fans because of Facebook and Instagram. Disintegrating the top-down relationship between celebrity and fan, supporters have initiated conversations with him directly on many occasions as a virtual friend: 'As long as I can read the messages, I will try my best to reply to them'. The convenience and interactivity facilitated by social media technology enables celebrities to gratify their fans' trophy-seeking wish and strengthen their emotional identification – a mutuality and reciprocity of co-present virtual interactions that could hardly be achieved in the Web 1.0 era (Ferris & Harris, 2011). However, it also heightens the problematic asymmetry of knowledge and power between a celebrity and a fan, as now the former can possess a much larger amount of information about their favourite stars, which intensifies their imagined relationship with that person. This may produce a compulsive, obsessive fandom, as well as a strong emotional burden for the celebrity. This is supported by a real case shared by Chau:

> Before I opened my Facebook account, there was a fan called Stacy. She used to write me letters every week. […]. Yet, from 2011 to 2013, she did not write me any letters. […] When I checked my Facebook [at a later date], I discovered that she had written me hundreds of private messages, saying that she was in the hospital because of diabetes […]. The condition was so bad that she had to amputate both legs […]. The last message was in fact written by her nurse, [who] informed me that Stacy had already passed away […]. I felt very sorry about that. […]. There was someone who […] was so supportive of me, yet I missed the chance to interact with her […] and the only thing I can do now is to remember her.

When asked about whether the replies on Instagram or Facebook are really written by him, Chau insisted that he wrote every reply to fans on his own, but he also admitted that his management company's colleagues also took up the role as administrators of his (and other affiliated artists') social media accounts to post feeds and disseminate their official news. This effectively explained that even social media theoretically facilitated instant and continuous communication between celebrities and fans at any time and any place. In reality, celebrities could scarcely manage this one-to-*too*-many mode of interaction.

Celebrity and paparazzi

According to van Krieken (2012a), the primary interest of the mass media is the attention capital of the celebrity concerned, and how that can be leveraged into sales and viewership. Although the paparazzi have always been a headache for many celebrities, Chau was optimistic about his method of handling them, as he now understood their respective roles. He also admitted that although some questions asked by the paparazzi were very offensive, most are very nice. Instead of resisting the matrix of media operation and its commercial logic, Chau chose to adapt to it:

> I clearly know my role as a public figure […]. If you choose to become a chef, you should already know that it could be super hot in the kitchen […]. If you can't stand the heat, just get out of the kitchen […]. When you choose to bear and give birth to a child, you can't innocently mourn and complain, 'Why is giving birth so painful?' […] If we are determined to enter the entertainment industry, we have to bear with them. […] Since we are a celebrity, people are curious about our everyday life, thereby creating a strong demand for the existence of paparazzi […]. I understand what the paparazzi want. After all, reporting the daily life of celebrities is their job. As long as they can give me a room to lead my private life, I really do not care.

Chau expressed that the time when he felt most uneasy was when he first entered showbiz: 'I was very cautious in the beginning […]. Not just with the paparazzi, but also with pedestrians. They took pictures of me directly without even asking for my permission'. To fight back, Chau stared at them or sometimes covered their camera lenses directly with his hands. Even now, Chau is still concerned about his parents' and friends' private lives being infringed upon, referring to the controversial media technique of taking advantage of a celebrity's attention capital by extending, fabricating and mystifying their public identity intertextually as attention-grabbing fables:

> I really care about my parents. If the paparazzi suddenly appeared when I was dining with my parents, I would definitely leave the restaurant in order to make my parents feel more comfortable. I need to protect everyone besides me.

Amid the rise of location tagging in social media, Chau developed a habit of securing his private life by not instantly uploading his photos in public:

> Many times, I demand a strong sense of safety [...]. Say when I was eating a piece of salmon sushi at a Japanese restaurant: I would definitely not upload the photo online as this might give hints to paparazzi about my location.

This demonstrates that Chau has been very cautious when using social networking sites to avoid revealing his physical location. Rather than enabling the subject to freely craft their own identity in virtual space, social media has a constraining side and a tendency to recentre a star's online identity to its idealized form. Furthermore, its (offline) ideological values and judgements can also be transferred to the online world (Miller, 2011). Under the tyranny of the digital panopticon, celebrities often engage in an 'impression management' process, continuously adjusting their online presence to accommodate the perceptions of audience judgement – from the media to paparazzi and the mass public – leading to a more centred and situated self (Goffman, 1959; van den Berg, 2009). Chau's case demonstrates how celebrities actually defend their multiple identities, and intentionally segregate their online and offline selves as an alternative strategy to resist the exploitative facet of the media system.

Bob Lam (林盛斌)

Bob Lam (林盛斌) is a television personality, a DJ and an actor. He is a seasoned master of ceremonies for banquets, weddings and corporate events, and a very popular celebrity endorser for various commercial products and services in Hong Kong. Lam began his career in the entertainment industry as a DJ for Metro Broadcast Corporation Limited's channel (FM 99.7–102). He joined TVB as a host for the talk show 兄弟幫/Big Boys Club (Tse, 2010) and rapidly attained fame. In 2015, he started to branch into the business field and established a production company called Chessman Entertainment Production (HK) Limited (棋人娛樂製作有限公司).

Celebrity as a form of rationalization
The development of celebrity as a concept can be understood by drawing on the concept of rationalization undertaken by the dominant classes and audience in making sense of their cultural world (Marshall, 1997). In contrast to traditional society, contemporary capitalist society emphasizes the importance of rationality and scientific discovery, in which 'consumer capitalism' is prevalent (Ritzer, 2008). In studying celebrity as a form of cultural power, it could be examined as a process of rationalization wherein people 'use celebrity to make sense of their own social world' in different ways (Marshall, 1997, p. 52). Marshall argued that members of the dominant culture – who control the majority of the forms of cultural

Figure 46: Bob Lam – a TV personality, a DJ and an actor – joined Television Broadcasts Limited (TVB) as a program host in 2010 and attained fame rapidly.

Figure 47: In 2015, Lam started to branch into the business field and established a production company named Chessman Entertainment Production (HK) Limited.

production – offer celebrity as the embodiment of cultural power and signs. In the process of the audience's rationalization, the audience sees the 'representations of personality in the celebrity as legitimate forms of identification and cultural value' (Marshall, 1997, p. 55).

At the beginning of the interview, Lam suggested that celebrity today is significantly attached to 'media values'. The presence of celebrity on media platforms enhances a celebrity's value, regardless of whether they have the presumed capabilities as a performer/artist. Citing the example of celebrity chefs, he indicated:

> A chef cooking food for his/her customers of a restaurant is not [regarded as] a celebrity. Only after he/she is interviewed by magazines or starts to have media values does he/she start to walk on the so-called 'path to celebrity'. He/she then starts to teach cooking on TV programmes…Having gained the attention, he/she has already stepped on the path to celebrity. So, being a celebrity, one can increase the values of his/her work. In other words, previously one might cook a dish of stir-fried rice noodle with beef which costs only HK$50. Having become a celebrity, the dish can cost HK$70. This is the impact that media value has on oneself.

Lam's remarks on the value of a celebrity's work corresponded with the view that celebrity carries additional values that are highly legitimized by the audience. In discussing the economic values of celebrity, Milner Jr. indicated that the economic aspects of celebrity, as a status system, define the value and prestige of celebrity 'in terms of their distinctiveness from "mere" economic exchange' (van Krieken, 2012b, p. 68). Apart from purely monetary values, however, celebrity also transforms other values to the audience. In Lam's view, Hong Kong's traditional broadcast and print media still play a key role in manufacturing different types of celebrity by generating positive news items about ordinary people doing something unique and meaningful in society. In the rationalization process, celebrity can function as a social model and spirit that 'celebrates the potential of the individual and the mass's support of the individual in mass society' (Marshall, 1997, p. 43). For Lam, Chan Cheuk-ming (陳焯明), the owner of Pei Ho Barbeque restaurant who gives free meals to the needy in Sham Shui Po, can be regarded as a celebrity of this sort:

> He has done a lot of good things to help poor people. Naturally, the media reported his doings and tried to understand the reasons behind that. He wanted to influence the people around us, which is absolutely something that a celebrity does no matter how much he does not want to be a celebrity or how much he wants to remain low profile. If you want to do something influential, you must rely on your level of reputation, your networks, social relationships, or the so-called media relations to spread it to people. If there were no TVB or magazines or newspapers reporting his free meals in Sham Shui Po, would there be any rich men paying several tens of thousands of dollars for the meal tickets?

Figure 48: In Lam's view, Hong Kong's traditional broadcast and print media still play a key role in manufacturing different 'types' of celebrity.

The examples of Chan and celebrity chefs demonstrate how identity and the meaning of celebrity are produced, perpetuated and shaped by the institutions of mass media and the cultural industry. During these processes of social construction, the legitimacy given by the audience and the public plays an important role in constructing celebrity as a cultural sign.

Manifesting multiple personae across different media
One of the most important developments of the media (according to media and communication studies) has been its ability to produce celebrity 'on its own'. Alongside this, the media plays an active role in constructing identity and desire (Turner, 2010). Turner (2010) asserted that the media acts more like authors than mediators in the star production process, playing a huge part in 'inventing, popularizing and distributing formations of identity and desire in our societies' (p. 224).

Lam's multiple roles across different media can be attributed to his extensive experience with radio and TV stations. The range of opportunities offered to him as a radio and television personality have allowed him to enhance his reputation, and meant he could develop multiple personae as a celebrity. Lam was particularly grateful that he received support from Metro Broadcast to explore his career in television. The producer of *Big Boys Club*, a TV programme on the TVB J2 channel, invited him to be the host of the programme, which was the starting point from which he was later able to appear on the broadcaster's TVB Jade channel. He was then given opportunities to be a guest on a variety of the channel's programmes, as well as to act in a drama series and be the master of ceremonies for big shows on a major local TV station. Such repeated exposure further accelerated his celebrity status and fame through the cross-media system.

To Lam, his ideal goal in the entertainment industry is to 'colour people's world', highlighting his perception that celebrities can establish their fame through media to manifest an entertaining and 'carnival' image – which is supposedly the *raison d'être* of the entertainment industry – rather than simply using their physical attractiveness and moral vision. In this regard, the notion of joy is often associated with celebrity. He admitted that one of his dreams is to be an icon like his idol, Eric Tsang Chi-wai (曾志偉), a long-standing and highly regarded local comedy actor and personality, who was voted the top celebrity associated with happiness by audiences in Hong Kong.

> I am very impressed by [the results of] a public opinion survey [...] regarding whom Hong Kongers will think of when asked to think of joy. I recall that the first place is Eric Tsang [曾志偉]. The Gods [福祿壽][1] came second place. And the programme *Super Trio Series* [超級無敵獎門人系列][2] (Television Broadcasts Limited, 2014) came in third or fourth place. So if one day I could be like that, it would be awesome. The most important goal of the entertainment industry is to entertain the mass audience. [I was thinking that] if I joined this industry, what I most wanted would not be just entertaining the mass audience and making them happy, but bringing some colour to their lives. Perhaps my attitudes toward life [–] like placing importance on family members, throwing myself into work and working seriously [–] so these attitudes are long lasting, but people cannot feel them easily in other places.

Lam's celebrity identity as a humorous and carnival figure was co-created and reinforced in and through his multiple roles and celebrated performances in several media fields, including his presence on radio programmes, television programmes and in motion pictures. Meanwhile, he has also developed a higher goal based on a commercial logic: to influence audiences' attitudes toward life through his crafted image as a hard-working and caring family man. However, in terms of his work for TV and radio programmes, as well as his endorsement of various brands, he insisted that he was not selective and would say yes to almost all types of work. He attributed this to his current celebrity status in the Hong Kong entertainment industry, which he compared to schooling. He believed that, as an emerging star comedian, he did not have much say or power to choose what he wanted to do because he was 'a primary sixth-grade student in transition to secondary school':

> Who am I? Do I think that I am that powerful? There are so many people who are more powerful than me, [...] who are at a level higher. In other words, I haven't reached the level

Figure 49: Lam's ideal goal is to 'colour people's world' – supposedly the *raison d'être* of the entertainment industry.

Figure 50: Advertisers are interested in linking Lam's 'family man/father' image as a public persona with their promotional strategies.

where I can have the autonomy to choose my work. I am being honest, not pretending to be humble.

Celebrities who are married and have kids are often invited to appear on television programmes or advertisements with their family members. Marketers and advertisers are interested in linking Lam's family man/father image as a public persona with the resonating themes of different promotional strategies, as these are deeply ingrained in the audiences' minds. Lam is sometimes asked to involve his daughters in his work, and he and his daughters have been regularly invited to participate in commercial photography or to walk the catwalk for events. Holding a more open stance toward involving family members in establishing his celebrity identity and career, Lam admitted that he would consider whether or not the monetary rewards are reasonable, discuss it with his family and seek their opinions before he agreed to accept those jobs:

I do not force them into doing this [i.e. commercial jobs]. I do not particularly enjoy [involving my family in these jobs]. I wasn't intending to involve them. But people invited us and I would say, 'It sounds fun, let me ask them first'. This is a way for stepping back. For example, some events [organizers] ask me and my daughter to perform catwalks.

[....]. I asked my daughter whether she wanted to do, saying that the pay is good – not just paying me but paying her. If she does not want to do it, then it will be a 'no'.

The impacts of new media on celebrity identity

Fan–star relationships

Arguably, electronic media may help develop a closer fan–celebrity relationship as it allows fans to glean the information they crave (Ferris & Harris, 2011). During the interview, Lam claimed that online media was a relatively insignificant facilitator in furthering the relationship; in fact, he had had more face-to-face contact and a closer relationship with his fans in the old days, when new media had not yet been introduced or popularly used. At that time, he was the presenter of an evening radio phone-in programme. Given that the nature of radio is audio-based, he was able to provide an imaginary space for the audience, and create a sense of intimacy with them both face-to-face and on-air, successfully building his fan base:

> In the night time, there was always the phone-in part for listeners pouring out their hearts. So the fan base was very large. Also, there were always chances for us to meet each other because there were many events or gatherings. Now we grow older and it's no longer [...]. I now have less contact with them and the number of people is smaller because they are older now [...]. Now I have more contacts with online fans. For example, I reply to them if they ask me questions. But it's not frequent unless they ask me something about my work [...]. I screen them and I will spend time to understand if it's related to work and earnings. If I have time, I will also try to reply to people pouring their hearts out – I am talking about those on Weibo and Facebook. But the relationship is not as close as it was before because online media has loosened the relationship.

Today, Lam no longer does the radio programme and is putting less time into his role as a television host than before. This might have contributed to his weaker bond with his fans. Although he still makes efforts to sustain the relationship with his fans, it is done mostly online and infrequently.

Celebrity, social media and the ethos of capitalism

Social media offers a new arena for celebrities actively promoting and selling themselves as products under the logic of capitalism, thereby propelling the marketing and promotion machine further. Celebrities are 'tied to the corporate world through their professional work' (Kapoor, 2013, p. 29). Social media has instrumentally deepened the entrenchment of celebrities in the corporate world by opening up more economic opportunities for them. For Lam, social media is important for his work and reputation:

> Without these [social networking sites], my reputation may not reach today's level. Although it might not be that high compared to that of superstars, [...] without social

networking sites, my income would be lowered because many job opportunities reach me through social networking sites.

In a way, social media has shaped Lam's relationship with the corporate and marketing worlds in positive ways. He has been very responsive when communicating with his clients online because he has strived to uphold his reputation and identity as a well-mannered artist, maintaining good relationships with the marketers and corporations he cared about:

> I am selective. Maybe there are some questions about work. I am just worried that, for example, I have a function to attend, and the company may have something to ask me and need my reply. I will reply to them quickly because it is for work and I don't want to destroy my own reputation. I may be regarded as being big-headed if I do not reply to them in a week's time.

When asked why he did not have an online fan page, he explained that the social media accounts he had were enough for him. He said he was not 'greedy' and would not use his number of followers as a bargaining tool when dealing with his clients.

Marketers have often approached him offering to pay him to post promotional feeds through his social media accounts. He accepted the jobs only if the reward was 'attractive'; in other words, he consciously considered his own market value in each case. His attitude toward such explicitly commercial jobs is positive: 'Isn't it quite decent? It requires releasing two posts only!'

Lam believed that people can easily reach him through social networking sites, but artists have the freedom to choose whether or not to reply. New media empowers artists, who no longer need to rely solely on traditional media, to decide how their social networking accounts should be used to release first-hand information:

> Without conducting interviews, media people can know what you have been up to through social networking sites. In the past two to three years, both online and printed magazines and newspapers cover artists' Weibo, Facebook, Instagram and Twitter. In the past, when a singer had a new song to release, he/she needed to have interviews on radio programmes, show up on TV programmes, and be published in magazines and newspapers, whereas now he/she can announce it on his/her page [online].

According to his view, social media offer a new platform for artists to bypass the traditional media system and be proactive in promoting their work to the public, without overly relying on traditional media to reach out to the audience.

Power of paparazzi and construction of celebrity image
Celebrity is closely tied to the circulation of information and networks of communication (Milner Jr., 2005). The media heavily emphasize visuality around celebrity stories so that

the moral dimensions of celebrity status are rendered relatively less important (Milner Jr., 2005). At the same time, tabloid-style celebrity stories can stimulate debate about moral and social issues (Johansson, 2006). In Hong Kong, it is common for paparazzi magazines to exaggerate a celebrity's negative sides, attempting to generate controversy in society in order to boost sales.

Lam believes that celebrities should avoid doing things that may create a negative image for themselves – a lesson he learned from his own personal experience with paparazzi. When asked about his feelings about the experience, Lam expressed:

> I think I am quite lucky. I am not really an idol or a superstar. So I do not have much feeling. The strongest one was that I was caught by paparazzi at an adult video shop and at a massage parlour with a 'not-so-decent [erotic] signboard'. [...] The worst thing that I have done was that I was not aware that I was already a so-called 'celebrity' and public figure, and did something 'non-celebrities' may do.

Lam sarcastically joked that the massage incident led him to appear on the front cover of a paparazzi magazine for the very first time. It was also the first time that he was followed by the paparazzi. The magazine magnified the incident by suggesting that Lam had gone to the parlour to receive an 'erotic service'. Although Lam claimed that he visited only for the normal massage service, he did not choose to clarify the incident in detail to the public in order to avoid further coverage of the incident. He felt that he was 'wrong' and 'did not handle it well' as he 'might have let down the people who believed that he was not a person doing such things'.

On the other hand, Lam assumed that the media's coverage of celebrities' private lives sometimes benefits both the celebrity and media. For the media, such coverage might increase the viewing rates of its news contents on its electronic platforms (e.g. mobile apps). As for celebrities, the coverage may enhance their name recognition in the public domain. Lam cited the example of Coffee Lam (林芊妤), a former TVB artist, to illustrate the mutual benefits for both parties:

> The scandal of Coffee's [sexual] gathering at a public accessible toilet with another man led to a sudden upsurge of download rates of the apps [a news application owned by the media corporation who released the story]. So who is the winner and who is the loser? The apps won, the company won and Coffee also won. She was nobody before. She is now having quite a good life... although she might feel unhappy at the press conference and was fired. But, what's next? She is having a good life.

Regardless of whether it is worthy and sustainable for a celebrity to use their negatively publicized image to build awareness and reputation, it is still controversial and judged differently. Generally, this kind of ambivalent relationship between the media and celebrities shapes the state of the entertainment industry. Still, Lam tended to believe that no artist or celebrity would like to be followed by paparazzi or have their secrets or faults disclosed.

Final insights

Denise Ho (何韻詩), Hilary Tsui (徐濠縈), Pakho Chau (周柏豪) and Bob Lam (林盛斌) hold rather different views toward their celebrity identity, how they construct it, the way they use it and the mechanism of identity construction in the media system. Five such views are:

1. During the interview, Ho demonstrated that her identity as a celebrity and her political, social and sexual identities are intertwined (Fuss, 1989). The complexities and contradictions in the identification process involve other externally imposed forces, such as the media's power and cultural dynamics, as well as struggles between its own subjectivity and the expectations of the public, the entertainment industry and the commercial markets (van Krieken, 2012a). Ho is clearly discontented with the present media system, which, according to her, aligns itself solely with the typical commercial and capitalist logic, while she, as a celebrity, is expected to be silent on sensitive issues such as equal sexual, civil and political rights. In the face of these mainstream expectations and constraints, Ho has taken a more subversive and rebellious stance. She resists the present system by negotiating a different, more idealistic role of celebrity by emphasizing celebrities' roles as charismatic spiritual leaders or, in some cases, political/cultural martyrs (Shils, 2010). The main concern for Ho has been to strike a balance between her entertainment career and her outspoken advocacy for the rights of Hong Kong's people. Although taking a marginal and less-travelled road is no comfortable job for Ho, the journey allows her to stay true to herself, and to further explore the possibilities of being both a celebrated public figure and an ordinary person who strives to pursue a better society (Dunn, 1998; Miller, 2011).

   Similarly, Tsui expressed her discontent with the media's inaccurate portrayal of her, judging her based on the mainstream expectations for a celebrity wife/mother (Turner, 2010). Tsui's negotiation of her star identity is not only based on the commercial logic of the entertainment industry, but also her desire for self-actualization, emotional fulfilment and radiating 'positive energy' to society. It also represents her resistance to the mass media holding her against social norms and ideological values by highlighting her unique traits, namely being married yet not overly domestic and feminine, being active and sporty, as well as her roles as a fashion consumer and trendsetter, 'cool hunter' and fashion entrepreneur (Lind, 2013). Her multiple, intertwined identities contest and expand the traditional notion of 'celebrity'; sometimes she even rejects identifying herself as a celebrity in order to escape the system (Miller, 2011).

In contrast, both Chau and Lam are more adapted to the mainstream media system in Hong Kong and strive to fit into it. Chau embraces the mainstream expectations of celebrities, and works hard to fulfil a celebrity's 'social responsibility' by having a positive outlook, promoting a healthy lifestyle and encouraging fans to contribute to society through volunteering (Gamson, 1992). He strives to be a good role model, and does not challenge or question the definition of celebrity. In a similar vein, Lam completely adopts the media system and the commodified notion of celebrity. He emphasizes how a celebrity's major role is as an entertainer, and makes no attempt to hide the commercial intent of the system nor his own economic pursuit (van Krieken, 2012a). Similar to Chau, he accepts without questioning the public's expectations (and even their double standards) by indicating it is wrong for him, as a celebrity, to do something which a non-celebrity may have done, such as visiting an adult video shop or a massage parlour offering erotic services.

2. When talking about the ideal role a celebrity should play in society, Chau conceived celebrity as a charismatic opinion leader for the public, especially amongst adolescents (Weber, 2006). One of the ultimate goals Chau wants to actualize is being positive, and using his fame and social influence to mobilize his supporters to contribute to society – from volunteering to playing sports (Shils, 2010). Ho had a more complex sentiment towards the celebrity's role as an opinion leader: she has become more outspoken socially and politically in terms of expressing her support for the Hong Kong people's equal sexual, civil and political rights. However, she found it difficult to go against mainstream waves and strike a balance between her multiple identities when facing the mass media and public, as well as in opposing the typical capitalist logic of the entertainment industry (van Krieken, 2012a). Both interviewees constantly negotiate their identities and reconcile the inevitable conflicts among them, while at the same time striving to help build a better society. Ultimately, being a positive and socially responsible artist who knows how to use their influence in a meaningful and constructive way concerned both Ho and Chau more than just excelling in the entertainment industry on economic terms (Kapoor, 2013). In addition to acting, singing and performing for their fans, a celebrity must make good use of their influence so as to benefit society; this continues to be a major endeavour for both of them.

3. Nowadays, consumers are no longer satisfied with a celebrity's public performances, and instead are more eager to discover their private life and authentic self. In order to maximize commercial profits, traditional media often respond to (or fuel) the public's desires by taking an active role in shaping the private image of celebrities and exposing their private lives, thereby delivering a seemingly more authentic self (Milner Jr., 2005). As a result, the boundary between the public and private spheres has become increasingly blurred (Horton & Wohl, 2010). Tsui's case raises concerns among celebrities about the problems derived from blurring the boundary between the public and private spheres, in addition to the tensions between the public's perception of celebrity and their self-identity. Tsui resists and differentiates her authentic self from the contrived

public image she holds in Hong Kong by lingering between her public and private life, thereby creating an acceptable façade of private life via social media, improvising new ways to 'collaborate' with paparazzi, and diversifying her identity as an entrepreneur and fashionista.

4. Although Ho and Chau have their respective hopes and fears regarding their position as celebrities and entertainment industry participants, they both face chances and challenges from the new media environment that affect how they manage their roles as public figures, maintain their multiple identities, and actualize their visions and missions (Théberge, 2005). Chau agrees that the emergence of social media provides an ideal platform from which the celebrities can interact with their fans directly at an unprecedented level (Ferris & Harris, 2011). Meanwhile, Ho indicated that the public could also use this interactive platform to criticize celebrities directly and openly, potentially triggering an unhealthy celebrity–public relationship (Lerman, 2007). Under digital surveillance, celebrities now tend to be very careful with their words and are more hesitant about speaking their mind; not being fearful of doing wrong, but of being seen as wrong and then extensively propagandized online (van Krieken, 2012a).

5. In order to expose the celebrities' private selves, the paparazzi in Hong Kong have adopted extreme methods and do not hesitate to intrude into a celebrity's private life (Horton & Wohl, 2010). Facing the intrusion of the media and the paparazzi, Tsui was confrontational at first. However, she has gradually adapted to the system, and improvised new strategies for protecting and upholding the 'authentic' image of herself and her family in front of the mass media (Johansson, 2006). She makes use of the media system tactfully for her personal ends. Social media has played a major role throughout this process, as demonstrated in the way she actively uses social media platforms to promote her fashion business and her image as a healthy marathon runner to the public (Turner, 2010). By using social media to her own ends, she can then selectively display her private life and seize control of her own attention capital as much as possible to elicit a positive public response. Similarly, Chau has made use of the freedom provided by social media platforms to craft his own identity. In order to conceal his private life, he often protects himself from the public by using indefinite words and sentences, as well as selectively exposing his life events and feelings on the platform (Langer, 2006).

In contrast to Tsui and Chau, who strive to draw a boundary between the public and private spheres via the use of social media, Lam does not intend to separate his public and private selves, and he is quite willing to share his private life, especially family life, with the public (van Krieken, 2012a). Sometimes he even involves his family members in public performances, such as television programmes, advertisements and media interviews (Hesmondhalgh, 2005; Marshall, 1997). Nonetheless, Lam perceives online media to be a relatively insignificant facilitator in furthering the celebrity–fan relationship, as he claims that he had a much closer relationship with fans long before the popularity of social media (Ferris & Harris, 2011).

In the 'good old days', celebrities were often portrayed as one-dimensional, glamorous and almost sacred stars beyond the reach of the common people (Lind, 2013). However, today a celebrity's identity is no longer stable or based on their presumed 'intrinsic' star qualities (Dunn, 1998). Multiple parties are often involved in crafting a celebrity's images, and in defining what it means to be a celebrity in Hong Kong and China, resulting in celebrities' multiple identities, which are easily changeable and sometimes even contradictory. In contrast to Tsui and Ho, who have actively reclaimed their authentic selves by posting on social media and advocated equal sexual/political rights, respectively, both Lam and Chau are seemingly undisturbed by their mystified mediated images, as they both realize it is something beyond their control. What they choose to do is to avoid dwelling on them and instead think in a positive way. They do not take great care to fight back or reclaim their 'authentic' selves, and Lam even believes these mystified mediated images – though sometimes negative in nature – may potentially boost a celebrity's popularity. In the contemporary entertainment industry environment, the line between good and bad publicity is elusive; wise use of the matrix of media that facilitates interactions between the celebrity and the masses generates attention capital, which is the key to managing a good public impression.

Notes

1 A personality group comprised of Louis Cheung (阮兆祥), Wong Cho Lam (王祖藍) and Johnson Lee (李思捷), who achieved fame in comedic performances in Hong Kong. The name of the group was appropriated from the three deities of Prosperity (Fu), Status (Lu), and Longevity (Shou) in Chinese mythology.

2 A personality trio of Eric Tsang (曾志偉) and his two 'lieutenants', Jerry Lamb (林曉峰) and Chin Kar-lok (錢嘉樂), who hosted the *Super Trio* game show series from 1995 to 2014.

Chapter 6

Conclusion

In this book, the authors conducted twelve interviews with famous celebrities and entertainment industry professionals in greater China, Hong Kong and South Korea. In the first two sections, we described the celebrity culture in the region; delineated the development of the celebrity creation system in Asia; contemplated the role of media and its influence in Hong Kong's entertainment business; discussed star identity and the use of celebrity in marketing communications/branding; and analysed the impacts of fame and celebrity culture in society. In doing so, there can be no doubt that the influence of celebrity is prevalent in today's society. As Marshall (1997) suggested, the presence of celebrities allows them a discursive power and a legitimately significant voice above others. Therefore, celebrities are capable of easily drawing public attention to a particular object or subject (for instance, the promotion of amyotrophic lateral sclerosis [ALS] through the Ice Bucket Challenge in 2014 [Reddy, 2014a]), and are believed to be influential in structuring meanings and providing sense to a particular culture (Marshall, 1997). They are also effective in generating profits for sponsoring companies. In this chapter, we draw conclusions by examining celebrities' influence via the perspectives of economic returns and societal impacts in society. By giving more vivid local examples in the Asian context, we hope that readers can critically analyse the diverse impacts of celebrities in our culture and society.

Economic values of celebrities in the commercial sector

Celebrities have enormous commercial potential and are profitable human brands that make money not only for themselves, but also for others surrounding them (Brockington, 2009; Turner, 2004). The star system was first adapted by film studios in the early twentieth century to add value to entertainment products, using its established actors and actresses to promote and market films (Gamson, 1992; Marshall, 1997). Nowadays, celebrities' economic values are even greater. Different media outlets have developed ways to capitalize on the celebrity phenomenon (Rein et al., 1997). For example, the presence of celebrities can bring significant increases in newspapers' and magazines' sales or in TV ratings (Turner, 2004).

Upon realizing celebrities' potential economic value, the use of public figures in marketing communications became increasingly common, and marketers believe that they are effective channels for promoting a corporation, product or brand with which they are associated (Pringle, 2004). Although some of our interviewees – like Anson and June – indicated that the actual economic implications of celebrity endorsement can be uncertain in specific cases, and that the economic influence of the use of celebrity is debatable, celebrities are undoubtedly attention-getting devices that are able to divert public and media attention to a product/brand, thereby leading to a significant increase in product/brand awareness (K. Chan et al., 2013; O'Mahony & Meenaghan, 1997; Rein et al., 1997; van Krieken, 2012a). They can give consumers confidence in a product or brand, and have considerable influence on consumers' purchase intentions (Atkin & Block, 1983; K. Chan et al., 2013; Elberse, 2013a; Petty et al., 1983). Therefore, the use of celebrities can bring great economic benefits for a corporation, and it has been proven that celebrity endorsements can increase the sales of a product and improve a firm's stock market valuation (Agrawal & Kamakura, 1995; K. Chung et al., 2013; Elberse & Verleun, 2012; Mathur et al., 1997).

Associating a celebrity with a brand or product is a common marketing strategy employed in Asia, which sometimes brings enormous benefits for those companies. In recent years, companies have made extensive use of the popularity of South Korean celebrity television programmes in Asia to publicize their products because of their substantial influence in the region. From 1999 to 2003, the value of South Korea's entertainment industry experienced a fivefold increase, surging from US$8.5 billion to US$43.5 billion (A. Chung, 2011). Besides local consumption, the industry is also exporting its products and spreading its influence extensively to Asia and beyond. The export of South Korean pop culture products grew more than 30 per cent between 2006 and 2010 (Yang, 2012), signifying its increasing popularity in the world. Beginning in the late 1990s, many people, especially those in Asian countries, became infatuated with South Korean popular culture and became ardent consumers of the country's media products. The unprecedented phenomenon attracted much media attention and was described as the 'Korean wave' or '*Hallyu*'.

The economic consumption of celebrity culture products can be further demonstrated by the South Korean television drama *My Love from the Star* (2013), which aired every Wednesday and Thursday night on Seoul Broadcasting System from 18 December 2013 to 27 February 2014. This fantasy romance involved an alien who landed on Earth during the Joseon dynasty and fell in love with a famous actress 400 years later. There are 21 episodes altogether and, according to AGB Nielsen (South Korea) (2014), the series was very popular in South Korea, reaching 24 per cent in its average ratings. The influence and popularity of *My Love from the Star* extended beyond its own country as well. In China, the online video portal 愛奇藝/iQIYI bought the broadcasting rights to the series and allowed Chinese viewers to watch each episode (with Chinese subtitles) several hours after it was broadcast in South Korea for free. The online ratings surpassed one billion viewers in China and the show was awarded the Silver Award for Best Foreign TV Series at the 20th Shanghai Television Festival Magnolia Awards (Xu, 2014), indicating its immense popularity. More interestingly, the influence of *My Love from the Star* (2013) did not end with the romantic love story. The series' high level of popularity provided a great opportunity for cultural marketing and triggered the consumption of related products. In the drama, the protagonists use several local South Korean brands: they talk and send texts using the Samsung's Galaxy Note smartphones and Line mobile app;

while the female protagonist, Cheon Song-yi (千頌伊), uses lotions and lipsticks from Amorepacific. The influence of the series was substantial and had an immediate effect on the sales of these products. The registered users of the Line mobile app increased tenfold in one day; products from local fashion brands such as Gentle Monster, Lucky Chouette and Rouge & Lounge became instant hits among consumers; while sales of Amorepacific's skincare products and lipsticks surged 75 per cent and 400 per cent, respectively (*Shanghai Daily,* 2014b).

The success of this type of cultural marketing has been supported in part by the South Korean government. In 2010, the national government loosened its control on product placement in television dramas, and encouraged entrepreneurs to invest by waiving the taxes on them. The effect was pronounced: the product placement market expanded to US$35 million, which was a tenfold increase in three years (Ngaai Wan, 2014).

Today, most of the product placement deals in South Korea involve domestic companies, which is also true in the case of *My Love from the Star* (2013). However, the economic potential of television dramas extends to foreign products as well. For example, the Hermès cape and Jimmy Choo shoes worn by Cheon Song-yi (千頌伊) were quickly sold out across Asia within days, while the Lolita Lempicka lip gloss and Yves Saint Laurent lipstick were termed 'Cheon Song-yi's lip gloss' (*Shanghai Daily,* 2014b). Given the substantial economic value brought about by television dramas, it is predicted that overseas firms will be increasingly attracted to invest in them (*Shanghai Daily,* 2014b).

The impacts of *My Love from the Star* (2013) on Korean food and tourism were also significant. Cheon Song-yi's (千頌伊) mention of her infatuation with *chimek* (fried chicken and beer) started a craze for the meal in mainland China and Hong Kong. Having *chimek* became trendy and the sudden surge in demand resulted in the opening of several fried chicken restaurants (Sito, 2014), with Korean restaurants witnessing a significant increase in business (He, 2014; L. Lin, 2014). The huge sales of fried chicken even boosted the poultry industry in China, which had been severely affected by the H7N9 bird flu crisis (Shanghai Daily, 2014a).

In addition to tasting what the characters eat, the ardent audience wanted to visit the sites where the story was filmed. In the past, South Korean television dramas have been effective in attracting foreign tourists to the country (S. Kim, Agrusa, Chon, & Cho, 2008; Y. Lin & Huang, 2010). Filming locations of popular Korean television dramas are continuously overrun by devoted fans, resulting in a significant boost to the tourism industry (A. Chung, 2011; W. Chung & Lee, 2011; D. Kim & Kim, 2011; D. Kim et al., 2009; S. Kim et al., 2008; Y. Lin & Huang, 2010). For example, a pronounced increase in foreign travellers visiting Nami Island was recorded after the broadcast of *Winter Sonata* (冬季戀歌) (Lee, 2002), while the outdoor set of the famous television drama *Jewel in the Palace* (大長今) (Lee, 2003) in the MBC Yangju Culture Valley was rebuilt into a theme park to attract tourists (A. Chung, 2011). The newest iconic landmark, Dongdaemun Design Plaza in South Korea, was opened in March 2014. Before its grand opening, it was chosen for the shooting location of *My Love from the Star* (2013), which attracted much publicity. The Plaza has even launched a special exhibition, and reconstructed the protagonists' apartments and several major settings of the television drama for fans to relive the story.

Without a doubt, the economic potential of celebrity culture is immense. With the emergence and spread of digital and mobile media, product placement has become a new trend in marketing. In order to better realize the economic potential of the use of celebrity in marketing communications or media in Asia, it is suggested that marketers invest more promotional efforts in stories with engaging and emotionally charged narratives, and target young consumers (especially females), who consume a great deal of South Korean dramas and programmes.

Values of celebrities in the non-profit sector

In addition to commercial sectors, celebrities are also widely used in non-profit sectors (Kapoor, 2013). Celebrities are perceived as effective messengers and persuaders in non-profit sectors because they can attract public attention, and raise money and awareness toward certain social issues (Salmones, Dominguez, & Herrero, 2013; Samman, McAuliffe, & MacLachlan, 2009). The use of celebrities is not uncommon in Hong Kong's non-profit sectors: Sammi Cheng (鄭秀文), a famous female singer in Hong Kong, shared her story about fighting depression and recorded a theme song for the HK Familylink Mental Health Advocacy Association in order to help educate the public about the seriousness of mental illness, as well as raise funds for the organization; in the past two decades, actress Sylvia Chang (張艾嘉) has joined World Vision Hong Kong as a 'lifetime volunteer' in an effort to raise funds and increase public awareness about the issues of global poverty; and famous local celebrities such as Karen Mok (莫文蔚), Daniel Wu (吳彥祖), Jade Kwan (關心妍) and Stephy Tang (鄧麗欣) have helped to raise funds for building projects in China, Nepal and the Philippines for the non-profit organization Habitat for Humanity Hong Kong, who work with families in need of improvements to their living environment.

Some celebrities are even setting up their own charitable foundations or pressure groups to direct public attention toward particular social issues and influence public policies (Brockington, 2009). For example, Bono is one of the founders of the non-government organization Debt, Aids, Trade, Africa (DATA), which aims to address and relieve the AIDS epidemic and poverty problems in Africa, while Leonardo DiCaprio has established a foundation to promote environmental protection. In Hong Kong, the well-known television personality Lam Kin-ming (林建明) founded the Joyful (Mental Health) Foundation, which aims to spread accurate information about mental illness and support mental health patients in the city (V. Chow, 2005). Hong Kong artists Anthony Wong (黃耀明) and Denise Ho (何韻詩) also set up the BigLove Alliance in January 2013, a non-profit charity organization that advocates and protects basic equal rights for the LGBT community in Hong Kong.

The increase in publicity may eventually attract more donations and make a campaign more successful. The Ice Bucket Challenge that originated in the United States in July 2014 is a good example of the effectiveness of using celebrity and social media in philanthropy. For the challenge, which became a global phenomenon, participants pour a bucket of ice and water over their heads. The whole process is filmed and posted on social media. People who have completed the challenge may then tag other friends and challenge them to do the same within 24 hours; otherwise, they have to donate money to organizations related to ALS. The Ice Bucket Challenge drew much attention to ALS and raised substantial donations: between 29 July and 29 August 2014, the biggest beneficiary, the US-based ALS Association, received US$100.9 million from more than three million donors around the world, compared to only US$2.8 million during the same period in 2013 (ALS Association, 2014). Other organizations related to ALS are also benefiting from the challenge. Boston-based ALS Therapy Development Institute received more than US$400,000 in two weeks, which was ten times the number of donations during the same period in 2013; Project ALS has also raised about US$116,000, compared to a mere US$1,000 in the same period the previous year (Reddy, 2014a, 2014b). People in Hong Kong are also enthusiastically responding to the Ice Bucket Challenge, where celebrities such as Joey Yung (容祖兒), Cheung Ka Fai (張家輝) and Kwai Lun Mei (桂綸鎂) have also responded to the event. The Hong Kong Neuromuscular Disease Association has received an astonishing HK$25 million in two weeks, which is more than the total donations received in the past eight years (Hong Kong Neuromuscular Disease Association, 2014).

Nowadays, the non-profit sector is becoming a very competitive promotional area (Wheeler, 2009), with organizations relying heavily on celebrities' fame to fundraise, attract people's attention and raise awareness of social issues. However, the use of celebrities in this sector is not without problems, with some celebrity activism raising concerns as to the motives of the endorsers (Salmones et al., 2013). According to motivation attribution (Kelley, 1967), the general public are sceptical about the credibility of those celebrities who endorse a non-profit company:

[T]he recipients [of the non-profit company] will perceive altruistic or intrinsic motives if they consider that the brand/endorser is supporting a cause because he/she wants to benefit society or raise awareness for that specific cause. On the other hand, consumers will perceive selfish or extrinsic motives if they think that the company/endorser is seeking only to make a profit, increase sales, boost their image.

(Salmones et al., 2013, p. 5)

With the Ice Bucket Challenge, some criticisms were made in regarding the intentions of celebrities who participated. In general, the celebrities/donors may draw too much focus and fail to raise awareness about ALS as effectively as suggested. Moreover, some Internet users/celebrities are doing the challenge without donating or even mentioning ALS in the videos (Jarvis, 2014); for example, Beyoncé and Joey Yung (容祖兒) just poured ice water over their heads and said nothing about ALS. Saxton and Wang (forthcoming) observed that this kind of 'slacktivism' is common in social media fundraising. As slacktivists, Internet users may put forth minimal personal effort in supporting a social cause (e.g. liking and promoting a cause without actually donating), but take much satisfaction in return from the feeling that they have contributed. It is thus perceived to be just an act of publicly praising themselves and satisfying their narcissistic egos in the form of 'likes' and public recognition (Jarvis, 2014). In addition, in the latter stages of the Ice Bucket Challenge, social networking sites were flooded with related video posts in which almost everyone was doing the same thing. As a result, people may become fed up or even find the campaign annoying, and potentially developed negative feelings toward ALS.

In the same vein, Kapoor (2013) argued that celebrity humanitarianism tends to individualize and isolate social problems, focusing on the outwardly visible and photogenic aspects of a crisis. It neglects the long-term structural causes of the problems, and rationalizes the global inequality, unevenness and social marginalization it seeks to address (Kapoor, 2013). Moreover, celebrities and their charity work are deeply entangled in capitalism, which is very often the root cause of the social problems they wish to address (Kapoor, 2013). Previous research was robust about the negative intentions of celebrity activism, which can normally be explained by the selfish motives of celebrities. Celebrities who joined a non-profit organization may want to increase their autonomy to promote their own personal brand, differentiate themselves, gain publicity and promote their image. Hence, both celebrities and non-profit organizations must be careful to find a way in which to coordinate the celebrity image with the social cause so as to enhance the elaboration of the message, as well as lower consumer doubt and scepticism (Salmones et al., 2013). To secure the effectiveness of communication in the non-profit sector, non-profit organizations may want to achieve the commitment of the celebrity to the cause off-camera; that is, engender genuine support (Magnini, Honeycutt, & Cross, 2008). The better the congruence of celebrity image and social causes, the higher the credibility of the celebrity and the more effective the communication.

Social values of celebrities

Celebrities can stimulate discussions about social and moral issues, and mediate cultural and ideological debates surrounding various social categories, such as national identity, race and class (Dyer, 2004; Johansson, 2006; Meeuf & Raphael, 2013). In some instances, celebrities may even provide a platform for the audience to negotiate the transforming of gender subjectivities and gendered norms (Dyer, 2004; Meeuf & Raphael, 2013). For example, in 1987, Agnes Chan (陳美齡), a Hong Kong-born Japanese celebrity, brought her newborn baby to work. Her action caught public attention and resulted in the well-known 'Agnes controversy', which ultimately raised public awareness about working mothers' situation. This provided a platform for various feminist scholars and social commentators to debate the related gender issues (Hambleton, 2012). In 2008, some obscene and private pictures of the Hong Kong celebrity Edison Chen (陳冠希), along with various female celebrities, were illegally distributed over the Internet. According to Y. Chow and Kloet (2013), the photo scandal propelled a moral discourse which suggested carnal desires are ultimately contained. Although Chen apologized for his act to the public and a number of ethical debates over his act emerged in society, it is obvious from this case that celebrities usually serve as characters in morality tales, and emblematize the moral values and constraints of the wider culture (Hinerman, 2006). The impact of their behaviour on- or off-camera has profound influence on society, especially when there is a close relationship between the celebrity and the audience.

Para-social relationship and identification

In contemporary culture, the ubiquitous existence of celebrities can be readily felt. These public personae are not merely mediated images or on-screen figures, and individuals may establish a wide range of relationships (sometimes conflicting in nature) with them in their daily lives. Horton and Wohl (1956) concluded that the audience establishes a para-social relationship (i.e. a complementary relationship to normal social life) with celebrities by watching television. In a similar vein, Hermes (2006) argued that celebrity news stories transform these public figures into familiar faces and, by reading these stories, consumers may come to see these familiar faces as acquaintances, friends or even family members. Communities may even be formed around these figures. For example, celebrity news stories can serve as talking points in various social situations and relationships, thereby contributing to the creation of a community experience (Johansson, 2006).

Through these para-social relationships, people easily identify with the idols/celebrities they like, and consequently mimic the behaviour and attitudes of the media image. For example, by reading celebrity stories, the audience can derive pleasure from vicariously identifying with the celebrities, thus enabling them to experience the world of glitter and glamour (Hermes, 2006; Johansson, 2006). Moreover, these glamorous figures often serve as role models and trendsetters in society, and the general public might imitate their fashion, speech, behaviour, etc., in order to harmonize with society and gain a sense of self-assurance (Payne, 2010; van Krieken, 2012a).

The influence of celebrities on their fans is even greater. Celebrities are believed to be sources for their followers' identity construction and personal transformation (Cashmore, 2014; Ward, 2011). They are figures whom fans aspire to be and imitate (Ward, 2011; Yue, 2007): for example, it is reported that Elvis Presley's fans have integrated their internal values and beliefs with those of their idol, and their construction of self-identity is closely associated with his mediated images (Fraser & Brown, 2002). Moreover, fans may review and reflect on themselves by comparing themselves with celebrities (van Krieken, 2012a), which may assist their self-development and enhance their self-knowledge, helping them better understand their feelings about themselves (Engle & Kasser, 2005). Having said that, Gilbert (2004) pointed out that celebrities are ultimately images of impossible perfection. The glamorous yet unattainable existence of celebrities emphasizes consumers' own insufficiency, and may arouse feelings of envy, frustration and even anger (Clark, 2008; Connor, 2005; Johansson, 2006). Thus, consumers might sometimes have an aggressive attitude toward celebrities and find it enjoyable to witness a celebrity's misfortune, through which they can experience a momentary vindication of injustice (Harper, 2006; Johansson, 2006).

Intense emotional attachments

As mentioned earlier, identification with celebrities can be intensified when the celebrity–audience relationship has evolved, as in the notion of celebrity worship. Yue (2007) pointed out that some adolescent fans in Hong Kong have strong emotional attachments to celebrities. He understood their emotions for their idols as a kind of 'hyperreal emotion', particularly as these figures lead a hyperreal existence themselves, and the celebrity lifestyle in which fans are indulging is dreamy and remote from reality (Yue, 2007). Some researchers have even examined the fans' emotional attachments from the perspective of clinical psychology. Maltby, Day, McCutcheon, Houran and Ashe (2006) classified celebrity worship into three categories according to the fans' attitudes and behaviours: (1) entertainment-social celebrity worship; (2) intense-personal celebrity worship; and (3) borderline-pathological celebrity worship. They asserted that intense-personal celebrity worship and borderline-pathological celebrity worship have clinical implications, and are associated with proneness to fantasy, as well as social-pathological attitudes and behaviours. Similarly, McCutcheon, Lange and Houran (2002) argued that the highest level of celebrity worship is accompanied by over-identification, compulsive behaviour and obsession.

These types of intense, emotional celebrity–audience relationships are not uncommon in Asia and are often negatively portrayed in mass media. For example, Yang Lijuan (楊麗娟) a well-known obsessive fan of Hong Kong singer/actor Andy Lau, quit school and repeatedly came to Hong Kong in order to get closer to her idol. Her father even sold his kidney and their house to financially support her fan activity. Unhappy about Lau's refusal to meet Yang in private, Yang's father eventually committed suicide after leaving behind a letter protesting Lau's 'cruelty'. In South Korea, these kind of obsessive fans are known as *sasaeng* fans (사생팬) – people who have a strong desire to establish a personal connection with their idols. They follow their favourite celebrities day and night, and may even use extreme methods, such as stalking and wiretapping, to intrude into the private lives of the celebrities.

Final thoughts

In this chapter, we outlined the economic and social values of the use of celebrities in Asia. The authors believe that celebrities are considered to be sources of great persuasive power. But there is no formula to envisage the effectiveness of celebrity endorsement in both the private and non-profit sectors. Given the nature of different markets and the needs of different consumer segments, we have concluded that a celebrity who is perceived as credible and trustworthy is more effective at getting consumers to respond positively to advertising messages. As suggested by Amos, Holmes and Strutton (2008), the success of advertising communications or endorsements is leveraged through a celebrity's perceived fit or image congruence. In general, a good fit (between the celebrity image and company/product) enhances celebrity credibility and, in turn, contributes to the effectiveness of the communication (Salmones et al., 2013). The authors presented first-hand, up-to-date insider stories about the celebrity culture in Asia via face-to-face interviews with industry professionals in the hopes of providing important insights for industry practitioners, academic professions and students to think and proactively question the significance of celebrity culture in society, as well as its symbolic and social meanings for younger generations. To reiterate, celebrities occupy a unique space in society. A celebrity is a person who is known for being well-known (Boorstin, 1962). Because of their high public recognition, celebrities are able to attract attention and communicate quickly with a comparatively large audience (van Krieken, 2012a). With the widespread ubiquity of the Internet and reality television shows, everyone can earn fame easily. To borrow Andy Warhol's maxim once again, 'In the future, everyone will be world-famous for fifteen minutes'. As such, everyone can exert an extent of influence on society, both positively and negatively.

References

AGB Nielsen (South Korea). (2014). 지상파/*Terrestrial ratings*. Retrieved from http://www. nielsenkorea.co.kr/tv_terrestrial_day.asp?menu=Tit_1&sub_menu=1_1&area=00. Accessed 3 July 2015.

Agrawal, J., & Kamakura, W. A. (1995). The economic worth of celebrity endorsers: An event study analysis. *Journal of Marketing, 59*(3), 56–62.

Almquist, E., & Roberts, K. J. (2000). A 'mindshare' manifesto: Common misconceptions squander the power of the modern brand. *Mercer Management Journal*, 9–20. Retrieved from http://membersonly.amamember.org/sales/pdf/1-Rethinking.pdf. Accessed 28 November 2015.

Alperstein, N. M., & Vann, B. H. (1997). Star gazing: A socio-cultural approach to the study of dreaming about media figures. *Communication Quarterly, 45*(3), 142–152.

ALS Association. (2014, August 29). The ALS Association expresses sincere gratitude to over three million donors. Retrieved from http://www.alsa.org/news/media/press-releases/ice-bucket-challenge-082914.html. Accessed 2 September 2014.

Altman, H. (2005). Celebrity culture: Are Americans too focused on celebrities? *CQ Press*. Retrieved from http://www.sagepub.com/upm-data/31937_1.pdf. Accessed 23 November 2015.

Amos, C., Holmes, G., & Strutton, D. (2008). Exploring the relationship between celebrity endorser effects and advertising effectiveness. *International Journal of Advertising, 27*(2), 209–234.

Arvidsson, A. (2006). *Brands: Meaning and value in media culture*. London & New York: Routledge.

Atkin, C., & Block, M. (1983). Effectiveness of celebrity endorsers. *Journal of Advertising Research, 23*(1), 57–62.

Belch, G. E., & Belch, M. A. (2014). *Advertising and promotion: An integrated marketing communications perspective* (10th ed.). Boston, MA: McGraw-Hill.

Bell, C. E. (2009). *American idolatry: Celebrity, commodity, and reality television* (Unpublished dissertation, University of Colorado, Boulder, CO).

Bell, D. (2001). Meat and metal. In R. Holliday & J. Hassard (Eds.), *Contested bodies* (pp. 168–178). London & New York: Routledge.

van den Berg, B. (2009). *The situated self: Identity in a world of ambient intelligence* (Unpublished doctoral dissertation, Erasmus Universiteit Rotterdam, Rotterdam).

Bernays, E. L. (1952). *Public relations*. Norman, OK: University of Oklahoma Press.

Biagi, S. (2012). *Media/impact: An introduction to mass media*. Australia & Boston, MA: Wadsworth Cengage Learning.

Boorstin, D. J. (1962). *The image, or what happened to the American dream*. Harmondsworth: Penguin.

—— (1971). *The image: A guide to pseudo-events in America*. New York: Atheneum.

Bordwell, D. (2000). *Planet Hong Kong: Popular cinema and the art of entertainment*. Cambridge, MA: Harvard University Press.

Boyd, D. (2008). *Taken out of context: American teen sociality in networked publics* (Doctoral dissertation, University of California, Berkeley, CA).

Boyd, D., & Heer, J. (2006). Profiles as conversation: Networked identity performance on Friendster. Proceeding of the *Hawaii International Conference on System Sciences (HICSS-39)*, IEEE Computer Society, 4–7 January.

Braudy, L. (1997). *Frenzy of renown*. New York: Vintage Books.

Brockington, D. (2009). *Celebrity and the environment: Fame, wealth and power in conservation*. London & New York: Zed Books.

Burgess, J., & Green, J. (2009). *YouTube: Online video and participatory culture*. Cambridge: Polity.

Burke, P. (1992). *The fabrication of Louis XIV*. New Haven, CT: Yale University Press.

Cai, J. (2008). China's first taste of the Korean wave. In *The Korea Herald* (Ed.), *Korean wave* (pp. 100–108). Gyeonggi-do, South Korea: Jimoondang.

Calvert, C. (2000). *Voyeur nation: Media, privacy, and peering in modern culture*. Boulder, CO: Westview Press.

Campbell, W. J. (2001). *Yellow journalism: Puncturing the myths, defining the legacies*. Westport, CT: Praeger Publishers.

Cashmore, E. (2006). *Celebrity/culture*. New York: Routledge.

—— (2014). *Celebrity culture*. Abingdon & New York: Routledge.

Castells, M. (1996). *The rise of the network society*. Malden, MA & Oxford: Blackwell Publishers.

—— (1997). *The power of identity*. Malden, MA & Oxford: Blackwell Publishers.

Centre for Communication and Public Opinion Survey. (2005). *Public opinion on the service of Radio Television Hong Kong (RTHK)*. Retrieved from http://www.com.cuhk.edu.hk/ccpos/b5/pdf/0509_rthk_research%20report_final_ex_summary.pdf. Accessed 23 November 2015.

Chan, J., Ma, E., & So, C. (1997). Back to the future: The retrospect and prospects of Hong Kong media. In J. Chan (Ed.), *The other Hong Kong report 1997* (pp. 475–482). Hong Kong: Chinese University Press.

Chan, J. M., & Fung, A. Y. H. (2010). Structural hybridization in film and television production in Hong Kong. *Visual Anthropology, 24*(1&2), 77–89.

Chan, J. M., Fung, A. Y. H., & Ng, C. H. (2009). *Policies for the sustainable development of the Hong Kong film industry*. Hong Kong: Hong Kong institute of Asia-Pacific Studies.

Chan, K. (2010). *Youth and consumption*. Hong Kong: City University of Hong Kong Press.

Chan, K., Ng, Y. L., & Luk, E. K. (2013). Impact of celebrity endorsement in advertising on brand image among Chinese adolescents. *Young Consumers, 14*(2), 167–179.

Chan, P. (Director). (2013). 中國合夥人/*American dreams in China* [Motion picture]. China: China Film Co.

Chan, P. (Creator). (1978). 孖生姊妹/*Between the twins* [Television broadcast]. Hong Kong: TVB Jade.

Chan, S. (Producer). (2009). 超級巨聲/*The voice* [Television series]. Hong Kong: TVB Jade.

Chan, S. H. (2010). Queering body and sexuality: Leslie Cheung's gender representation in Hong Kong popular culture. In Y. Ching (Ed.), *As normal as possible: Negotiating sexuality and gender in mainland China and Hong Kong* (pp. 113–150). Hong Kong: Hong Kong University Press.

Chang, T. Y. (Producer). (2013). 별에서 온 그대/*My love from the star* [Television series]. Seoul: HB Entertainment (SBS).

Charbonneau, J., & Garland, R. (2010). Product effects on endorser image: The potential for reverse image transfer. *Asia Pacific Journal of Marketing and Logistics, 22*(1), 101–110.

Chau, P. (2007). 同天空/*Same sky. Beginning.* Hong Kong: Warner Music Hong Kong Ltd.

Cheung, C. M. (Producer). (2013). 求愛大作戰/*Bachelors at war* [Television series]. Hong Kong: TVB Jade.

Ching, T. (Director). (1989). 秦俑/*A terracotta warrior* [Motion picture]. China: China Film Co-Production Corporation.

Choi, S. M., Lee, W., & Kim, H. (2005). Lessons from the rich and famous: A cross-cultural comparison of celebrity endorsement in advertising. *Journal of Advertising, 34*(3), 85–98.

Chow, V. (2005, April 1). I had no goals. I hated meeting people. *South China Morning Post*, p. city1.

——— (2015, May 18). Singer says job drought after supporting Occupy worth the sacrifice. *South China Morning Post.* Retrieved from http://www.scmp.com/news/hong-kong/article/1800853/singer-says-job-drought-after-supporting-occupy-worth-sacrifice. Accessed 23 November 2015.

Chow, Y. F., & Kloet, J. (2013). *Sonic multiplicities: Hong Kong pop and the global circulation of sound and image.* Bristol & Chicago, IL: Intellect.

Chu, D. (2013). Kong girls and Lang mo: Teen perceptions of emergent gender stereotypes in Hong Kong. *Journal of Youth Studies, 17*(1), 134–147.

Chu, K. (Director). (2014). 販賣．愛/*I sell love* [Motion picture]. China: Ignite Productions Limited.

Chu, S. Y. W. (2007). *Before and after the fall: Mapping Hong Kong cantopop in the global era.* Hong Kong: David C. Lam Institute of East-West Study.

Chua, B. H. (2004). Conceptualizing an East Asian popular culture. *Inter-Asia Cultural Studies, 5*(2), 200–221.

Chung, A. Y. (2011). *K-drama: A new TV genre with global appeal.* Sejong-si, South Korea: Korean Culture and Information Service.

Chung, K. Y. C., Derdenger, T. P., & Srinivasan, K. (2013). Economic value of celebrity endorsements: Tiger Woods' impact on sales of Nike golf balls. *Marketing Science, 32*(2), 271–293.

Chung, W., & Lee, T. D. (2011). Hallyu as a strategic marketing key in the Korean media content industry. In D. K. Kim & M. S. Kim (Eds.), *Hallyu: Influence of Korean popular culture in Asia and beyond* (pp. 431–460). Seoul: Seoul National University Press.

Clark, H. (2008). Confessions of a celebrity mom: Brooke Shields's *Down came the rain: My journey through postpartum depression. Canadian Review of American Studies, 38*(3), 449–461.

Connor, S. (2005). Defiling celebrity. Paper presented at *A Cultural History of Celebrity, Humanities Research Centre Interdisciplinary Seminar*, University of Warwick. Retrieved from http://stevenconnor.com/defiling/DefilingCelebrity.pdf. Accessed 15 August 2015.

Consumer Search Group. (2010). Opinion survey on the mid-term review of sound broadcasting licenses. Retrieved from http://ba_archives.ofca.gov.hk/cn/doc/es_opinionsurvey_c.pdf. Accessed 23 November 2015.

Couldry, N. (2003). *Media rituals: A critical approach.* London: Routledge.

——— (2012). *Media, society, world: Social theory and digital media practice.* Cambridge: Polity.

Croteau, D., & Hoynes, W. (2003). Media organizations and professionals. In *Media/society: Industries, images, and audiences* (pp. 113–150). London: SAGE.

Daschmann, G. (2007). Der preis der prominenz: Medienpsychologische überlegungen zu den wirkengen von medienberichterstattung auf die dargestellten akteure. In T. Schierl (Ed.), *Prominenz in den medien: Zur genese und verwertung von prominenten in sport, wirtschaft und kultur* (pp. 184–211). Köln: Halem Verlag.

Davisson, A. L. (2013). *Lady Gaga and the remaking of celebrity culture.* Jefferson, NC: McFarland and Company, Inc.

Debord, G. (1983). *Society of the spectacle.* Detroit, MI: Black and Red.

DeCordova, R. (2007). The emergence of the star system in America. In S. Redmond & S. Holmes (Eds.), *Stardom and celebrity: A reader* (pp. 132–140). London: SAGE.

Derrida, J. (1984). *Signéponge/signsponge* (R. Rand, Trans.). New York: Columbia University Press.

van Dijk, W. W., Ouwerkerk, J. P., van Koningsbruggen, G. M., & Wesseling, Y. M. (2012). 'So you wanna be a pop star?' Schadenfreude following another's misfortune on TV. *Basic and Applied Social Psychology, 34*(2), 168–174.

Ding, H., Molchanov, A. E., & Stork, P. A. (2011). The value of celebrity endorsements: A stock market perspective. *Marketing Letters, 22*(2), 147–163.

Doss, S. K. (2011). The transference of brand attitude: The effect on the celebrity endorser. *Journal of Management and Marketing Research, 7,* 1–11.

Drake, P., & Miah, A. (2010). The cultural politics of celebrity. *Cultural Politics, 6*(1), 49–64.

Driessens, O. (2012). The celebritization of society and culture: Understanding the structural dynamics of celebrity culture. *International Journal of Cultural Studies, 16*(6), 641–657.

Dunn, R. G. (1998). *Identity crises: A social critique of postmodernity.* Minneapolis, MN: University of Minnesota Press.

Dyer, R. (2004). *Heavenly bodies: Film stars and society* (2nd ed.). London & New York: Routledge.

Economist, The. (2012, August 18). Top of the K-pops: South Korea's music industry. Retrieved from http://www.economist.com/node/21560605. Accessed 23 November 2015.

Edwards, L., & Jeffreys, E. (Eds.) (2010). *Celebrity in China.* Hong Kong: Hong Kong University Press.

Elberse, A. (2013a). *Blockbusters: Hit-making, risk-taking, and the big business of entertainment.* New York: Henry Holt and Company.

——— (2013b). *Blockbusters: Why big hits – and big risks – are the future of the entertainment business.* London: Faber and Faber.

Elberse, A., & Verleun, J. (2012). The economic value of celebrity endorsements. *Journal of Advertising Research, 52*(2), 149–165.

Endemol. (Producer). (2011). *Superhirn* [Television series]. Germany: ZDF.

—— (2014). 最强大脑/*The brain* [Television series]. Nanjing: Jiangsu TV.

Engle, Y., & Kasser, T. (2005). Why do adolescent girls idolize male celebrities? *Journal of Adolescent Research, 20*(2), 263–283.

Erdogan, B. Z. (1999). Celebrity endorsement: A literature review. *Journal of Marketing Management, 15*(4), 291–314.

Esch, M. (2013). Sociology of celebrity from Franz Liszt to Lady Gaga. *Journal of Mass Media Ethics, 28*(1), 70–72.

Evans, J. (2005). Celebrity, media and history. In J. Evans & D. Hesmondhalgh (Eds.), *Understanding media: Inside celebrity* (pp. 11–55). Maidenhead & New York: Open University Press.

Ferle, C. L., & Choi, S. M. (2005). The importance of perceived endorser credibility in South Korean advertising. *Journal of Current Issues and Research in Advertising, 27*(2), 67–81.

Ferris, K., & Harris, S. R. (2011). *Stargazing: Celebrity, fame, and social interaction.* New York & London: Routledge.

FFx UTO. (2015). 香港4人女子跳唱組合*FFx SUGAR BABY MV (Official).* Retrieved from https://www.youtube.com/watch?v=yNDWRa8CV8U. Assessed 21 November 2015.

Fisher, M. (2007). *Something in the air: Radio, rock, and the revolution that shaped a generation.* New York: Random House.

Fleming, C. (2010). *The radio handbook.* London & New York: Routledge.

Forbes. (2015). 2015 Forbes China celebrity list (full list). Retrieved from http://www.forbes.com/sites/russellflannery/2015/05/13/2015-forbes-china-celebrity-list-full-list/. Accessed 19 November 2015.

Foucault, M. (1970). *The order of things: An archaeology of the human sciences.* New York: Pantheon Books.

Fraser, B. P., & Brown, W. J. (2002). Media, celebrities, and social influence: Identification with Elvis Presley. *Mass Communication and Society, 5*(2), 183–206.

Frater, P. (2008). HK police arrest 7 in porn scandal. *Variety Asia.* Retrieved from http://variety.com/2008/film/asia/hk-police-arrest-7-in-porn-scandal-1117980073/. Accessed 23 November 2015.

Fridae.asia. (2012, December 29). Denise Ho talking about coming out: We need to strive for same-sex marriage. Retrieved from http://www.fridae.asia/tc/gay-news/2012/12/29/12223. Accessed 15 September 2014.

Fuller, S., Lythgoe, N., Holloway, R., & Warwick, K. (Producers). (2001–03). *Pop idol* [Television series]. London: Thames Television & 19 Entertainment.

Fung, A. (2004). Coping, cloning and copying: Hong Kong in the global television format business. In A. Moran & M. Keane (Eds.), *Television across Asia: Television industries, programme formats and globalization* (pp. 74–87). London & New York: RoutledgeCurzon.

Furedi, F. (2010). Celebrity culture. *Sociology, 47*, 493–497.

Fuss, D. (1989). *Essentially speaking: Feminism, nature and difference.* New York & London: Routledge.

Gabler, N. (n.d.). *Toward a new definition of celebrity*. Los Angeles, CA: The Norman Lear Centertainment, USC Annenberg.

Galbraith, P. W., & Karlin, J. G. (2012). Introduction: The mirror of idols and celebrity. In P. W. Galbraith & J. G. Karlin (Eds.), *Idols and celebrity in Japanese media culture* (pp. 1–32). Houndmills & New York: Palgrave Macmillan.

Gamson, J. (1992). The assembly line of greatness: Celebrity in twentieth-century America. *Critical Studies in Mass Communication, 9*(1), 1–24.

——— (1994). *Claims to fame: Celebrity in contemporary America*. Berkeley, CA: University of California Press.

Garthwaite, C. L. (2014). Demand spillovers, combative advertising, and celebrity endorsements. *American Economic Journal: Applied Economics, 6*(2), 76–104.

Gazi, A., Starkey, G., & Jedrzejewski, S. (Eds.). (2011). *Radio content in the digital age: The evolution of a sound medium*. Bristol & Chicago, IL: Intellect.

Gergen, K. J. (1996). Technology and the self: From the essential to the sublime. In D. Gordin & T. Lindlof (Eds.). *Constructing the self in a mediated world* (pp. 127–140). London: SAGE.

Giddens, A. (1991). *Modernity and self-identity: Self and society in the late modern age*. Cambridge: Polity Press.

Gilbert, J. (2004). Small faces: The tyranny of celebrity in post-oedipal culture. *MediActive, 2*, 86–109.

Giles, D. (2000). *Illusions of immortality: A psychology of fame and celebrity*. Basingstoke & New York: Macmillan Press & St. Martin's Press.

Gilovich, T., Keltner, D., & Nisbett, R. E. (2010). *Social psychology* (Vol. 2). New York: W. W. Norton and Co.

Goffman, E. (1959). *The presentation of self in everyday life*. Garden City, NY: Doubleday Anchor Books.

Gold, D. L. (2001). English paparazzo, Italian paparazzo = commonization of the charactonym paparazzo (in Federico Fellini's *La dolce vita*). *Neophilologus, 85*, 111–119.

Gorin, V., & Dubied, A. (2011). Desirable people: Identifying social values through celebrity news. *Media Culture & Society, 33*(4), 599–618.

Gregory, K. (2008). *Celebrities: Who they are, how they gain popularity, and why society is so fascinated with them and their court cases*. (Unpublished senior honours theses, Eastern Michigan University, Ypsilanti, MI).

Guo, J. M. (Director). (2013). 小時代/*Tiny times* [Motion picture]. China: EE-Media.

Hall, S. (1990). Cultural identity and diaspora. In J. Rutherford (Ed.), *Identity: Community, culture, difference* (pp. 222–237). London: Lawrence and Wishart.

Hambleton, A. (2012). Idol as accidental activist: Agnes Chan, feminism, and motherhood in Japan. In P. W. Galbraith & J. G. Karlin (Eds.), *Idols and celebrity in Japanese media culture* (pp. 153–165). Houndmills & New York: Palgrave Macmillan.

Harper, S. (2006). Madly famous: Narratives of mental illness in celebrity culture. In S. Holmes & S. Redmond (Eds.), *Framing celebrity: New directions in celebrity culture* (pp. 311–327). London & New York: Routledge.

He, W. (2014, February 18). Korean culture rides in on mobile technology. *China Daily*, p. P07.

Hellmueller, L. C., & Aeschbacher, N. (2010). Media and celebrity: Production and consumption of 'well-knownness'. *Communication Research Trends, 29*(4), 3–35.

Hermes, J. (2006). Reading gossip magazines: The imagined communities of 'gossip' and 'camp'. In P. D. Marshall (Ed.), *The celebrity culture reader* (pp. 291–310). New York & London: Routledge.

Hesmondhalgh, D. (2005). Producing celebrity. In J. Evans & D. Hesmondhalgh (Eds.), *Understanding media: Inside celebrity* (pp. 97–134). Maidenhead: Open University Press.

Hinerman, S. (2006). (Don't) leave me alone: Tabloid narrative and the Michael Jackson child-abuse scandal. In P. D. Marshall (Ed.), *The celebrity culture reader* (pp. 454–469). New York & London: Routledge.

Hing, Y. K. (Producer). (1977). 家變/*A house is not a home* [Television series]. Hong Kong: TVB.

Ho, D. (2015, March 23). My declaration of independence in 2015. *Apple Daily*. Retrieved from http://hk.apple.nextmedia.com/enews/realtime/20150323/53560989. Accessed 23 November 2015.

Hollander, P. (2010). Michael Jackson, the celebrity cult, and popular culture. *Society, 47*(2), 147–152.

Holmes, S., & Redmond, S. (2006). *Framing celebrity: New directions in celebrity culture*. Abingdon & New York: Routledge.

——— (2010). A journal in 'celebrity studies'. *Celebrity Studies, 1*(1), 1–10.

Hong Kong Neuromuscular Disease Association. (2014, September 1). *About ice bucket challenge: Notice*. Retrieved from http://www.hknmda.org.hk/index.php. Accessed 2 September 2014.

Hong Kong Television Entertainment Ltd. (Producer). (2009). 娛樂頭條/*Entertainment headline* [Television broadcast/series]. Hong Kong: HD Jade.

Horton, D., & Wohl, R. R. (1956). Mass communication and para-social interaction: Observations on intimacy at a distance. *Journal of Psychiatry, 19*(3), 215–229.

——— (2010). Mass communication and para-social interaction: Observations on intimacy at a distance. In C. Rojek (Ed.), *Celebrity: Critical concepts in sociology* (Vol. 2) (pp. 35–55). London & New York: Routledge.

Hoskins, C., & Mirus, R. (1988). Reasons for the US dominance of the international trade in television programmes. *Media Culture and Society, 10*, 499–515.

Hovland, C. I., Janis, I. L., & Kelley, H. H. (1953). *Communication and persuasion: Psychological studies of opinion change*. New Haven, CT: Yale University Press.

Hsia, H. (2015, June 1). Mandy Lieu and Alvin Cha not on speaking terms?. *Yahoo News*. Retrieved from http://news.yahoo.com/mandy-lieu-alvin-chau-not-speaking-terms-035500194.html. Accessed 23 November 2015.

Hsu, C. K., & McDonald, D. (2002). An examination on multiple celebrity endorsers in advertising. *Journal of Product and Brand Management, 11*(1), 19–29.

Hui, K. & Yeung, V. (Directors). (2016). *3D* 封神榜/*Legend of the gods* [Motion picture]. China: China Star Entertainment Group.

Hung, K., Chan, K. W., & Tse, C. H. (2011). Assessing celebrity endorsement effects in China: A consumer-celebrity relational approach. *Journal of Advertising Research, 51*(4), 608–623.

Ibrahim, A. M. A. (2010). The influence of using celebrities on consumers buying behavior. *Interdisciplinary Journal of Contemporary Research in Business, 2*(1), 257–282.

Ilicic, J., & Webster, C. M. (2011). Effects of multiple endorsements and consumer-celebrity attachment on attitude and purchase intention. *Australasian Marketing Journal, 19*, 230–237.

Im, H. T. (Producer). (2014). 奔跑吧兄弟/*Hurry up, brother* [Television series]. Seoul: Seoul Broadcasting System.

Jarvie, I. C. (1977). *Window on Hong Kong: A sociological study of the Hong Kong film industry and its audience.* Hong Kong: Centre of Asian Studies, University of Hong Kong.

Jarvis, J. (2014). The problem with the ALS ice bucket challenge. *University Wire.* Retrieved from http:// search.proquest.com/docview/1553746609?accountid=11440. Accessed 15 September 2014.

Jermyn, D. (2006). Bring out the star in you: SJP, Carrie Bradshaw and the evolution of television stardom. In S. Holmes & S. Redmond (Eds.), *Framing celebrity: New directions in celebrity culture* (pp. 67–85). London & New York: Routledge.

Jiang, J., Huang, Y. H., Wu, F., Choy, H. Y., & Lin, D. (2015). At the crossroads of inclusion and distance: Organizational crisis communication during celebrity-endorsement crises in China. *Public Relations Review, 41*, 50–63.

Johansson, S. (2006). 'Sometimes you wanna hate celebrities': Tabloid readers and celebrity coverage. In S. Holmes & S. Redmond (Eds.), *Framing celebrity: New directions in celebrity culture* (pp. 341–358). London & New York: Routledge.

Johnson, J. (2004). The secret: Sex and celebs. *British Journalism Review, 15*(3), 51–56.

Kahle, L. R., & Homer, R. M. (1985). Physical attractiveness of the celebrity endorser: A social adaptation perspective. *Journal of Consumer Research, 11*(4), 954–961.

Kam, K.-L. (Director). (1987). 神奇兩女俠/*Wonder women* [Motion picture]. Hong Kong: D & B Films Co.

——— (Director). (2012). 熱愛島/*Passion island* [Motion picture]. China: China Film Group Corporation.

Kamins, M. A. (1990). An investigation into the 'match-up' hypothesis in celebrity advertising: When beauty may be only skin deep. *Journal of Advertising, 19*(1), 4–13.

Kapoor, I. (2013). *Celebrity humanitarianism: The ideology of global charity.* New York: Routledge.

Keller, K.-L. (2008). *Strategic brand management: Building, measuring and managing brand equity.* Upper Saddle River, NJ: Prentice Hall.

Kelley, H. H. (1967). Attribution theory in social psychology. In D. Levine (Ed.), *Nebraska symposium on motivation* (pp. 192–238), Lincoln, NE: University of Nebraska Press.

Kelman, H. (1961). Process of opinion change. *Public Opinion Quarterly, 25*(1), 57–78.

Kengo [Ip, K. H.] (2010). 星光大戰：娛樂文化青筋暴現評論集/*Stars war: A commentary collection revealing entertainment culture.* Hong Kong: Wenhua Gongfang.

Kim, C. N. (2012). *K-pop: Roots and blossoming of Korean popular music.* Elizabeth, NJ: Hollym International Corporation.

Kim, D. K., & Kim, S. J. (2011). Hallyu from its origin to present: A historical overview. In D. K. Kim & M. S. Kim (Eds.), *Hallyu: Influence of Korean popular culture in Asia and beyond* (pp. 13–34). Seoul: Seoul National University Press.

Kim, D. K., Singhal, A., Hanaki, T., Dunn, J., Chitnis, K., & Han, M. W. (2009). Television drama, narrative engagement and audience buying behavior. *International Communication Gazette, 71*(7), 595–611.

Kim, J. H., Lee, H. J., & Jung, C. M (Producers). (2010). 런닝맨/*Running-man* [Television series]. South Korea: SBS.

Kim, S. S., Agrusa, J., Chon, K., & Cho, Y. (2008). The effects of Korean pop culture on Hong Kong residents' perceptions of Korea as a potential tourist destination. *Journal of Travel and Tourism Marketing, 24*, 163–183.

Knittel, C. R., & Stango, V. (2011). Celebrity endorsements, firm value, and reputation risk: Evidence from the Tiger Woods scandal. *Management Science, 60*(1), 21–37.

Korea Herald, The. (Ed.). (2008). *Korean wave.* Gyeonggi-do, South Korea: Jimoondang.

van Krieken, R. (2012a). *Celebrity society.* London & New York: Routledge.

———— (2012b). Celebrity as a social form: Status, charisma and power. In *Celebrity society* (pp. 62–80). London & New York: Routledge.

Kuei, C. H. (Director). (1974). 蛇殺手/*Killer snake* [Motion picture]. Hong Kong: Shaw Brothers.

Laclau, E. (1994). *The making of political identities.* New York: Verso.

Lafferty, B. A., Goldsmith, R. E., & Newell, S. J. (2002). The dual credibility model: The influence of corporate and endorser credibility on attitudes and purchase intentions. *Journal of Marketing Theory and Practice, 10*(3), 1–12.

Langer, J. (2006). Television's 'personality system'. In P. D. Marshall (Ed.), *The celebrity culture reader* (pp. 181–195). New York & London: Routledge.

Lee, B. H. (Producer). (2003). 대장금/*Jewel in the palace* [Television series]. Seoul: Munhwa Broadcasting Corporation.

Lee, H. M. (Producer). (2002). 겨울연가/*Winter sonata* [Television broadcast]. Seoul: KBS2.

Lerman, K. (2007). Social networks and social information filtering on Digg. Proceeding of the *International Conference on Weblogs and Social Media*, Boulder, CO. Retrieved from http://arxiv.org/PS_cache/cs/pdf/0612/0612046v1.pdf. Accessed 4 July 2015.

Liao, K. (Producer). (2005). 超級女聲/*Super voice girls* [Interactive reality game show]. Changsha, China: Hunan Satellite Television.

Lin, L. (2014, February 26). Korean TV show sparks chicken and beer craze in China. *The Wall Street Journal.* Retrieved from http://blogs.wsj.com/chinarealtime/2014/02/26/korean-tv-show-sparks-chicken-and-beer-craze-in-china/. Accessed 23 July 2015.

Lin, Y. S., & Huang, J. Y. (2010). Analyzing the use of TV miniseries for Korea tourism marketing. *Journal of Travel and Tourism Marketing, 24*(2&3), 223–227.

Lind, A. (2013). Heteronormativity and sexuality. In G. Waylen, K. Celis, J. Kantola & L. Weldon (Eds.). *Oxford handbook of gender and politics* (pp. 189–213). New York: Oxford University Press.

Longhetti, C. (2015). First day of our honeymoon! Loved-up Hugh Jackman shares throwback picture of him and wife of 19 years, Deborra-Lee Furness, from back in 1996. *Daily Mail Australia.* Retrieved from http://www.dailymail.co.uk/tvshowbiz/article-3187386/Hugh-Jackman-shares-throwback-picture-wife-19-years-Deborra-Lee-Furness-1996.html. Accessed 23 November 2015.

Luk, K. C., & Leung. L. M. (Directors). (2015). 赤道/*Helios* [Motion picture]. China: Media Asia Films.

Lyu, H. B., Zhang, H. L., & Li, H. (Producers). (2013). 爸爸去哪兒/*Where are we going, Dad?* [Television series]. Changsha: HBS Hunan Television.

Magnini, V. P., Honeycutt, E. D., & Cross, A. M. (2008). Understanding the use of celebrity endorsers for hospitality firms. *Journal of Vacation Marketing, 14*(1), 57–70.

Mak, J. (Producer). (2013). 星夢傳奇/*The voice of the stars* [Television series]. Hong Kong: TVB Jade.

Maltby, J., Day, L., McCutcheon, L. E., Houran, J., & Ashe, D. (2006). Extreme celebrity worship, fantasy proneness and dissociation: Developing the measurement and understanding of celebrity worship within a clinical personality context. *Personality and Individual Differences, 40*, 273–283.

Marshall, P. D. (1997). *Celebrity and power: Fame in contemporary culture.* Minneapolis, MN: University of Minnesota Press.

—— (2006a). Intimately intertwined in the most public way: Celebrity and journalism. In P. D. Marshall (Ed.), *The celebrity culture reader* (pp. 315–323). New York & London: Routledge.

—— (2006b). New media – new self: The changing power of celebrity. In P. D. Marshall (Ed.), *The celebrity culture reader* (pp. 634–644). New York & London: Routledge.

—— (2010). The promotion and presentation of the self: Celebrity as marker of presentational media. *Celebrity Studies, 1*(1), 35–48.

—— (2016). Comparative persona: Transnational and national flows of the public self. In P. D. Marshall, *Persona in formation.* Minneapolis, MN: University of Minnesota Press.

Marshall, P. D., & Barbour, K. (2015). Making intellectual room for persona studies. *Persona Studies, 1*(1), 1–12. https://ojs.deakin.edu.au/index.php/ps/article/view/464.

Marshall, P. D., Moore, C., & Barbour, K. (2015). Persona as method: Exploring celebrity and the public self through persona studies. *Celebrity Studies, 6*(3), 288–305.

Marwick, A., & Boyd, D. (2011). To see and be seen: Celebrity practice on Twitter. *Convergence, 17*(2), 139–158.

Marx, W. D. (2012). The jimusho system: Understanding the production logic of the Japanese entertainment industry. In P. W. Galbraith & J. G. Karlin (Eds.), *Idols and celebrity in Japanese media culture* (pp. 35–55). Houndmills & New York: Palgrave Macmillan.

Mathur, L. K., Mathur, I., & Rangan, N. (1997). The wealth effects associated with a celebrity endorser: The Michael Jordan phenomenon. *Journal of Advertising Research, 37*(3), 67–73.

Mazdon, L. (2006). The Cannes Film Festival as transnational space. *Post Script, 25*(2), 19–30.

McCarthy, T. (2009, Fall). Shooting stars. *TIME Style & Design.* Retrieved from https://web.archive.org/web/20051226032035/http://www.time.com/time/2005/style/091305/shooting_stars_paparazz39a.html. Accessed 4 July 2015.

McCracken, G. (1989). Who is the celebrity endorser? Cultural foundations of the endorsement process. *Journal of Consumer Research, 16*(3), 310–321.

McCutcheon, L. E., Lange, R., & Houran, J. (2002). Conceptualization and measurement of celebrity worship. *British Journal of Psychology, 93*, 67–87.

McGuire, W. J. (1985). Attitudes and attitude change. In G. Lindzey & E. Aronson (Eds.), *Handbook of Social Psychology* (Vol. 2) (pp. 233–346). New York: Random House.

McNamara, K. (2011). The paparazzi industry and new media: The evolving production and consumption of celebrity news and gossip websites. *International Journal of Cultural Studies, 14*(5), 515–530.

Meeuf, R., & Raphael, R. (2013). Introduction. In R. Meeuf & R. Raphael (Eds.), *Transnational stardom: International celebrity in film and popular culture* (pp. 1–16). New York: Palgrave Macmillan.

Mendelson, A. L. (2007). On the function of the United States paparazzi: Mosquito swarm or watchdogs of celebrity image control and power. *Visual Studies, 22*(20), 169–183.

Miller, V. (2011). *Understanding digital culture*. London: SAGE.

Milner Jr., M. (2005). Celebrity culture as a status system. *Hedgehog Review, 7*(1), 66–77.

——— (2010). Is celebrity a new kind of status system. *Society, 47*(5), 379–387.

Miramax Television. (Producer). (2004). *Project runway* [Television series]. US: Lifetime.

Mirrlees, T. (2013). *Global entertainment media: Between cultural imperialism and cultural globalization*. New York: Routledge.

Montgomery, L. (2010). *China's creative industries: Copyright, social network markets and the business of culture in a digital age*. Cheltenham & Northampton, MA: Edward Elgar.

Mowen, J. C., & Brown, S. W. (1981). On explaining and predicting the effectiveness of celebrity endorsers. *Advances in Consumer Research, 8*, 437–441.

Muntean, N., & Petersen, A. H. (2009). Celebrity Twitter: Strategies of intrusion and disclosure in the age of technoculture. *M/C Journal, 12*(5). Retrieved from http://journal.media-culture.org.au/index.php/mcjournal/article/viewArticle/194. Accessed 4 July 2015.

Murray, A. M. (2009). *Your public is online: Public relations in an online world* (Unpublished master's thesis, University of Southern California, Los Angeles, CA). Retrieved from http://digitallibrary.usc.edu/cdm/ref/collection/p15799coll127/id/205569. Accessed 28 July 2015.

Ngaai, Wan [艾雲]. (2014, March 7). Money views: 分析「劇毒」商機/Money views: Analyzing the economic potential of the 'toxic TV dramas'. *Oriental Daily*, p. B06.

Noh Kelsey, S. (2014). Between hallyu and han: Global celebrities, local narratives, and melodramatic sensibility. *Ewha Journal of Social Sciences, 30*(2). Retrieved from http://ssrn.com/abstract=2581369. Assessed 28 November 2015.

O'Keefe, D. J. (1990). *Persuasion theory and research*. Newbury Park, CA: SAGE.

O'Mahony, S., & Meenaghan, T. (1997). The impact of celebrity endorsements on consumers. *Irish Marketing Review, 10*(2), 15–24.

Ohanian, R. (1991). The impact of celebrity spokesperson's perceived image on consumers' intention to purchase. *Journal of Advertising Research, 31*(1), 46–52.

On-Tou [Law, W. S.]. (2012). 當大學遇上周秀娜/When university meets with Chrissie Chau. In C. H. Ng., C. W. Cheung, & C. K. Tsang (Eds.), 閱讀香港普及文化, 2000–2010/Pop Hong Kong 2: Reading Hong Kong popular culture 2000–2010 (pp. 160–163). Hong Kong: Hong Kong Educational Press.

Park, S. (2004). China's consumption of Korean television dramas: An empirical test of the 'cultural discount' concept. *Korea Journal, 44*(4), 265–290.

Payne, T. (2010). *Fame: What the classics tell us about our cult of celebrity*. New York: Picador.

Penfold, R. (2004). The star's image, victimization and celebrity culture. *Punishment and Society, 6*(3), 289–302.

Percy, L., & Rossiter, J. R. (1997). *Advertising communications and promotion management.* Irwin, VA: McGraw-Hill International.

Petty, R. E., Cacioppo, J. T., & Schuman, D. (1983). Central and peripheral routes to advertising effectiveness: The moderating role of involvement. *Journal of Consumer Research, 10*(2), 135–146.

Petty, R. E., Ostrom, T. M., & Brock, T. C. (1981). Historical foundations of the cognitive response approach to attitudes and persuasion. In R. E. Petty, T. M. Ostrom, & T. C. Brock (Eds.), *Cognitive responses in persuasion* (pp. 5–29). Hillsdale, NJ: Lawrence Erlbaum Associates.

Poster, M. (1995). *The second media age*, New York: Polity.

Pringle, H. (2004). *Celebrity sells.* Chichester & Hoboken, NJ: Wiley.

Puente, M. (2014, March 28). Celebs push back against the paparazzi. *USA Today.* Retrieved from http://www.usatoday.com/story/life/people/2014/03/22/celebs-push-back-against-the-paparazzi/6186163/. Accessed 4 July 2015.

Rak, J. (2005). The digital queer: Weblogs and internet identity. *Biography, 28*(1), 166–182.

Ravitz, J. (2012, February 23). National Enquirer's Whitney Houston casket pic: Did they go too far?. *US Weekly.* Retrieved from http://www.usmagazine.com/celebrity-news/news/national-enquirers-whitney-houston-casket-pic-did-they-go-too-far-2012232. Accessed 23 November 2015.

Reddy, S. (2014a, August 14). How the ice-bucket challenge got its start: Celebrities raise money for Lou Gehrig's disease in a social-media stunt that exploded. *Wall Street Journal.* Retrieved from http://online.wsj.com/articles/how-the-ice-bucket-challenge-got-its-start-1408049557. Accessed 2 September 2014.

——— (2014b, August 18). Charities seek ice buckets to ride own viral wave. *Wall Street Journal.* Retrieved from http://online.wsj.com/news/articles/SB200014240529702043925045800999100994669940. Accessed 2 September 2014.

Rein, I., Kotler, P., & Stoller, M. (1997). *High visibility: The making and marketing of professionals into celebrities.* Lincolnwood, IL: NTC Business Books.

Rheingold, H. (1993). *The virtual community: Homesteading on the electronic frontier.* Reading, MA: Addison-Wesley.

Ritzer, G. (2008) *The McDonaldization of society.* Thousand Oaks, CA: Pine Forge Press. (Original work published 1993).

Roberts, I. D. (2010). China's internet celebrity: Furong Jiejie. In L. Edwards & E. Jeffreys (Eds.), *Celebrity in China* (pp. 217–236). Hong Kong: Hong Kong University Press.

Rockwell, D., & Giles, D. (2009). Being a celebrity: A phenomenology of fame. *Journal of Phenomenological Psychology, 40*(2), 178–210.

Rojek, C. (2001). *Celebrity.* London: Reaktion.

——— (2012). *Fame attack: The inflation of celebrity and its consequences.* London: Bloomsbury.

Rossiter, J. R., & Smidts, A. (2012). Print advertising: Celebrity presenters. *Journal of Business Research, 65*(6), 874–879.

Rudin, R. (2011). *Broadcasting in the 21st century.* Basingstoke & New York: Palgrave Macmillan.

Salmones, M. D. G. de los, Dominguez, R., & Herrero, A. (2013). Communication using celebrities in the non-profit sector: Determinants of its effectiveness. *International Journal of Advertising, 32*(1), 101–119.

Salup, M. (2014, February 24). The evolution of celebrity endorsements. *Huffington Post.* Retrieved from http://www.huffingtonpost.com/marni-salup/the-evolution-of-celebrit_b_4830864.html. Accessed 23 November 2014.

Samman, E., McAuliffe, E., & MacLachlan, M. (2009). The role of celebrity in endorsing poverty reduction through international aid. *International Journal of Nonprofit and Voluntary Sector Marketing, 14*, 137–148.

Saner, E. (2009, May 4). Have celebrities finally snapped? *The Guardian.* Retrieved from http://www.theguardian.com/media/2009/may/04/celebrities-paparazzi. Accessed 4 July 2015.

Saxton, G. D., & Wang, L. (forthcoming). The social network effect: The determinants of giving through social media. *Nonprofit and Voluntary Sector Quarterly.*

Schickel, R. (1985). *Intimate strangers: The culture of celebrity.* New York: Doubleday.

Schierl, T. (2007). *Ökonomie der prominenz: Celebrity sells.* Köln: Halem.

Schmidt, J. (2007). Blogging practices: An analytical framework. *Journal of Computer-Mediated Communication, 12*, 1419–1427.

Schmitz, A. (2012). *A primer on communication studies.* Retrieved from http://2012books.lardbucket.org/books/a-primer-on-communication-studies/. Accessed 4 July 2015.

Seifert, A. (2010). *Das model(l) Heidi Klum. Celebrities als kulturelles Phänomen.* Konstanz: UVK Verlag.

Semsel, G. S., Chen, X., & Xia, H. (Eds.). (1993). *Film in contemporary China: Critical debates, 1979–1989.* Westport, CT: Praeger.

Senft, T. M. (2008). *Camgirls: Celebrity and community in the age of social networks.* New York: Lang.

Shanghai Daily. (2014a, February 16). 3 new H7N9 cases as controls tightened. *Shanghai Daily,* p. A2.

——— (2014b, June 23). Korean TV dramas trigger Asian urge to splurge. *Shanghai Daily,* p. A8.

Shils, E. (2010). Charisma, order, and status. In C. Rojek (Ed.), *Celebrity: Critical concepts in sociology* (Vol. 3) (pp. 83–103). London & New York: Routledge.

Shoemaker, P. J., & Vos, T. P. (2009). *Gatekeeping theory.* New York: Routledge.

Shum, Y. (Director). (2012). 盛女愛作戰/*Bride wannabes* [Television series]. Hong Kong: TVB Jade.

Sina News (2012). Revealing the process of TVB artist training program. *Sina News.* Retrieved from http://dailynews.sina.com/bg/ent/tv/sinacn/v/h/2012-10-14/10293763191.html. Accessed 23 November 2015.

Sito, P. (2014, May 21). S Korea rides cultural wave into HK stores. *South China Morning Post,* p. PPT3.

Star, D. (Creator). (1998). *Sex and the city* [Television series]. US: HBO.

Stephens, A., & Rice, A. (1998). Spicing up the message. *Finance Week, 76*(26), 46–47.

Stevenson, N. (2010). New media, popular culture and social theory. In A. Elliott (Ed.), *The Routledge companion to social theory* (pp. 156–172). London & New York: Routledge.

Stever, G., & Lawson, K. (2013). Twitter as a way for celebrities to communicate with fans: Implications for the study of parasocial interaction. *North American Journal of Psychology, 15*(2), 339–354. Retrieved from http://www.researchgate.net/profile/Gayle_Stever/publication/263257850_Twitter_as_a_Way_for_Celebrities_to_Communicate_with_Fans_Implications_for_the_Study_of_Parasocial_Interaction/links/00b4953a44862a8747000000.pdf. Accessed 20 August 2015.

Stokes, J. (2013). *How to do media and cultural studies*. Los Angeles, CA: SAGE.

Stone, R. A. (1995). *The war of desire and technology at the close of the mechanical age*. Cambridge, MA: MIT Press.

Suen, S. M. J. (2000). *Tina Ti as sex symbol: A challenge to dominant culture* (Unpublished master's thesis, University of Hong Kong, Hong Kong).

Sun, Z. (2010). Chinese celebrity-endorsed TV commercials: A content analysis. *China Media Research, 6*(2), 34–46.

Canxing Productions. (Producer). (2012). 中國好聲音/*The voice of China* [Television series]. Hangzhou: Zhejiang Television.

Telecommunication Development Sector, The (ITU-D). (2015). *Percentage of individuals using the Internet.* (n.p.).

Television Broadcasts Limited. (Producer). (2009). 娛樂頭條/*Entertainment headline* [Telelvision series]. Hong Kong: TVB.

——— (Producer). (2014). 超級無敵獎門人/*Super trio series* [Telelvision series]. Hong Kong: TVB.

Temptalia. (2011). Do celebrity endorsements impact your beauty purchases? Retrieved from http://www.temptalia.com/do-celebrity-endorsements-impact-your-beauty-purchases. Accessed 18 June 2015.

Teo, S. (1997). *Hong Kong cinema: The extra dimensions*. London: British Film Institute.

Théberge, P. (2005). Everyday fandom: Fan clubs, blogging, and the quotidian rhythms of the internet. *Canadian Journal of Communication, 30*(4). Retrieved from http://www.cjc-online.ca/index.php/journal/article/view/1673/1810. Accessed 5 July 2015.

Tinkcom, M., & Villarejo, A. (Eds.). (2003). *Keyframes: Popular cinema and cultural studies*. London: Routledge.

TMZ Staff (2012, February 13). Whitney Houston – Family told she died from Rx not drowning. *TMZ*. Retrieved from http://www.tmz.com/2012/02/13/whitney-houston-cause-of-death-prescription-drugs-drowning-atlanta. Accessed 23 November 2015.

Trewin, J. (2003). *Presenting on TV and radio: An insider's guide*. Oxford: Focal.

Tripp, C., Jensen, T. D., & Carlson, L. (1994). The effects of multiple product endorsements by celebrities on consumers' attitudes and intentions. *Journal of Consumer Research, 20*, 535–547.

Tsang, C. (Producer). (2012). 愛回家/*Come home love* [Television series]. Hong Kong: TVB Jade.

Tse, Y. W. (Producer). (2010). 兄弟幫/*Big boys club* [Television series]. Hong Kong: TVB J2.

Turkle, S. (1995). *Life on the screen: Identity in the age of the internet*. New York: Simon & Schuster.

Turner, G. (2004). *Understanding celebrity*. London: SAGE.

——— (2006). The mass production of celebrity: 'Celetoids', reality TV and the 'demotic turn'. *International Journal of Cultural Studies, 9*(2), 153–165.

—— (2007). The economy of celebrity. In *Stardom and Celebrity: A reader* (pp. 193–206). London: SAGE.

—— (2010). The mass production of celebrity: 'Celetoids', reality TV and the 'demotic turn'. In C. Rojek (Ed.), *Celebrity: Critical concepts in sociology* (Vol. 3) (pp. 216–227). London & New York: Routledge.

Turner, G., Bonner, F., & Marshall, P. D. (2000). Producing celebrity. In *Fame games: The production of celebrity in Australia* (pp. 61–91). Cambridge: Cambridge University Press.

Turtle, S. (2013, December 13). PR insider: The changing relationship between celebrities and brands. *PRNews*. Retrieved from http://www.prnewsonline.com/featured/2013/12/13/pr-insider-the-romance-of-celebrity-and-brand-partnerships/. Accessed 23 November 2015.

Vaid, H. (2003). *Branding: Brand strategy, design, and implementation of corporate and product identity*. New York: Watson-Guptill.

Van den Bulck, H., & Tambuyzer, S. (2008). *The celebrity supermarket*. Berchem, Belgium: EPO.

Wang, Y. M. (2007). A star is dead: A legend is born: Practicing Leslie Cheung's posthumous fandom. In S. Redmond & S. Holmes (Eds.), *Stardom and celebrity: A reader* (pp. 326–340). London: SAGE.

Ward, P. (2011). *Gods behaving badly: Media, religion, and celebrity culture*. Waco, TX: Baylor University Press.

Warhol, A. (n.d.). *Everyone will be famous for 15 minutes*. Retrieved from http://www.justquotes.com/authors/andy_warhol/166396. Accessed 15 September 2015.

Weber, M. (2006). The sociology of charismatic authority: The nature of charismatic authority and its routinization. In P. D. Marshall (Ed.), *The celebrity culture reader* (pp. 55–71). New York & London: Routledge.

Wheeler, R. T. (2009). Nonprofit advertising: Impact of celebrity connection, involvement and gender on source credibility and intention to volunteer time or donate money. *Journal of Nonprofit and Public Sector Marketing, 21*(1), 80–107.

Wolf, N. (2009, December 22). Carrie Bradshaw – Icons of the decade. *The Guardian*. Retrieved from http://www.theguardian.com/world/2009/dec/22/carrie-bradshaw-icons-of-decade. Accessed 28 November 2015.

Wong, J. (Director). (2015). 小姐誘心/*S for sex, s for secret* [Motion picture]. China: Sundream Motion Pictures.

Wong, J., & Kong, P. (Directors). (2011). 猛鬼愛情故事/*Hong Kong ghost stories* [Motion picture]. China: Jing's Production Limited.

Wong, L. L., & Trumper, R. (2002). Global celebrity athletes and nationalism: Futbol, hockey, and the representation of nation. *Journal of Sport and Social Issues, 26*(2), 168–194.

Woo, J. (Director). (1986). 英雄本色/*A better tomorrow* [Motion picture]. Hong Kong: Cinema City Company Limited.

Xu, W. (2014, June 5). US, Korean TV series win top awards at Shanghai TV Festival. *Shanghai Daily*. Retrieved from http://www.shanghaidaily.com/metro/entertainment-and-culture/US-Korean-TV-series-win-top-awards-at-Shanghai-TV-Festival/shdaily.shtml. Accessed 2 July 2015.

Yang, J. (2012). The Korean wave (Hallyu) in East Asia: A comparison of Chinese, Japanese, and Taiwanese audiences who watch Korean TV dramas. *Development and Society, 41*(1), 103–147.

Yue, X. D. (2007). 追星與粉絲：青少年偶像崇拜探析/*My favorite idol your die-hard fans – The study of adolescent idol worship*. Hong Kong: City University of Hong Kong Press.

Yue, X. D., & Cheung, C. K. (2000). 青少年偶像與榜樣之比較:香港、廣州和長沙三 地大學生的調查分析/Selection of favorite idols and models among Chinese young people: A comparative study in Hong Kong and Guangzhou and Changsha. 青年研究學報/*Journal of Youth Studies, 5*(2), 133–145.

Yuen, E. (2007, August 10). Erica's blog. Retrieved from http://ericayuen.blogspot.com/2007/08/blog.html. Accessed 23 November 2015.

Zhang, H. (2013). Gender reconstruction in post-Mao urban China: The interplay between modernity and popular culture. In L. Fitzsimmons & J. A. Lent (Eds.), *Popular culture in Asia: Memory, city, celebrity* (pp. 165–182). Houndmills & New York: Palgrave Macmillan.

Zhang, H. X., & Zhang, Y. (2010). Is nationality important? A new perspective on the relationship between celebrity endorsement and advertising effects. *Acta Psychologica Sinica, 42*(2), 304–316.

Zhang, Y. (2004). *Chinese national cinema*. New York: Routledge.

Zhao, S., Grasmuck, S., & Martin, J. (2008). Identity construction on Facebook: Digital empowerment in anchored relationships. *Computers in Human Behavior, 24*(5), 1816–1836.

Zhao, W. (Director). (2013). 致我們終將逝去的青春/*So young* [Motion picture]. China: China Film Group Corporation.

Authors' biographies

Vivienne Leung is a senior lecturer and the programme director of public relations and advertising major at the Communication Studies Department at Hong Kong Baptist University (HKBU). She received her Ph.D. in communication studies from HKBU, and has been teaching in communication and advertising for more than ten years. Previously, she held positions at Grey Advertising and Fallon Asia/Hong Kong, and also worked in advertising as a strategic planner. Her clients include United Airlines, P&G, Wrigley, Audi, PCCW, McDonald's and Bank of China. Her research interests include advertising, celebrity effects, health communication, social service marketing and consumer behaviour. Her work has been published in *Service Marketing Quarterly*, the *Journal of Nonprofit and Public Sector Marketing*, *Intercultural Communication Studies*, the *Asian Journal of Business Research*, the *Journal of Consumer Marketing*, the *Chinese Journal of Communications*, the *Patient Experience Journal* and the *International Journal of Health Promotion and Education*.

Kimmy Cheng is a lecturer and programme director of public speaking at the Communication Studies Department at HKBU. She graduated from Western Michigan University with a BA in organizational communication, and received her MA and Ph.D. in communication studies at HKBU. Her primary research area of interest includes health communication, public relations, crisis management, public speaking and gender studies. Previously, she worked as a PR consultant at various agencies, where her clients included Harry Winston, Gucci, Swarovski, Chevignon, SK-II, KFC, Citi Group and The Oriental Spa. Her works have appeared in the *Journal of Communication in Healthcare*, the *Patient Experience Journal*, the *International Journal of Health Promotion and Education* and *Motherhood – Pakistan's First Parenting Magazine*. She has also taught at the Culture and Media Domain at HKU SPACE.

Tommy Tse is an assistant professor in the Department of Sociology at The University of Hong Kong (HKU), specializing in literary and cultural theory, fashion communication and the creative industries in East Asia. His work has appeared in the *Asian Journal of Business Research*, *Journal of Business Anthropology*, *Clothing Cultures*, the *International Journal of Fashion Studies*, the *International Journal of Fashion Design, Technology and Education* and

Young Consumers. Tse has experience in marketing and advertising with various media companies and creative agencies, including ADO and TBWA. He has taught at the School of Communication at HKBU, the Department of Fashion and Image Design at the Hong Kong Design Institute, and the Culture and Media Domain at HKU School of Professional and Continuing Education.

Foreword biographies

Kineta Hung is a professor and head of the Department of Communications Studies at Hong Kong Baptist University. Her research interests include celebrity endorsement, managing national images, communication engagement and advertising in China. Her works have appeared in the *Journal of Marketing, Journal of Advertising, Journal of International Business Studies, Journal of Advertising Research, Journal of Retailing* and *Journal of International Marketing*. Professor Hung serves on the editorial boards of the *Journal of Advertising* and the *International Journal of Advertising*. She is also a member of the research committee at the American Academy of Advertising. She is the recipient of five major research grants, as well as several awards, including the Emerald Management Reviews Citations of Excellence. She has given academic and executive talks on various advertising topics in Hong Kong, China and overseas. She is currently co-authoring the book *Chinese Firms Going Global: Their Impacts, Best Practices, and Implications* (Cambridge University Press, forthcoming), and editing a volume on advertising and branding in China under Routledge's 'Major Works on China Marketing'. Kineta Hung is an honorary professor at the Communication University of China, and is a research fellow at the Chinese Management Centre at Hong Kong University.

P. David Marshall is a research professor and holds a personal chair in new media, communication and cultural studies at Deakin University. He has published widely in two areas: public personality/celebrity and new media culture. His books include *Companion to Celebrity* (2015), *Celebrity and Power* (1997; second edition, 2014), *Fame Games* (2000), *Web Theory* (2003), *New Media Cultures* (2004) and *The Celebrity Culture Reader* (2006). He has been a keynote speaker at many international conferences, and has been interviewed for articles and many broadcast media programmes, from CNN, Fox News, the BBC and ABC/Radio National to the *Sydney Morning Herald, New York Times* and *Toronto Star*. His previous academic positions have been at Northeastern University in Boston, the University of Queensland in Brisbane and Carleton University in Ottawa, along with visiting positions at New York University, York University and Karlstad University. He is also Visiting Distinguished Foreign Expert in the School of Journalism and Communication at Central China Normal University (CCNU) in Wuhan China. His current writing and research has focused on some key areas in contemporary popular culture. In particular, he has been developing the idea of persona studies, where the presentation of the public self has expanded well beyond celebrity culture via particular online forms to the point where it now structures and patterns reputation and value across many professions, as well as through many recreational and leisure pursuits. He has developed three related concepts to help explore this change in contemporary culture: (1) presentational media; (2) the intercommunication industry; and (3) the personalization complex. His forthcoming books include *Promotional Vistas* (Palgrave, 2016), *Contemporary Publics* (2016) and *Persona Studies: Celebrity, Identity and the Transformation of the Public Self* (Palgrave, forthcoming), and *Persona in Formation* (University of Minnesota Press, 2016). He is also the founder of the *Persona Studies Journal* and *M/C*. His personal blog can be found at www.pdavidmarshall.com, which lists many of his most recent keynote and public addresses that he has given around the world.